AUTHORS
OF THE
ENLIGHTENMENT
1660 TO 1800

AUTHORS
OF THE
ENLIGHTENMENT
1660 TO 1800

EDITED BY J.E. LUEBERING , DIRECTOR, CORE REFERENCE

Britannica®
Educational Publishing

IN ASSOCIATION WITH

ROSEN
EDUCATIONAL SERVICES

Published in 2014 by Britannica Educational Publishing
(a trademark of Encyclopædia Britannica, Inc.)
in association with Rosen Educational Services, LLC
29 East 21st Street, New York, NY 10010.

First Edition

Britannica Educational Publishing
J.E. Luebering: Director, Core Reference Group
Adam Augustyn: Assistant Manager, Core Reference Group
Marilyn L. Barton: Senior Coordinator, Production Control
Steven Bosco: Director, Editorial Technologies
Lisa S. Braucher: Senior Producer and Data Editor
Jennifer Sale: Production Coordinator
Kathy Nakamura: Manager, Media Acquisition

Rosen Educational Services
Hope Lourie Killcoyne: Executive Editor
Nelson Sá: Art Director
Cindy Reiman: Photography Manager
Brian Garvey: Designer
Introduction by Joseph Kampff

Library of Congress Cataloging-in-Publication Data

Authors of the Enlightenment : 1660 to 1800/edited by J.E. Luebering.
    pages cm. — (The Britannica Guide to Authors)
"In association with Britannica Educational Publishing, Rosen Educational Services."
Includes bibliographical references and index.
ISBN 978-1-61530-999-3 (library binding)
1. Authors—17th century—Biography. 2. Authors—18th century—Biography. 3. Literature—
17th century—Bio-bibliography. 4. Literature—18th century—Bio-bibliography. 5.
Authorship—History—17th century. 6. Authorship—History—18th century. I. Luebering, J.
E., editor of compilation.
PN451.A965 2014
809'.03—dc23
[B]

                                                                    2013008886

On the cover, p.iii   : Voltaire, marble bust by Jean-Antoine Houdon; in the Hermitage, St.
Petersburg. Voltaire, considered to be one of the finest French writers of the Enlightenment
and indeed of all time, may well be remembered best as an advocate of human rights.
SuperStock/Getty Images

CONTENTS

Introduction   x
Paul Scarron   1
Samuel Butler   2
John Cleveland   5
François VI, duke de La
Rochefoucauld   6
John Evelyn   13
Andrew Marvell   15
Jean de La Fontaine   18
Hans Jacob Christoph von
Grimmelshausen   25
Molière   26
Gabriel-Joseph de Lavergne,
viscount of Guilleragues   36
Zhu Yizun   37
John Dryden   38
Samuel Pepys   46
Nicolas Boileau   52
Jean Racine   54
Mariana Alcoforado   63
Aphra Behn   64
William Wycherley   67
Ihara Saikaku   68
Thomas Shadwell   70
Bashō   71
Jean de La Bruyère   75
John Wilmot, 2nd earl of Rochester 76
Sor Juana Inés de la Cruz   78
Thomas Otway   84
Chikamatsu Monzaemon   85
Daniel Defoe   88
John Arbuthnot   96
Jonathan Swift   97
William Congreve   106

Colley Cibber   111
Joseph Addison   113
Sir Richard Steele   120
Ahmed Nedim   124
Ludvig Holberg, Baron
Holberg   125
John Gay   129
Allan Ramsay   131
Pierre Marivaux   133
Alexander Pope   135
Lady Mary Wortley Montagu   145
Samuel Richardson   147
Philip Dormer Stanhope,
4th earl of Chesterfield   153
Voltaire   154
Richard Savage   165
James Thomson   166
Henry Brooke   167
Antônio José da Silva   168
Benjamin Franklin   169
Carlo Goldoni   178
Henry Fielding   180
Antiokh Dmitriyevich
Kantemir   188
Jean-Baptiste-Louis Gresset   189
Samuel Johnson   190
Sarah Fielding   202
Laurence Sterne   203
Thomas Gray   208
Buson   210
Horace Walpole,
4th earl of Orford   211
Tobias Smollett   213
William Collins   217

Goronwy Owen   218
Friedrich Gottlieb Klopstock   220
Giovanni Giacomo Casanova   221
Mercy Otis Warren   223
Gotthold Ephraim Lessing   226
Charlotte Lennox   232
Oliver Goldsmith   233
Lucy Terry   237
William Cowper   238
Sophie von La Roche   241
Christoph Martin Wieland   242
Ueda Akinari   243
Michel Guillaume-Saint-Jean
de Crèvecoeur   244
James Macpherson   247
Thomas Paine   248
Edward Gibbon   253
Hester Lynch Piozzi   259
Marquis de Sade   260
James Boswell   265
Basílio da Gama   271
Johannes Ewald   272
Olaudah Equiano   274
Hannah More   276
Vittorio, Count Alfieri   278
Robert Fergusson   279
Richard Brinsley Sheridan   280
Philip Freneau   286
Fanny Burney   287
Thomas Chatterton   290
Phillis Wheatley   292
George Crabbe   295
Julian Ursyn Niemcewicz   296
Royall Tyler   298

Gâlib Dede   298
Robert Burns   299
Mary Wollstonecraft   306
William Beckford   309
André de Chénier   311
Jean Paul   312
Ann Radcliffe   314
William Hill Brown   317
Maria Edgeworth   318

Glossary   320
Bibliography   328
Index   331

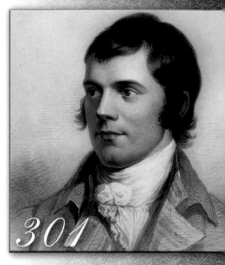

301

INTRODUCTION

The term *Enlightenment* usually refers to an intellectual movement that originated in Europe in the 17th century and had a wide influence on life across Europe and North America during the 18th century. The literature, philosophy, and politics of this period were marked to a large extent by a belief in the capacity of human reason to achieve knowledge, freedom, and happiness for all humankind, and history was conceived as a progression toward these ends. This new emphasis on the efficacy of human rationality led to tremendous advances in science, radical social reform, an intolerance of abuses committed by church and state, and an emphasis on individual agency and inalienable human rights. Indeed, the Enlightenment culminated in the American and French revolutions and produced such important documents as the United States Bill of Rights and the French Declaration of the Rights of Man and the Citizen. Freedom, democracy, and reason are the crucial terms of the Enlightenment. *Authors of the Enlightenment: 1660 to 1800* provides in-depth and authoritative biographical, contextual, bibliographical, and other critical information on the authors whose literary (and not so literary) works not only helped to produce and spread the Enlightenment but, by doing so, also laid the foundations for modern life. This volume encompasses such important figures as Molière, Daniel Defoe, Jonathan Swift, Voltaire, Benjamin Franklin, and Thomas Paine, who both wrote about and lived the struggles central to the Enlightenment. But it also contains descriptions of authors from the same historical period not usually associated with the Enlightenment, such as the Japanese master of the haiku, Bashō, and the Mexican poet Sor Juana Inés de la Cruz, in whose writings many of the same ideas are circulating. While the Enlightenment was a European phenomenon, its concerns were universal ones that were being addressed at the same time by authors around the world.

Jean-Baptiste Poquelin, better known by his stage name, Molière, was an actor and playwright whose works are considered the greatest comedies in the history of French theatre. Born into an affluent Parisian family in 1622, Molière received his education at the prestigious Collège de Clermont—the same place at which Voltaire would later study. Despite his father's wishes, Molière was determined to pursue a career in the theatre and organized his first comedic acting company, the Illustre-Théâtre, in 1643. Molière's theatrical ventures were not immediately successful, however, and he was sent to prison twice in 1645 because he could not pay his debts. Unable to compete with the better-established companies in Paris, Molière spent the next 13 years touring the provinces, honing his skills as a playwright, actor, and manager. Molière's break came in 1658 when his company greatly impressed King Louis XIV in an impromptu performance in the guardroom of the Louvre. Afterward, he quickly acquired a reputation among Parisian theatregoers as a writer with a scathing wit for whom nothing was off-limits. Often causes of public scandal, his plays were censored by the church—*Dom Juan* was not staged during his lifetime. Nevertheless, until his death in 1673, Molière devoted his life to theatre, both charming and outraging audiences with comic masterpieces such as *Le Misanthrope* (*The Misanthrope*), *Tartuffe; ou, l'imposteur* (*Tartuffe; or, The Imposter*), and *L'École des femmes* (*The School for Wives*).

Although the early English novelist Daniel Defoe (1660–1731) was also a notable pamphleteer and journalist, he is best remembered today for his outstanding novels *Robinson Crusoe* and *Moll Flanders*. Defoe was not only a writer, however. Soon after completing his studies at the academy for Dissenters (English

Protestants who did not conform to the Church of England) at Newington Green, Defoe established himself as a merchant dealing in a diverse range of goods. His various business ventures led him to travel extensively and ushered him into the world of politics—although, because religion and politics were practically inextricable at this time, that meant also an introduction to religious politics. He produced a number of influential political pamphlets and a periodical, *The Review*, which he wrote almost entirely by himself from 1704 to 1713. But Defoe was not always successful in his commercial and political enterprises. Frequently in debt, he went bankrupt in 1692. Defoe's politics often contributed to his failings in business, although he was no political idealist. Early in his career, he was an outspoken critic of the politically powerful High-Church Tories, and his Whiggish views landed him in Newgate Prison in 1703, which caused his business to suffer. Once released, however, he served the Tories, who were in control of the British government, as a pamphleteer and spy. In 1714, when the Whigs ascended to power, Defoe continued in the same role for the new government. Only after 1714, though, was Defoe was able to commit himself to the longer prose works for which he is celebrated. He published *Robinson Crusoe* in 1719 and *Moll Flanders* in 1722.

Jonathan Swift (1667–1745), the Anglo-Irish satirical writer most famous for his 1726 novel *Gulliver's Travels* and the bitingly satiric essay "A Modest Proposal" (1729), was also active in politics in England. A Whig by birth, but devoted to the Anglican Church, Swift early on drew the attention of a circle of Whig writers, but he spent the years from 1710 to 1714 working as the foremost political writer for the Tory party, producing pamphlets and editing the Tory journal *The Examiner*. When the Tory government collapsed in 1714, Swift was appointed dean of the St. Patrick's Cathedral in Dublin. After a period of inactivity in Dublin, Swift returned to public life and writing. The 1720s were a productive time for Swift. In addition to writing numerous verses, he produced a number of important pamphlets that addressed the urgent social and economic problems Ireland was facing. While he tended to blame English governance for Ireland's woes, he consistently urged the Irish not to wallow in their misfortune, but to do what they could to resolve their own problems. Swift's prose often shifted from tones of biting irony to gentle humour to straightforward exhortation—whatever served his ideas best at the time. "A Modest Proposal," through its acidly ironic recommendation that Irish children be sold as food to English landlords, attacks policies regarding the poor. Swift's masterpiece, *Gulliver's Travels* (published soon after the appearance of Defoe's *Robinson Crusoe*), was an immediate success that has remained a favourite of adults and children alike, although the piercing satire of the novel is likely lost on the latter.

The French writer François-Marie Arouet (1694–1778), working under the pseudonym Voltaire, is one of the most important figures in European history. Although his best-known literary work is his 1759 satirical novel, *Candide*—a work which famously, and perhaps cynically, suggests that in order to be happy in a corrupt world such as ours, "we must cultivate our garden"—Voltaire, buoyed by his belief in human progress, devoted much of his life to advocating for human rights. Born into a middle-class family, Voltaire attended the Lycée Louis-le-Grand (formerly the Collège de Clermont) where, along with a love of literature and theatre, he acquired a healthy skepticism toward religious authority. Voltaire was a free thinker whose confidence in human reason and sardonic wit combined to garner him notoriety in Paris. A controversial figure, as a young man Voltaire was both a successful court poet and an outcast from French society, spending time in prison and in exile in England. Voltaire's international celebrity was secured late in his life when, denied access to Paris by King Louis XV, he sought asylum first in Geneva then at Ferney, a property he bought on the French and Swiss border. Ferney quickly gained a reputation as a gathering place for many of Europe's most eminent literary, philosophical, and political figures. Meanwhile, Voltaire, the "Innkeeper of Europe," was more active than ever, often speaking out against *l'infâme*—his term for the church's intolerance—and on behalf of those who were unjustly persecuted.

The life of one of the most celebrated Americans of the 18th century, Benjamin Franklin—from his inauspicious birth as the 10th son of 17 children in 1706, to his death in 1790—is impossible to summarize without doing him some injustice. Among other achievements, Franklin was a successful author, publisher, inventor, diplomat, and statesman. As one of the founding fathers of the United States, he was one of the principal authors of the Declaration of Independence. To Franklin can be traced proposals that gave rise to institutions from the American Philosophical Society to the University of Pennsylvania. His diplomacy in France secured French aid for America during the American Revolution and was central to bringing about the Peace of Paris treaties that signified the end of that war with Great Britain. Franklin was also an accomplished inventor—inventing bifocal glasses, the Franklin stove (which was in widespread use by Americans for more than 200 years), the odometer, and the glass harmonica—and he conducted early and important experiments with electricity. Had he done nothing else, Franklin's scientific work alone would have garnered him international recognition. He published a profitable and well-regarded newspaper, the *Pennsylvania Gazette*, and his *Poor Richard's* almanac gave us such wonderful maxims as, "Early to bed, early to rise, makes a man healthy, wealthy, and wise." It is no surprise, therefore, that Franklin's autobiography stands as one of the most influential and widely read ever written.

When Thomas Paine died, in 1809, a widely reproduced obituary remarked that "[h]e had lived long, did some good and much harm." Posterity has been kinder to Paine, however, and in 1937 the *Times* of London described him as "the English Voltaire." Born in England in 1737, Paine had a rudimentary education of reading, writing, and arithmetic before going to work with his father when he was 13 years old. Although Paine worked at many trades in England, none of them brought him financial success or happiness. After working for a time for the excise office, collecting taxes on liquor and tobacco, Paine was fired for publishing an article in 1772 arguing for better pay and working conditions for excise workers. Paine may have accomplished very little had he not met Benjamin Franklin in London. With Franklin's encouragement and letters of introduction, Paine arrived in America in 1774, at a crucial point in the conflict between the colonies and Great Britain. In his most famous early work, the 50-page pamphlet *Common Sense* (1776), he argued compellingly that independence should be the primary goal of the American Revolution. This work was enormously influential to the authors of the Declaration of Independence. After some success in America, Paine again found himself in need of employment and departed for Europe in 1787. There, Paine was captivated by the French Revolution, publishing two defenses of the French people's actions within the span of one year, *Rights of Man* and *Rights of Man, Part II*. These works were exceedingly popular and came out in numerous editions both in Europe and in the United States. Although Paine was in favour of the abolition of the French monarchy, he was opposed to the way the revolutionary regime treated the royalists, speaking out forcefully against the execution of King Louis XVI. He was imprisoned for his principles in 1793. There, he composed his pamphlet opposing organized religion, *The Age of Reason*.

In Japan, far from the regions usually associated with the Enlightenment, Matsuo Bashō (1644–94) was the most important poet of his era. He continues to be regarded as a master of the haiku form today, and his poetry is read around the world. A haiku consists of 17 syllables in three lines and is notable for its simplicity and clarity. Although Bashō was always drawn to poetry, early in his life he held the status of samurai. After his master's death in 1666, however, he moved to Edo (modern-day Tokyo) to devote his life to writing. In his poetry, Bashō often creates imagery that describes the tension between a conception of identity as an act of performance and as a display of one's true essence:

> *year after year*
> *the monkey wears*
> *a monkey mask*

(Translation from Stephen Addiss, The Art of Haiku in History Through Poems and Paintings by Japanese Masters [2012])

While playful, such imagery is also as deeply philosophical as any of Volatire's meditations on what it means to be human. Late in his life, Bashō traveled throughout Japan, taking inspiration for his poetry, advising younger poets, and writing beautiful travel sketches. Bashō's work contributed greatly not only to the haiku's structure but also to its lasting reputation.

The poet, dramatist, scholar, and nun Sor Juana Inés de la Cruz, was born out of wedlock near modern-day Mexico City, likely in 1651. While living with her uncle in Mexico City, Juana—who was almost certainly self-taught —greatly impressed the viceroy, Antonio Sebastián de Toledo, with her intelligence, and she went to live in his court in 1664, where he had her knowledge tested by 40 scholars. Showing what she herself called a "total disin-clination to marriage," Juana joined the Convent of Santa Paula in 1669, where she devoted her life to writing and scholarship. Sor Juana may be regarded as an early femi-nist for her insistence on women's right to education and knowledge. Her most famous poem, "Hombres necios" ("Foolish Men") begins, "You foolish and unreasoning men / who cast all blame on women, / not seeing you yourselves are cause / of the same faults you accuse" (translation from Electa Arenal and Amanda Powell, *The Answer/La Respuesta* [1994]). In addition to her prodigious poetic out-put, which she composed in every available genre, Sor Juana composed a number of religious dramas and cloak-and-dagger plays. She died in her convent in 1695 while nursing other nuns during an epidemic.

The Enlightenment was a fascinating time of pro-found political and social transformation across Europe and in North America. Sustained by an unfaltering belief in the efficacy of human rationality, many authors of the Enlightenment worked hard to make the ideals of indi-vidual freedom and social justice a reality, often suffering grave injustices themselves in the process. These authors created enduring literary works whose political effects are still with us today.

PAUL SCARRON

(baptized July 4, 1610, Paris, France—d. October 7, 1660, Paris)

The French writer Paul Scarron contributed significantly to the development of three literary genres: the drama, the burlesque epic, and the novel. He is best known today for *Le Roman comique* ("The Comic Novel") and as the first husband of Françoise d'Aubigné, marquise de Maintenon, the influential second wife of King Louis XIV.

Scarron's origins were bourgeois, and it was originally intended that he should enter the church. After a period in Brittany and a visit to Rome, however, Scarron settled back in Paris and devoted himself to writing. His first works were burlesques, or comic imitations of serious literature. The poet Marc-Antoine Girard de Saint-Amant had already started the vogue for parodies of the classics, but Scarron is mainly responsible for making the burlesque one of the characteristic literary forms of the mid-17th century. His seven-volume *Virgile travesty* (1648–53) was a tremendous success. Modern readers, perhaps because they are less impressed than Scarron's contemporaries by the daring of parodying the *Aeneid*, often find the humour facile and too drawn out.

Scarron, who married d'Aubigné in 1652, was also a considerable figure in the theatrical life of Paris in the years immediately preceding the actor and playwright Molière's arrival in the capital. He often wrote with particular actors in mind; for example, *Le Jodelet* (produced

1645) was written to include a starring role for the popular comedian of the same name. Scarron's plots are usually based upon Spanish originals, and even his most successful comedy, *Dom Japhet d'Arménie* (produced 1647), owes a good deal to a play by Castillo Solórzano. Though no longer performed, Scarron's plays are of real historical importance, and Molière took many hints from them.

Scarron's profound practical experience of the theatre is reflected in *Le Roman comique*, 3 vol. (1651–59). This novel, composed in the style of a Spanish picaresque romance, recounts with gusto the comical adventures of a company of strolling players. The humour of *Le Roman comique* has lasted better than that of the parodies, probably because it is more human and less literary. The realism of the novel makes it an invaluable source of information about conditions in the French provinces in the 17th century.

SAMUEL BUTLER

(baptized February 8, 1612, Strensham, Worcestershire, England — d. September 25, 1680, London)

The poet and satirist Samuel Butler is famous as the author of *Hudibras*, the most memorable burlesque poem in the English language and the first English satire to make a notable and successful attack on ideas rather than on personalities. It is directed against the fanaticism, pretentiousness, pedantry, and hypocrisy that Butler saw in militant Puritanism, extremes that he attacked wherever he saw them.

Butler, the son of a farmer, was educated at the King's school, Worcester. He afterward obtained employment in the household of the Countess of Kent, at Wrest,

Bedfordshire, where he had access to a fine library. He then passed into the service of Sir Samuel Luke, a rigid Presbyterian, a colonel in the Parliamentary army, and scoutmaster general for Bedfordshire. In his service Butler undoubtedly had firsthand opportunity to study some of the fanatics who attached themselves to the Puritan army and whose antics were to form the subject of his famous poem. At the restoration of the monarchy he obtained a post as secretary to Richard Vaughan, earl of Carbery, lord president of Wales, who made him steward of Ludlow castle, an office he held throughout 1661. About this time he is said to have married a woman with a "competent fortune" that was, however, squandered through "being put out on ill securities."

The first part of *Hudibras* was apparently on sale by the end of 1662, but the first edition, published anonymously, is dated 1663. Its immediate success resulted in a spurious second part appearing within the year; the authentic second part, licensed in 1663, was published in 1664. The two parts, plus "The Heroical Epistle of Hudibras to Sidrophel," were reprinted together in 1674. In 1677 King Charles II, who delighted in the poem, issued an injunction to protect Butler's rights against piratical printers and awarded him an annual pension. In 1678 a third (and last) part was published.

The hero of *Hudibras* is a Presbyterian knight who goes "a-coloneling" with his squire, Ralpho, an Independent. They constantly squabble over religious questions and, in a series of grotesque adventures, are shown to be ignorant, wrongheaded, cowardly, and dishonest. Butler had derived his outline from *Don Quixote*—a novel published in two parts (1605, 1615) by the Spanish writer Miguel de Cervantes—and his burlesque method (making everything "low" and undignified) from Paul Scarron. However, his brilliant handling of the octosyllabic (eight-syllable) metre, his witty, clattering rhymes, his delight in strange words and esoteric learning, and his enormous zest and vigour create effects that are entirely original. Its pictures of low life are perhaps the most notable of their kind in English poetry between John Skelton, whose most important work, written during the early 16th century, bridged the medieval and Renaissance periods, and George Crabbe, who was born more than 70 years after Butler's death. Butler has a certain affinity with both.

According to John Aubrey, the 17th-century antiquary, after the appearance of *Hudibras* King Charles and the lord chancellor, Clarendon, promised Butler considerable compensation that never seem to have materialized. In the latter part of his life he was attached to the suite of George Villiers, 2nd duke of Buckingham; but there seems little doubt that Butler died a poor and disappointed man who, at the end of an apparently successful literary career, in the words of a contemporary, "found nothing left but poverty and praise."

Butler's other works include "The Elephant in the Moon" (1676), mocking the solemnities of the newly founded Royal Society; and "Repartees between Puss and Cat at a Caterwalling," laughing at the absurdities of contemporary rhymed heroic tragedy. *The Genuine Remains in Verse and Prose of Mr. Samuel Butler*, in two volumes (1759), was edited by Robert Thyer from Butler's papers and includes more than 100 brilliant prose "Characters" in the manner of the ancient Greek philosopher Theophrastus, as well as a satiric analysis of the duke of Buckingham, "Duke of Bucks," that bears comparison with the "Zimri" characterization in *Absalom and Achitophel* by John Dryden, the most influential literary figure of late 17th-century England.

JOHN CLEVELAND

(b. June 16, 1613, Loughborough, Leicestershire, England —
d. April 29, 1658, London)

John Cleveland was the most popular English poet of his era but became in later times the most commonly abused of the Metaphysical poets, a label used to describe those poets in 17th-century England inclined to personal and intellectual complexity and concentration.

Educated at Cambridge, Cleveland became a fellow there before joining the Royalist army at Oxford in 1643, during the English Civil Wars. In 1645–46 he was judge advocate with the garrison at Newark until it surrendered to the Parliamentary forces, after which he lived with friends. When Charles I put himself in the hands of the Scots' army and they turned him over to the Parliamentary forces, Cleveland excoriated his enemies in a famous satire, *The Rebel Scot*. Imprisoned for "delinquency" in 1655, Cleveland was released on appeal to Britain's lord protector, Oliver Cromwell, but he did not repudiate his royalist convictions.

Cleveland's poems first appeared in *The Character of a London Diurnal* (1647) and thereafter in some 20 collections in the next quarter century; this large number of editions attests to his great popularity in the mid-17th century. Cleveland carried obscurity and conceit to their limits, and many of his poems have been decried as mere intellectual gymnastics. From the time of John Dryden's deprecatory criticism of the Metaphysical poets, Cleveland has been a whipping boy for them, largely because his conceits are profuse and cosmetic rather than integral to his thought. Cleveland's real achievement lay in his political poems, which satirized contemporary persons and issues and were mostly written in heroic couplets (couplets of rhyming iambic pentameters). Cleveland's political satires influenced his friend Samuel Butler (in *Hudibras*), and his use of heroic couplets foreshadowed that of Dryden.

FRANÇOIS VI, DUKE DE LA ROCHEFOUCAULD

(b. September 15, 1613, Paris, France—d. March 16/17, 1680, Paris)

François VI, duke de La Rochefoucauld, was a French classical author. Before he became the leading exponent of the *maxime*, a French literary form of epigram that expresses a harsh or paradoxical truth with brevity, he had been one of the most active rebels of the Fronde, a series of civil wars in France during the mid-17th century.

Heritage and Political Activities

La Rochefoucauld was the son of François, Count (comte) de La Rochefoucauld, and his wife, Gabrielle du Plessis-Liancourt. In 1628 he was married to Andrée de Vivonne, with whom he had four sons and three daughters. He served in the army against the Spaniards in Italy in 1629, in the Netherlands and Picardy in 1635–36, and again in Flanders in 1639. The public lives of both father and son were conditioned by the policies of Louis XIV's government, which by turns threatened and flattered the nobility. Though his father was made duke and then governor of Poitou, he was later deprived of that post when the loyalty of the family was called into question. The younger La Rochefoucauld was allowed by Cardinal Mazarin, the

François VI, duke de La Rochefoucauld, 17th-century portrait; in the Palace of Versailles, France. Charles Ciccione/Gamma-Rapho/ Getty Images

infant king's chief minister, to resume the governorship in 1646. The fact that his château at Verteuil was demolished by the crown, apparently without notice, in 1650 throws light on a main cause of the revolts between 1648 and 1653 known as the Fronde: the distrust and fear felt by the monarchy for the local independence of the nobility.

La Rochefoucauld was more vulnerable than most of his contemporaries, because throughout his life he seems to have been susceptible to feminine charm. In 1635 the Duchess (duchesse) de Chevreuse had lured him into intrigues against Cardinal de Richelieu, the chief minister of Louis XIII, an adventure that only procured for La Rochefoucauld a humiliating interview with Richelieu, eight days of imprisonment in the Bastille, and two years of exile at Verteuil. Later, his hatred for Mazarin and his devotion to Anne de Bourbon, duchess de Longueville, sister of the Great Condé, who was the leader of the Fronde, led to an even more disastrous outcome. His own account of the weary alternation of plots and campaigns of the mutinous nobles throughout the revolts may be read in his *Mémoires.* His loyalty to the House of Condé did not increase his popularity with the crown and prevented him from pursuing any single policy for reform of royal or ministerial government. How far toward treason he allowed himself to be led, when the intentions of the reforming princes and nobility were superseded by personal ambitions, is shown by the draft of the so-called Treaty of Madrid of 1651, which laid down conditions of Spanish help to the French nobility. La Rochefoucauld not only signed the treaty but is thought by one scholar to have drafted it.

Two other features of La Rochefoucauld's public career deserve mention, since they explain much of his writing—courage and litigation. The man who was to pen the aphorisms on courage and cowardice had certainly been in the forefront of battle. Within six years he was wounded in no fewer than three engagements. The injuries to his face and throat were such that he retired from the struggle, his health ruined and his peace of mind lost.

His financial difficulties were no doubt intensified by war, his lands were heavily mortgaged, and but for the astute help of his agent he might not have been able to keep his establishment in central Paris, as he did from 1660 onward. He was forced to pay not only for fine living but for endless litigation. There is evidence of no fewer than five lawsuits in the space of three years, chiefly against other noble families, over questions of precedence and court ceremonial.

Yet in 1655 his literary endeavours were still before him. Thanks to the lasting and intellectually stimulating friendships with Mme de Sablé, one of the most remarkable women of her age, and Mme de Lafayette, he seems to have avoided politics for a while and gradually won his way back into royal favour, a feat sealed by his promotion to the knightly order of the Saint-Esprit at the end of 1661. Reading and intellectual conversation occupied his time as well as that of other men and women of a circle who listened to private readings of Pierre Corneille's classical tragedies and Nicolas Boileau's didactic poem on the principles of poetic composition, *L'Art poétique*. The circle was enlivened by a new game that consisted of discussing epigrams on manners and behaviour, expressed in the briefest, most pungent manner possible. The care with which La Rochefoucauld kept notes and versions of his thoughts on the moral and intellectual subjects of the game is clear from the surviving manuscripts. When the clandestine publication of one of them in Holland forced him to publish under his own name, it was clear that he had satisfied public taste: five editions of the *Maximes*, each of them revised and enlarged, were to appear within his lifetime.

The Maximes

The first edition of the *Maximes*, published in 1665, was called *Réflexions ou sentences et maximes morales* ("Reflections or Aphorisms and Moral Maxims") and did not contain epigrams exclusively; the most eloquent single item, which appeared only in the first edition and was thereafter removed by the author, is a three-page poetic description of self-interest, a quality he found in all forms of life and in all actions. The manuscripts also contain epigrams embedded in longer reflections; in some cases the various versions show the steps by which a series of connected sentences was filed down to the point of ultimate brevity. Beneath the general single statement, however, can be found a personal reaction to the Fronde, or to politics, often violent in its expression. For example:

> *Les crimes deviennent innocents, même glorieux, par leur nombre et par leurs qualités; de là vient que les voleries publiques sont des habiletés, et que prendre des provinces injustement s'appelle faire des conquêtes. Le crime a ses héros, ainsi que la vertu. (Crimes are made innocent, even virtuous, by their number and nature; hence public robbery becomes a skillful achievement and wrongful seizure of a province is called conquest. Crime has its heroes no less than virtue has.)*

It may have been hostile reception or the fear of revealing a political attitude that made him abandon this kind of epigram except for the almost unrecognizable No. 185: "*Il y a des héros en mal comme en bien*" ("Evil as well as good has its heroes"). Modern readers often forget that La Rochefoucauld's contemporaries would read recent history into statements that appear cryptic and opaque to posterity.

The Fronde was to La Rochefoucauld one of those moments of history that seemed to reveal men's motives at their worst. His exposure of the self-seeking that lay beneath conventional homage to morality has earned for him the reputation of a cynic, but his keener contemporaries are no less severe. The pungency and absence of explanation make his epigrams seem more scornful than similar statements embedded in memoirs. But La Rochefoucauld was concerned with conveying something more than scorn, and beneath his professions of idealism he pinpointed a restless and unquenchable thirst for self-preservation. Virtue in the pure state was something he did not find:

> *Les vertus se perdent dans l'intérêt comme les fleuves se perdent dans la mer. (Virtues are lost in self-interest as rivers are lost in the sea.)*

This image of the sea recurred:

> *Voilà la peinture de l'amour-propre, dont toute la vie n'est qu'une grande et longue agitation; la mer en est une image sensible; et l'amour-propre trouve dans le flux et reflux de ses vagues continuelles une fidèle expression de la succession turbulente de ses pensées et de ses éternels mouvements. (Such is the picture of self-love, of which all life is one continuous and immense ferment. The sea is its visible counterpart and self-love finds in the ebb and flow of the sea's endless waves a true likeness of the chaotic sequence of its thoughts and of its everlasting motion.)*

La Rochefoucauld has been called an Epicurean, but his imaginative insights attached him to no doctrine. Like the essayist Michel de Montaigne and the philosopher and scientist Blaise Pascal, he was aware of the mystery around humans that dwarfs their efforts and mocks their knowledge, of the gap between thinking and being, between what an individual is and what that individual does: *"La nature fait le mérite et la fortune le met en oeuvre"* ("Nature gives us our good qualities and chance sets them to work"). Some epigrams show a respect for the power of indolence, and others reveal a respect for strength. All these insights seem common to the French classical school of which La Rochefoucauld is so brilliant a member—though as an aristocrat he disdained being called a writer. These insights also accounted for his fame and influence on his disciples: in England Lord Chesterfield, the orator and man of letters, and the novelist and poet Thomas Hardy; in Germany the philosophers Friedrich Nietzsche and Georg Christoph Lichtenberg; in France the writers and critics Stendhal, Charles-Augustin Sainte-Beuve, and André Gide.

Yet La Rochefoucauld's chief glory perhaps is not as thinker but as artist. In the variety and subtlety of his arrangement of words he made the *maxime* into a jewel. It is not always the truth of the maxim that is so striking, but its exaggeration which can surprise one into a new aspect of the truth. He describes and defines—he has no time for more—but of the single metallic image he makes amazing use. He handles paradox to such effect that a final words can reverse the rest:

> *On ne donne rien si libéralement que ses conseils (We give nothing so generously as...advice). C'est une grande folie de vouloir être sage tout seul (It is great folly to seek to be wise...on one's own).*

La Rochefoucauld authorized five editions of the *Maximes* from 1665 to 1678. Two years after the last publication, he died in Paris.

Though he did a considerable amount of writing over the years La Rochefoucauld actually published only two works, the *Mémoires* and the *Maximes*. In addition, about 150 letters have been collected and 19 shorter pieces now known as *Réflexions diverses*. These, with the treaties and

conventions that he may have drawn up personally, constitute his entire work and of these only the *Maximes* stand out
as a work of genius. Like his younger contemporary, Jean de
La Bruyère, La Rochefoucauld was a man of one book.

JOHN EVELYN

(b. October 31, 1620, Wotton, Surrey, England—d. February 27, 1706,
Wotton)

The English country gentleman John Evelyn was the
author of some 30 books on the fine arts, forestry, and
religious topics. His *Diary*, kept all his life, is considered
an invaluable source of information on the social, cultural,
religious, and political life of 17th-century England.

Son of a wealthy landowner, after studying in the Middle
Temple, London, and at Balliol College, Oxford, Evelyn
decided not to join the Royalist cause in the English Civil
War for fear of endangering his brother's estate at Wotton,
then in parliamentary territory. In 1643, therefore, he went
abroad, first to France and then to Rome, Venice, and
Padua, returning to Paris in 1646, where the following year
he married Mary, daughter of Sir Richard Browne, Charles
I's diplomatic representative to France. In 1652, during the
Commonwealth, he returned to England and acquired his
father-in-law's estate, Sayes Court, at Deptford. In 1659 he
published two Royalist pamphlets.

At the Restoration of the monarchy in 1660, Evelyn
was well received by Charles II; he served on a variety of commissions, including those concerned with
London street improvement (1662), the Royal Mint
(1663), and the repair of old St. Paul's (1666). Far more

important was the commission for sick and wounded mariners and for prisoners of war in Charles II's Dutch Wars (1665–67, 1672–74), during which Evelyn exposed himself to plague and incurred personal expenses, reimbursement for which he was still petitioning in 1702. At that time he received help from Samuel Pepys (a navy official and, likewise, a diarist), with whom he formed a lifelong friendship.

Evelyn served on a council for colonial affairs from 1671 to 1674. He was appointed to the council of the Royal Society by its first and second charters in 1662 and 1663 and remained a lifelong member. In this capacity in 1664 he produced for the commissioners of the navy *Sylva, or a Discourse of Forest-trees, and the Propagation of Timber*, a description of the various kinds of trees, their cultivation, and uses. The study, with numerous modifications, had gone through 10 editions by 1825. In 1662 Evelyn produced *Sculptura,* a small book on engraving and etching, in which he announced a new process, the mezzotint.

About 1670 Evelyn formed a paternal affection for Margaret Blagge, a maid of honour at court, who later secretly married Sidney Godolphin, future lord high treasurer. She died after giving birth to a child in 1678; Evelyn's *Life of Mrs. Godolphin* (first published in 1847, long after Evelyn's death) is one of the most moving of 17th-century biographies.

In 1685, a few months after James II's accession, Evelyn was appointed one of three commissioners for the privy seal, an office he held for 15 months. Evelyn's last important book, *Numismata*, was published in 1697.

His *Diary*, begun when he was 11 years old and first published in 1818, was written for himself alone but with relatively little about himself in it. It ranges from bald memoranda to elaborate set pieces. With its descriptions of places and events, characters of contemporaries, and many reports of sermons, it bears witness to more than 50 years of English life and, as such, is of great historical value.

ANDREW MARVELL

(b. March 31, 1621, Winestead, Yorkshire, England—
d. August 18, 1678, London)

The political reputation of English poet Andrew Marvell overshadowed that of his poetry until the 20th century. He is now considered to be one of the best Metaphysical poets.

Marvell was educated at Hull grammar school and Trinity College, Cambridge, taking a B.A. in 1639. His father's death in 1641 may have ended Marvell's promising academic career. He was abroad for at least five years (1642–46), presumably as a tutor. In 1651–52 he was tutor to Mary, daughter of Lord Fairfax, the Parliamentary general, at Nun Appleton, Yorkshire, during which time he probably wrote his notable poems "Upon Appleton House" and "The Garden" as well as his series of Mower poems.

Although earlier opposed to Oliver Cromwell's Commonwealth government, he wrote "An Horatian Ode upon Cromwell's Return from Ireland" (1650), and from 1653 to 1657 he was a tutor to Cromwell's ward William Dutton. In 1657 he became assistant to John Milton as Latin secretary in the foreign office. "The First Anniversary" (1655) and "On the Death of O.C." (1659) showed his continued and growing admiration for Cromwell. In 1659 he was elected member of Parliament for Hull, an office he held until his death, serving skillfully and effectively.

After the restoration of Charles II in 1660, Marvell turned to political verse satires—the most notable was

Andrew Marvell. Archive Photos/Getty Images

Last Instructions to a Painter, against Lord Clarendon, Charles's lord chancellor—and prose political satire, notably *The Rehearsal Transpros'd* (1672–73). Marvell is also said to have interceded on behalf of Milton to have him freed from prison in 1660. He wrote a commendatory poem for the second edition of Milton's *Paradise Lost*. His political writings favoured the toleration of religious dissent and attacked the abuse of monarchical power.

At Marvell's death, his housekeeper-servant Mary Palmer claimed to be his widow, although this was undoubtedly a legal fiction. The first publication of his poems in 1681 resulted from a manuscript volume she found among his effects.

While Marvell's political reputation has faded and his reputation as a satirist is on a par with others of his time, his small body of lyric poems, first recommended in the 19th century by Charles Lamb, has since appealed to many readers, and in the 20th century he came to be considered one of the most notable poets of his century. In "To His Coy Mistress," which is one of the most famous poems in the English language, the impatient poet urges his mistress to abandon her false modesty and submit to his embraces before time and death rob them of the opportunity to love:

> *Had we but world enough, and time,*
> *This coyness, lady, were no crime....*
> *But at my back I always hear*
> *Time's wingèd chariot hurrying near;*
> *And yonder all before us lie*
> *Deserts of vast eternity...*
> *The grave's a fine and private place,*
> *But none, I think, do there embrace....*

JEAN DE LA FONTAINE

(b. July 8?, 1621, Château-Thierry, France — d. April 13, 1695, Paris)

Jean de La Fontaine was a poet whose *Fables* rank among the greatest masterpieces of French literature.

La Fontaine was born in the Champagne region into a bourgeois family. There, in 1647, he married an heiress, Marie Héricart, but they separated in 1658. From 1652 to 1671 he held office as an inspector of forests and waterways, an office inherited from his father. It was in Paris, however, that he made his most important contacts and spent his most productive years as a writer. An outstanding feature of his existence was his ability to attract the goodwill of patrons prepared to relieve him of the responsibility of providing for his livelihood. In 1657 he became one of the protégés of Nicolas Fouquet, the wealthy superintendent of finance. From 1664 to 1672 he served as gentleman-in-waiting to the duchess of Orléans, a widow, in Luxembourg. For 20 years, from 1673, he was a member of the household of Mme de La Sablière, whose salon was a celebrated meeting place of scholars, philosophers, and writers. In 1683 he was elected to the French Academy after some opposition by the king to his unconventional and irreligious character.

The Fables

The *Fables* unquestionably represent the peak of La Fontaine's achievement. The first six books, known as the *premier recueil* ("first collection"), were published in 1668 and were followed by five more books (the *second recueil*)

Jean de La Fontaine. DEA/G. Dagli Orti/De Agostini Picture Library/Getty Images

in 1678–79 and a twelfth book in 1694. The *Fables* in the second collection show even greater technical skill than those in the first and are longer, more reflective, and more personal. Some decline of talent is commonly detected in the twelfth book.

La Fontaine did not invent the basic material of his *Fables*; he took it chiefly from the tradition established by the ancient Greek fables attributed to Aesop and, in the case of the second collection, from the East Asian. He enriched immeasurably the simple stories that earlier fabulists had in general been content to tell perfunctorily, subordinating them to their narrowly didactic intention. He contrived delightful miniature comedies and dramas, excelling in the rapid characterization of his actors, sometimes by deft sketches of their appearance or indications of their gestures and always by the expressive discourse he invented for them. In settings usually rustic, he evoked the perennial charm of the countryside. Within the compass of about 240 poems, the range and the diversity of subject and of treatment are astonishing. Often he held up a mirror to the social hierarchy of his day. Intermittently he seems inspired to satire, but, sharp though his thrusts are, he had not enough of the true satirist's indignation to press them home. The *Fables* occasionally reflect contemporary political issues and intellectual preoccupations. Some of them, fables only in name, are really elegies, idylls, epistles, or poetic meditations. But his chief and most comprehensive theme remains that of the traditional fable: the fundamental, everyday moral experience of humankind throughout the ages, exhibited in a profusion of typical characters, emotions, attitudes, and situations.

Countless critics have listed and classified the morals of La Fontaine's *Fables* and have correctly concluded that they amount simply to an epitome of more or less proverbial wisdom, generally prudential but tinged in the second collection with a more genial embrace of pleasure and high living. Simple countryfolk and heroes of Greek mythology and legend, as well as familiar animals of the fable, all play their parts in this comedy, and the poetic resonance of the *Fables* owes much to these actors who, belonging to no century and to every century, speak with timeless voices.

What disconcerts many non-French readers and critics is that in the *Fables* profundity is expressed lightly. La Fontaine's animal characters illustrate the point. They are serious representations of human types, so presented as to hint that human nature and animal nature have much in common. But they are also creatures of fantasy, bearing only a distant resemblance to the animals the naturalist observes, and they are amusing because the poet skillfully exploits the incongruities between the animal and the human elements they embody. Moreover—as in his collection of tales known as the *Contes*, but with far more delicate and lyrical modulations—the voice of La Fontaine himself can constantly be heard, always controlled and discreet, even when most charged with emotion. Its tones change swiftly, almost imperceptibly: they are in turn ironical, impertinent, brusque, laconic, eloquent, compassionate, melancholy, or reflective. But the predominant note is that of *la gaieté*, which, as he says in the preface to the first collection, he deliberately sought to introduce into his *Fables*. "Gaiety," he explains, is not that which provokes laughter but is "a certain charm...that can be given to any kind of subject, even the most serious." No one reads the *Fables* rightly who does not read them with a smile—not only of amusement but also of complicity with the poet in the understanding of the human comedy and in the enjoyment of his art.

To the grace, ease, and delicate perfection of the best of the *Fables*, even close textual commentary cannot hope to do full justice. They represent the quintessence of a century of experiments in prosody and elevated poetic language in France. The great majority of the *Fables* are composed of lines of varying metre and, from the unpredictable interplay of their rhymes and of their changing rhythms, La Fontaine derived the most exquisite and diverse effects of tone and movement. His vocabulary harmonizes widely different elements: the archaic, the precious and the burlesque, the refined, the familiar and the rustic, the language of professions and trades and the language of philosophy and mythology. But for all this richness, economy and understatement are the chief characteristics of his style, and its full appreciation calls for a keen sensitivity to the overtones of the 17th-century French, a sensitivity that has naturally ebbed and faded with the passing centuries.

Miscellaneous Writings and the Contes

La Fontaine's many miscellaneous writings include much occasional verse in a great variety of poetic forms and dramatic or pseudodramatic pieces such as his first published work, *L'Eunuque* (1654; "The Eunuch"), and *Climène* (1671), as well as poems on subjects as different as *Adonis* (1658, revised 1669), *La Captivité de saint Malc* (1673; "The Captivity of Saint Malc"), and *Le Quinquina* (1682; the title refers to bark from trees of the genus *Cinchona*, which is a source of the drugs quinine and quinidine). All these are, at best, works of uneven quality. In relation to the perfection of the *Fables*, they are no more than poetic exercises or experiments. The exception is the leisurely narrative of *Les Amours de Psiché et de Cupidon* (1669; *The Loves of Cupid and Psyche*), notable for the lucid elegance of its prose, its skillful blend of delicate feeling and witty banter, and some sly studies of feminine psychology.

As with his miscellaneous works, La Fontaine's *Contes et nouvelles en vers* (*Tales and Novels in Verse*) considerably exceed the *Fables* in bulk. The first of them was published in 1664, the last posthumously. He borrowed them mostly from Italian sources, in particular Giovanni Boccaccio, but he preserved none of the 14th-century poet's rich sense of reality. The essence of nearly all his *Contes* lies in their lack of moral and sexual restraint, which is not presented with energetic frankness but is transparently and flippantly disguised. Characters and situations are not meant to be taken seriously; they are meant to amuse and are too monotonous to amuse for long. The *Contes* are the work far less of a poet than of an ingenious stylist and versifier. The accent of La Fontaine the narrator enlivens the story with playfully capricious comments, explanations, and digressions.

Personality and Reputation

Though he never secured the favour of Louis XIV, La Fontaine had many well-wishers close to the throne and among the nobility. He moved among churchmen, doctors, artists, musicians, and actors. But it was literary circles that he especially frequented. Legend has exaggerated the closeness of his ties with Molière, Nicholas Boileau, and Jean Racine, but he certainly numbered them among his friends and acquaintances, along with La Rochefoucauld, Mme de Sévigné, Mme de La Fayette, and many other, albeit less-well-remembered, writers.

The true nature of La Fontaine the man remains enigmatic. He was intensely and naively selfish, unconventional in behaviour, and impatient of all constraint; yet he charmed countless friends—perhaps by a naturalness of manner and a sincerity in social relationships that were rare in his age—and made apparently only one enemy (a fellow academician, Antoine Furetière). He was a parasite without servility, a sycophant without baseness, a shrewd schemer who was also a blunderer, and a sinner whose errors were, as one close to him observed, "full of wisdom." He was accommodating, sometimes to the detriment of proper self-respect, but he was certainly not the lazy, absent-minded simpleton that superficial observers took him for. The quantity and the quality of his work show that this legendary description of him cannot be accurate: for at least 40 years La Fontaine, in spite of his apparent aimlessness, was an ambitious and diligent literary craftsman of subtle intelligence and meticulous conscientiousness.

He was an assiduous and discriminating reader whose works abound in judicious imitations of both the matter and the manner of his favourite authors. He was influenced by so many 16th- and 17th-century French writers that it is almost pointless to mention only François Rabelais, Clément Marot, François de Malherbe, Honoré d'Urfé, and Vincent Voiture. The authors of classical antiquity that he knew best were Homer, Plato, Plutarch—these he almost certainly read in translation—Terence, Virgil, Horace, and Ovid. Boccaccio, Niccolò Machiavelli, Ludovico Ariosto, and Torquato Tasso were his favourites among the Italians. La Fontaine was no romantic; his work derives its substance and its savour less from his experience of life than from this rich and complex literary heritage, affectionately received and patiently exploited.

HANS JACOB CHRISTOPH VON GRIMMELSHAUSEN

(b. 1621/22, Gelnhausen, near Frankfurt am Main [Germany]—
d. August 17, 1676, Renchen, Strasbourg [France])

Hans Jacob Christoph (or Jakob Christoffel) von Grimmelshausen was a German novelist whose *Simplicissimus* series is one of the masterworks of his country's literature. Satiric and partially autobiographical, it is a matchless social picture of the often grotesque Thirty Years' War (1618–48).

Apparently the son of an innkeeper of noble descent, Grimmelshausen was orphaned at an early age. While still a child, he was drawn (or kidnapped) into the Thirty Years' War by Hessian and Croatian troops. He served as a musketeer, formally joined the imperial army, and in 1639 became secretary to Reinhard von Schauenburg, commandant at Offenburg. After the war, as steward for the Schauenburg family, Grimmelshausen collected taxes from peasants, dragged defaulters into court, and served as host at a Schauenburg tavern. To supplement his income, he sold horses. He left in 1660 when it was found that he had bought land with money belonging to the family. Afterward he was successively a steward for a wealthy physician and art lover, Johannes Rüffen of Strasbourg; a tavernkeeper at Gaisbach; and a bailiff at Renchen, where he survived an invasion.

Grimmelshausen, who had begun writing in his army days, published two minor satires (in 1658 and 1660) and then (in 1669) the first part of *Simplicissimus* (full title *Der abenteuerliche Simplicissimus Teutsch* ["The Adventurous Simplicissimus Teutsch"]). Grimmelshausen's authorship, however, was not established until 1837 from the initials HJCVG, which he used in a sequel to identify himself merely as editor.

Modeled on the 16th-century Spanish picaresque novel, *Simplicissimus* tells the story of an innocent child brought into contact with life through his experiences of the Thirty Years' War. The novel traces the development of a human soul against the depraved background of a Germany riven by war, depopulation, cruelty, and fear. *Simplicissimus* gives full rein to Grimmelshausen's power of narration, eye for realistic detail, coarse humour, social criticism, and gift for creating convincing characters.

Grimmelshausen's continuations of *Simplicissimus* include *Die Lanstörtzerin Courage* (1669; *Courage, the Adventuress*)—which inspired Bertolt Brecht's play *Mutter Courage und ihre Kinder* (1941; *Mother Courage and Her Children*)—and *Das wunderbarliche Vogelnest* (1672; "The Magical Bird's Nest"). One part of the latter, translated as *The False Messiah* (1964), is about an adventurer whose pose as the messiah enables him to steal a wealthy Jew's money and daughter; it is a satire on gullibility and greediness.

MOLIÈRE

(baptized January 15, 1622, Paris, France—d. February 17, 1673, Paris

The French actor and playwright Molière remains the greatest of all writers of French comedy. Despite the frequent opposition of sacred and secular authorities, he succeeded in inventing a new style of comedy that was based on a double vision of normal and abnormal seen in relation to each other. Molière's works also demonstrate that he was incapable of visualizing any situation without animating and dramatizing it, often beyond the limits of probability. Though living in an age of reason, his own good sense led him not to proselytize but rather to animate the absurd, as in such masterpieces as *Tartuffe; ou, l'imposteur* (*Tartuffe; or, The Imposter*), *L'École des femmes* (*The School for Wives*), *Le Misanthrope* (*The Misanthrope*), and many others.

Beginnings in Theatre

Molière was born Jean-Baptiste Poquelin in the heart of Paris. His mother died when he was 10 years old; his father, one of the appointed furnishers of the royal household, gave him a good education at the Collège de Clermont (the school that, as the Lycée Louis-le-Grand, was to train so many brilliant Frenchmen, including Voltaire). Although his father clearly intended him to take over his royal appointment, the young man renounced it in 1643, apparently determined to break with tradition and seek a living on the stage. That year he joined with nine others to produce and play comedy as a company under the name of the Illustre-Théâtre. His stage name, Molière, is first found in a document dated June 28, 1644.

A talented actress, Madeleine Béjart, persuaded Molière to establish a theatre, but she could not keep the young company alive and solvent. In 1645 Molière was twice sent to prison for debts on the building and properties. The number of theatregoers in 17th-century Paris was small, and the city already had two established theatres, so that a continued existence must have seemed impossible to a young company. From the end of 1645, for no fewer

Molière, oil painting by Pierre Mignard. Roger Viollet Collection/ Getty Images

than 13 years, the troupe sought a living touring the provinces. These unchronicled years must have been of crucial importance to Molière's career, forming as they did a rigorous apprenticeship to his later work as actor-manager and teaching him how to deal with authors, colleagues, audiences, and authorities. His rapid success and persistence against opposition when he finally got back to Paris is inexplicable without these years of training. His first two known plays date from this time: *L'Étourdi ou les contretemps (The Blunderer)*, performed at Lyon in 1655, and *Le Dépit amoureux (The Amorous Quarrel)*, performed at Béziers in 1656.

The path to fame opened for him on the afternoon of October 24, 1658, when, in the guardroom of the Louvre and on an improvised stage, the company presented French playwright Pierre Corneille's *Nicomède* before the king, Louis XIV, and followed it with what Molière described as one of those little entertainments that had won him some reputation with provincial audiences. This was *Le Docteur amoureux* ("The Amorous Doctor"); whether it was in the form still extant is doubtful. It apparently was a success and secured the favour of the king's brother Philippe, duc d'Orléans. It is difficult to know the extent of Orléans's patronage, which lasted seven years, until the king himself took over the company known as "Troupe du roi." No doubt the company gained a certain celebrity and prestige, invitations to great houses, and subsidies (usually unpaid) to actors, but not much more.

Molière's first Paris play, *Les Précieuses ridicules (The Affected Young Ladies)*, prefigured what was to come. It centres on two provincial girls who are exposed by valets masquerading as masters in scenes that contrast, on the one hand, the girls' desire for elegance coupled with a lack of common sense and, on the other, the valets' plain speech seasoned with cultural clichés. *Les Précieuses*, as well as *Sganarelle* (first performed in October, 1660), probably had its premiere at the Théâtre du Petit-Bourbon, adjacent to the Louvre. The Petit-Bourbon was demolished (apparently without notice), and the company moved early in 1661 to a hall in the Palais-Royal, built as a theatre by Richelieu. Here it was that all Molière's "Paris" plays were staged, starting with *Dom Garcie de Navarre; ou, le prince jaloux* ("Don Garcia of Navarre; or, The Jealous Prince") in February 1661, a heroic comedy of which much was hoped; it failed on the stage and succeeded only in inspiring Molière to work on *Le Misanthrope*. Such failures were rare and eclipsed by successes greater than the Paris theatre had known.

Scandals and Successes

The first night of *L'École des femmes*, December 26, 1662, caused a scandal as if people suspected that here was an emergence of a comic genius that regarded nothing as sacrosanct. Some good judges have thought this to be Molière's masterpiece, as pure comedy as he ever attained. Based on Paul Scarron's version of a Spanish story, it presents a pedant, Arnolphe, who is so frightened of femininity that he decides to marry a girl entirely unacquainted with the ways of the world. The delicate portrayal in this girl of an awakening temperament, all the stronger for its absence of convention, is a marvel of comedy. Molière crowns his fantasy by showing his pedant falling in love with her, and his elephantine gropings toward lovers' talk are both his punishment and the audience's delight.

From 1662 onward the Palais-Royal theatre was shared by Italian actors, each company taking three playing days in each week. Molière also wrote plays that were privately commissioned and thus first performed elsewhere: *Les Fâcheux* (*The Impertinents*) at Vaux in August 1661; the first version of *Tartuffe* at Versailles in 1664; *Le Bourgeois Gentilhomme* (*The Bourgeois Gentleman*) at Chambord in 1670; and *Psyché* in the Tuileries Palace in 1671.

On February 20, 1662, Molière married Armande Béjart. It is not certain whether she was Madeleine's sister, as the documents state, or her daughter, as some contemporaries suggest. There were three children of the marriage; only a daughter survived to maturity. It was not a happy marriage; flirtations of Armande are indicated in hostile pamphlets, but there is almost no reliable information.

Molière cleverly turned the outcry produced by *L'École des femmes* to the credit of the company by replying to his critics on the stage. *La Critique de L'École des femmes* (*The Critique of the School of Wives*, or *The School for Wives Criticized*) in June 1663 and *L'Impromptu de Versailles* (*The Impromptu at Versailles*) in October were both single-act discussion plays. In *La Critique* Molière allowed himself to express some principles of his new style of comedy, and in the other play he made theatre history by reproducing with astonishing realism the actual greenroom, or actors' lounge, of the company and the backchat involved in rehearsal.

The quarrel of *L'École des femmes* was itself outrun in violence and scandal by the presentation of the first version of *Tartuffe* in May 1664. The history of this great play sheds much light on the conditions in which Molière had to work and bears a quite remarkable testimony to his persistence and capacity to show fight. He had to wait five years and risk the livelihood of his actors before his reward, which proved to be the greatest success of his career.

Molière made matters worse, however, by staging a version of *Dom Juan; ou, le festin de Pierre* (*Don Juan; or, The Feast of Stone*) with a spectacular ending in which an atheist is committed to hell—but only after he had amused and scandalized the audience. *Dom Juan* was meant to be a quick money raiser, but it was a costly failure, mysteriously removed after 15 performances and never performed again or published by Molière. It is a priceless example of his art. The central character, Dom Juan, carries the aristocratic principle to its extreme by disclaiming all types of obligation, either to parents or doctors or tradesmen or God. Yet he assumes that others will fulfill their obligations to him. His servant, Sganarelle, is imagined as his opposite in every point, earthy, timorous, superstitious. These two form the perfect French counterpart to Cervantes's Don Quixote and Sancho.

Harassment by the Authorities

While engaged in his battles against the authorities, Molière continued to hold his company together single-handedly. He made up for lack of authors by writing more plays himself. He could never be sure either of actors or authors. In 1664 he put on the first play of Jean Racine, *La Thébaïde* (Eng. trans. *The Fatal Legacy*), but the next year Racine transferred his second play, *Alexandre le Grand* (*Alexander the Great*), to a longer-established theatre while Molière's actors were actually performing it. He was constantly harassed by the authorities. These setbacks may have been offset in part by the royal favour conferred upon Molière, but royal favour was capricious. Pensions were often promised and not paid. The court wanted more light plays than great works. The receipts of his theatre were uncertain and fluctuating. In his 14 years in Paris, Molière wrote 31 of the 95 plays that were presented on his stage. To meet the cumulative misfortunes of his own illness, the closing of the theatre for seven weeks upon the death of the Queen Mother, and the proscription of *Tartuffe* and *Dom Juan*, he wrote five plays in one season (1666–67). Of the five, only one, *Le Médecin malgré lui* (*The Doctor in Spite of Himself*), was a success.

In the preceding season, however, *Le Misanthrope*, almost from the start, was treated as a masterpiece by discerning playgoers, if not by the entire public. It is a drawing-room comedy, without known sources, constructed from the elements of Molière's own company. Molière himself played the role of Alceste, a fool of a new kind, with high principles and rigid standards, yet by nature a blind critic of everybody else. Alceste is in love with Célimène (played by Molière's wife, Armande), a superb comic creation, equal to any and every occasion, the incarnate spirit of society. The structure of the play is as simple as it is poetic. Alceste storms moodily through the play, finding no "honest" men to agree with him, always ready to see the mote in another's eye, blind to the beam in his own, as ignorant of his real nature as a Tartuffe.

The church nearly won its battle against Molière: it prevented public performance, both of *Tartuffe* for five years and of *Dom Juan* for the whole of Molière's life. A five-act version of *Tartuffe* was played in 1667, but once only; it was promptly banned. Molière's reply was to lobby the king repeatedly, even in a military camp, and to publish a defense of his play called *Lettre sur la comédie de l'Imposteur* ("Letter on the Comedy of the Imposter"). He kept his company together through 1668 with *Amphitryon* (January 13), *George Dandin* (Versailles, July 18), and *L'Avare* (*The Miser*; September 9). The last of his three 1668 plays, *L'Avare*, is composed in prose that reads like verse; the stock situations are all recast, but the spirit is different from Molière's other works. His miser is a living paradox, inhuman in his worship of money, all too human in his need of respect and affection. In breathtaking scenes his mania is made to suggest cruelty, pathological loneliness, even insanity.

His second play of 1668, *George Dandin*, often dismissed as a farce, may be one of Molière's greatest creations. It centres on a fool, who admits his folly while suggesting that wisdom would not help him because, if things in fact go against us, it is pointless to be wise. As it happens he is in the right, but he can never prove it. The subject of the play is trivial, the suggestion is limitless; it sketches a new range of comedy altogether. In 1669, permission was somehow obtained, and the long run of *Tartuffe* at last began. More than 60 performances were given that year alone. The theme for this play, which brought Molière more trouble than any other, may have come to him when a local hypocrite seduced his landlady. At the time it was common for lay directors of conscience to be placed in families to reprove and reform conduct. When this "holy" man is caught making professions of love to his employer's wife, he recovers by masterly self-reproach and persuades the master not only to pardon him but also to urge him to see as much of his wife as possible. Molière must have seen even greater comic possibilities in this theme, for he made five acts out of it. The final version contains two seduction scenes and a shift of interest to the comic paradox in Tartuffe himself, posing as an inhuman ascetic while by nature he is an all-too-human lecher. It is difficult to think of a theme more likely to offend pious minds.

Last Plays

The struggle over *Tartuffe* probably exhausted Molière to the point that he was unable to stave off repeated illness and supply new plays; he had, in fact, just four years more to live. Yet he produced in 1669 *Monsieur de Pourceaugnac* for the king at Chambord and in 1670 *Le Bourgeois Gentilhomme*.

Le Bourgeois Gentilhomme treated a contemporary theme—social climbing among the bourgeois, or upper middle class—but it is perhaps the least dated of all his comedies. The protagonist Jourdain, rather than being an unpleasant sycophant, is as delightful as he is fatuous, as genuine as he is naive; his folly is embedded in a bountiful disposition, which he of course despises. This is comedy in Molière's happiest vein.

Continuing to write despite his illness, he produced *Psyché* and *Les Fourberies de Scapin* (*The Cheats of Scapin*) in 1671. *Les Femmes savantes* (Eng. trans. *The Blue-Stockings*) followed in 1672; in rougher hands this subject would have been (as some have thought it) a satire on women of affected learning, but Molière has imagined a sensible bourgeois who goes in fear of his masterful and learned wife. *Le Malade imaginaire* (Eng. trans. *The Imaginary Invalid*), about a hypochondriac who fears death and doctors, was performed in 1673 and was Molière's last work. It is a powerful play in its delineation of medical jargon and professionalism, in the fatuity of a would-be doctor with learning and no sense, in the normality of the young and sensible lovers, as opposed to the superstition, greed, and charlatanry of other characters. During the fourth performance of the play, on February 17, Molière collapsed on stage and was carried back to his house in the rue de Richelieu to die. As he had not been given the sacraments or the opportunity of formally renouncing the actor's profession, he was buried without ceremony and after sunset on February 21.

GABRIEL-JOSEPH DE LAVERGNE, VISCOUNT OF GUILLERAGUES

(b. November 18, 1628, Bordeaux, France—d. March 4, 1685, Constantinople, Ottoman Empire [now Istanbul, Turkey])

The French author and diplomat Gabriel-Joseph de Lavergne, viscount of Guilleragues, is considered by most modern authorities to be the author of the *Lettres portugaises* (1669; "Portuguese Letters"), a vivid account of a nun's feelings of betrayal after a French officer seduces and abandons her. These purported letters remained widely popular from the 17th century onward.

Guilleragues was educated at the Collège de Navarre and subsequently remained in Paris to study law. He later returned to his place of birth, Bordeaux, to become a lawyer in the *parlement* (high court) there. In 1651 he met Armand I de Bourbon, prince de Conti, and five years later became his steward, a post he occupied until Conti's death. Guilleragues then moved to Paris, where he frequented Mme de Sablé's salon and was on friendly terms with the writers Molière, Nicolas Boileau (who called him "the most agreeable man in France"), and La Rochefoucauld. Guilleragues entered the service of King Louis XIV in 1669 as his private secretary, and 10 years later he was appointed French ambassador at Constantinople, where the scholar Antoine Galland served as his secretary.

In 1669 Guilleragues published the two works that appear to constitute his entire literary oeuvre: *Valentins*

(1668), a collection of rhymed poems, and the *Lettres por-tugaises*, a claimed translation into French of five letters written by a Portuguese nun, who in the early 19th century was identified as Mariana Alcoforado. They were accepted as Alcoforado's until the 1920s, when Guilleragues was identified as their probable author, although debate over their authorship continued into the 21st century.

ZHU YIZUN

(b. October 7, 1629, Xiushui [now Jiaxing], Zhejiang province,
China—d. November 14, 1709, Xiushui)

Zhu Yizun (in an earlier transliteration system spelled Chu Yi-tsun or Chu I-tsun) was a Chinese scholar and poet who lived during the early Qing dynasty (1644–1911/12).

Although Zhu's family had been prominent under the Ming dynasty, the collapse of that dynasty in 1644 forced him to spend much of his life as a private tutor and personal secretary to various local officials and men of letters. His considerable intellectual accomplishments, however, won him a summons to a special Qing examination in 1678 and eventually an appointment to the prestigious Hanlin Academy at the court in Beijing, where he became an editor on the official Ming history project. While at the capital he wrote a number of other histories, including a noted history of Beijing and its environs (*Rixia jiuwen*, 1688; "Legends and Places of Beijing"), and produced his *Jingyikao* (1701; expanded ed. 1755; "General Bibliography of the Classics"), a massive descriptive catalog of both lost and extant works in the Confucian canon.

Zhu was also a prolific poet, regarded as one of the greatest of the early Qing. He is best known for his role in the revival of *ci* poetry, a lyric form that had flourished during the Song dynasty (960–1279) and then had fallen out of fashion. He edited a definitive anthology of *ci* and urged a return to the refined elegance of the form; his efforts influenced a new generation of poets. His own *ci* were traditional in their emphasis on tonal rules, though somewhat obscure and allegorical in approach.

JOHN DRYDEN

(b. August 9 [August 19, New Style], 1631, Aldwinkle, Northamptonshire, England—d. May 1 [May 12], 1700, London)

The English poet, dramatist, and literary critic John Dryden so dominated the literary scene of his day that it came to be known as the Age of Dryden.

Youth and education

The son of a country gentleman, Dryden grew up in the country. When he was 11 years old the Civil War broke out. Both his father's and mother's families sided with Parliament against the king, but Dryden's own sympathies in his youth are unknown.

About 1644 Dryden was admitted to Westminster School, where he received a predominantly classical education under Richard Busby, the celebrated and longtime head of Westminster. Dryden's easy and lifelong familiarity with classical literature begun at the school later resulted in idiomatic English translations.

John Dryden in an engraving after Thomas Hudson. Photos.com/
Thinkstock

In 1650 he entered Trinity College, Cambridge, where he took a B.A. degree in 1654. What Dryden did between leaving the university in 1654 and the restoration of Charles II in 1660 is not known with certainty. In 1659 his contribution to a memorial volume for Oliver Cromwell marked him as a poet worth watching. His "heroic stanzas" were mature, considered, and sprinkled with those classical and scientific allusions that characterized his later verse. This kind of public poetry was always one of the things Dryden did best.

When in May 1660 Charles II was restored to the throne, Dryden joined the poets of the day in welcoming him, publishing in June *Astraea Redux,* a poem of more than 300 lines in rhymed couplets. For the coronation in 1661, he wrote *To His Sacred Majesty.* These two poems were designed to dignify and strengthen the monarchy and to invest the young monarch with an aura of majesty, permanence, and even divinity. Thereafter, Dryden's ambitions and fortunes as a writer were shaped by his relationship with the monarchy. On December 1, 1663, he married Elizabeth Howard, the youngest daughter of Thomas Howard, 1st earl of Berkshire. In due course she bore him three sons.

Dryden's longest poem to date, *Annus Mirabilis* (1667), was a celebration of two victories by the English fleet over the Dutch and the Londoners' survival of the Great Fire of 1666. In this work Dryden was once again gilding the royal image and reinforcing the concept of a loyal nation united under the best of kings. It was hardly surprising that when the poet laureate, Sir William Davenant, died in 1668, Dryden was appointed poet laureate in his place and two years later was appointed royal historiographer.

Writing for the Stage

Soon after his restoration to the throne in 1660, Charles II granted two patents for theatres, which had been closed by the Puritans in 1642. Dryden soon joined the little band of dramatists who were writing new plays for the revived English theatre. His first play, *The Wild Gallant*, a farcical comedy with some strokes of humour and a good deal of licentious dialogue, was produced in 1663. It was a comparative failure, but in January 1664 he had some share in the success of *The Indian Queen*, a heroic tragedy in rhymed couplets in which he had collaborated with Sir Robert Howard, his brother-in-law. Dryden was soon to successfully exploit this new and popular genre, with its conflicts between love and honour and its lovely heroines before whose charms the blustering heroes sank down in awed submission. In the spring of 1665 Dryden had his own first outstanding success with *The Indian Emperour*, a play that was a sequel to *The Indian Queen*.

In 1667 Dryden had another remarkable hit with a tragicomedy, *Secret Love, or the Maiden Queen*, which appealed particularly to the king. The part of Florimel, a boisterous and witty maid of honour, was played to perfection by the king's latest mistress, Nell Gwynn. In Florimel's rattling exchanges with Celadon, the Restoration aptitude for witty repartee reached a new level of accomplishment. In 1667 Dryden also reworked for the stage Molière's comedy *L'Étourdi* (translated by William Cavendish, duke of Newcastle) under the title *Sir Martin Mar-all*.

In 1668 Dryden published *Of Dramatick Poesie, an Essay*, a leisurely discussion between four contemporary writers of whom Dryden (as Neander) is one. This work is a defense of English drama against the champions of both ancient Classical drama and the Neoclassical French theatre; it is also an attempt to discover general principles of dramatic criticism. By deploying his disputants so as to break down the conventional oppositions of ancient and modern, French and English, Elizabethan and Restoration, Dryden deepens and complicates the discussion. This is the first substantial piece of modern dramatic criticism; it is sensible, judicious, and exploratory and combines general principles and analysis in a gracefully informal style. Dryden's approach in this and all his best criticism is characteristically speculative and shows the influence of detached scientific inquiry. The prefaces to his plays and translations over the next three decades were to constitute a substantial body of critical writing and reflection.

In 1668 Dryden agreed to write exclusively for Thomas Killigrew's company at the rate of three plays a year and became a shareholder entitled to one-tenth of the profits. Although Dryden averaged only a play a year, the contract apparently was mutually profitable. In June 1669 he gave the company *Tyrannick Love*, with its blustering and blaspheming hero Maximin. In December of the next year came the first part of *The Conquest of Granada by the Spaniards*, followed by the second part about a month later. All three plays were highly successful; and in the character Almanzor, the intrepid hero of *The Conquest of Granada*, the theme of love and honour reached its climax. But the vein had now been almost worked out, as seen in the 1671 production of that witty burlesque of heroic drama *The Rehearsal*, by George Villiers, 2nd duke of Buckingham, in which Dryden (Mr. Bayes) was the main satirical victim. *The Rehearsal* did not kill the heroic play, however; as late as November 1675, Dryden staged his last and most intelligent example of the genre, *Aureng-Zebe*. In this play he abandoned the use of rhymed couplets for that of blank verse (unrhymed iambic pentameter).

In writing those heroic plays, Dryden had been catering to an audience that was prepared to be stunned into admiration by drums and trumpets, rant and extravagance, stage battles, rich costumes, and exotic scenes. His abandonment of crowd-pleasing rant and bombast was symbolized in 1672 by his brilliant comedy *Marriage A-la-Mode*, in which the Restoration battle of the sexes was given a sophisticated and civilized expression that, among playwrights whose careers overlapped with Dryden's, only Sir George Etherege and William Congreve at their best would equal. Equally fine in a different mode was his tragedy *All for Love* (1677), based on William Shakespeare's *Antony and Cleopatra* and written in a flowing but controlled blank verse. He had earlier adapted *The Tempest* (1667), and later he reworked yet another Shakespeare play, *Troilus and Cressida* (1679). Dryden had now entered what may be called his Neoclassical period, and, if his new tragedy was not without some echoes of the old extravagance, it was admirably constructed, with the action developing naturally from situation and character.

By 1678 Dryden was at loggerheads with his fellow shareholders in the Killigrew company, which was in grave difficulties owing to mismanagement. Dryden offered his tragedy *Oedipus*, a collaboration with Nathaniel Lee, to a rival theatre company and ceased to be a Killigrew shareholder.

Verse Satires

Since the publication of *Annus Mirabilis* 12 years earlier, Dryden had given almost all his time to playwriting. If he had died in 1680, it is as a dramatist that he would be chiefly remembered. Now, in the short space of two years, he was to make his name as the greatest verse satirist that England had so far produced. In 1681 the king's difficulties—arising from political misgivings that his brother, James, the Roman Catholic duke of York, might succeed him—had come to a head. Led by the earl of Shaftesbury, the Whig Party leaders had used the Popish Plot to try to exclude James in favour of Charles's illegitimate Protestant son, the duke of Monmouth (The Popish Plot being a fictitious but widely believed plot in which it was alleged that Jesuits were planning the assassination of King Charles II in order to bring the Duke of York to the throne.) But the king's shrewd maneuvers eventually turned public opinion against the Whigs, and Shaftesbury was imprisoned on a charge of high treason.

As poet laureate in those critical months Dryden could not stand aside, and in November 1681 he came to the support of the king with his *Absalom and Achitophel*, so drawing upon himself the wrath of the Whigs. Adopting as his framework the Hebrew Bible story of King David (Charles II), his favourite son Absalom (Monmouth), and the false Achitophel (Shaftesbury), who persuaded Absalom to revolt against his father, Dryden gave a satirical version of the events of the past few years as seen from the point of view of the king and his Tory ministers and yet succeeded in maintaining the heroic tone suitable to the king and to the seriousness of the political situation. As anti-Whig propaganda, ridiculing their leaders in a succession of ludicrous satirical portraits, Dryden's poem is a masterpiece of confident denunciation; as pro-Tory propaganda it is equally remarkable for its serene and persuasive affirmation. When a London grand jury refused to indict Shaftesbury for treason, his fellow Whigs voted him a medal. In response Dryden published early in 1682 *The Medall*, a work full of unsparing invective against the Whigs, prefaced by a vigorous and plainspoken prose "Epistle to the Whigs." In the same year, anonymously and apparently without Dryden's authority, there also appeared in print his famous extended lampoon, *Mac Flecknoe*, written about four years earlier. What triggered this devastating attack on the Whig playwright Thomas Shadwell has never been satisfactorily explained; all that can be said is that in *Mac Flecknoe* Shadwell's abilities as a literary artist and critic are ridiculed so ludicrously and with such good-humoured contempt that his reputation has suffered ever since. The basis of the satire, which represents Shadwell as a literary dunce, is the disagreement between him and Dryden over the quality of the wit of Ben Jonson, the most important of the playwrights contemporary to Shakespeare. Dryden thinks Jonson deficient in this quality, while Shadwell regards him with uncritical reverence. This hilarious comic lampoon was both the first English mock-heroic poem and the immediate ancestor of Alexander Pope's *The Dunciad*.

Late Works

In 1685, after the newly acceded king James II seemed to be moving to Catholic toleration, Dryden was received into the Roman Catholic church. In his longest poem, the beast fable *The Hind and the Panther* (1687), he argued the case for his adopted church against the Church of England and the sects. His earlier *Religio Laici* (1682) had argued in eloquent couplets for the consolations of Anglicanism and against unbelievers, Protestant dissenters, and Roman Catholics. Biographical debate about Dryden has often focused on his shifts of political and religious allegiance; critics, like his hostile contemporaries, have sometimes charged him with opportunism.

The abdication of James II in 1688 destroyed Dryden's political prospects, and he lost his laureateship to Shadwell. He turned to the theatre again. The tragedy *Don Sebastian* (1689) failed, but *Amphitryon* (1690) succeeded, helped by the music of Henry Purcell. Dryden collaborated with Purcell in a dramatic opera, *King Arthur* (1691), which also succeeded. His tragedy *Cleomenes* was long refused a license because of what was thought to be the politically dangerous material in it, and with the failure of the tragicomedy *Love Triumphant* in 1694, Dryden stopped writing for the stage.

In the 1680s and '90s Dryden supervised poetical miscellanies and translated the works of the ancient

Roman poets Juvenal and Persius for the publisher Jacob Tonson with success. In 1692 he published *Eleonora*, a long memorial poem commissioned for a handsome fee by the husband of the Countess of Abingdon. But his great late work was his complete translation of Virgil, the greatest poet of ancient Rome and the author of the *Aeneid*; Dryden's work was contracted by Tonson in 1694 and published in 1697. Dryden was now the grand old man of English letters and was often seen at Will's Coffee-House chatting with younger writers. His last work for Tonson was *Fables Ancient and Modern* (1700), which consisted mainly of verse adaptations from the works of the ancient Roman poet Ovid and the medieval poets Geoffrey Chaucer and Giovanni Boccaccio, introduced with a critical preface. He died in 1700 and was buried in Westminster Abbey between Chaucer and Abraham Cowley in the Poets' Corner.

Besides being the greatest English poet of the later 17th century, Dryden wrote almost 30 tragedies, comedies, and dramatic operas. He also made a valuable contribution in his commentaries on poetry and drama, which are sufficiently extensive and original to entitle him to be considered, in the words of the 18th-century critic and biographer Samuel Johnson, as "the father of English criticism."

SAMUEL PEPYS

(b. February 23, 1633, London, England—d. May 26, 1703, London)

Samuel Pepys (pronounced "peeps") was an English diarist and naval administrator who is celebrated for his *Diary* (first published in 1825), which gives a fascinating picture of the official and upper-class life of Restoration London from January 1, 1660, to May 31, 1669. Though of humble parentage, Pepys rose to be one of the most important men of his day, becoming England's earliest secretary of the Admiralty. He was the trusted confidant of two kings, Charles II and James II, and the friends of his old age included some of the greatest men of his era.

Early Career

Pepys was the son of a tailor, and his mother, Margaret Kite, was the sister of a Whitechapel butcher. He was sent, after early schooling at Huntingdon, to St. Paul's School, London. In 1650 he was entered at Trinity Hall, Cambridge, but instead went to Magdalene College. In March 1653 he took a B.A. degree and in 1660 received an M.A. Little is known of his university career save that he was once admonished for being "scandalously overserved with drink."

In December 1655 he married a penniless beauty of 15, Elizabeth Marchant de Saint-Michel, daughter of a French Huguenot refugee. At this time he was employed by his cousin Admiral Edward Montagu, later 1st earl of Sandwich, who was high in the lord protector Oliver Cromwell's favour. But it was while working in the office of George Downing, one of the tellers of the Exchequer, that on January 1, 1660, Pepys began his diary. A few months later he sailed, as his cousin's secretary, with the fleet that brought back Charles II from exile. Appointed, through Montagu's interest at court, clerk of the acts of the navy, he became in the next few years a justice of the peace, a commissioner for and, later, treasurer of, Tangier, and surveyor of naval victualling. When he entered upon his functions, he was ignorant of almost everything that belonged to them. His chief use of his position was to

Samuel Pepys, oil painting by John Hayls, 1666; in the National Portrait Gallery, London. DEA Picture Library/De Agostini/ Getty Images

enjoy his newfound importance and the convivial companionship of his colleagues, admirals Sir William Batten and Sir William Penn. But early in 1662 there came a change. His colleagues' insistence on their superior experience and status galled Pepys's pride, and he sought for ways by which he could show himself their equal. He had not far to look, for his fellow officers were anything but attentive to business. "So to the office," Pepys wrote, "where I do begin to be exact in my duty there and exacting my privileges and shall continue to do so." He had found his vocation.

Naval Administration

It was not in Pepys's nature to do things by halves. Having resolved to do his duty, he set out to equip himself for its performance. In the summer of 1662 he occupied his leisure moments by learning the multiplication table, listening to lectures on shipbuilding, and studying the prices of naval stores. At the same time, he began his habit of making careful entries of all contracts and memoranda in large vellum books—beautifully ruled by Elizabeth Pepys and her maids—and of keeping copies of his official letters.

The qualities of industry and devotion to duty that Pepys brought to the service of the Royal Navy became realized during the Second Dutch War of 1665–67. Before trouble with his eyesight caused him to discontinue his diary in 1669—an event followed by the death of his wife—these qualities had won him the trust of the king and his brother James, the duke of York, the lord high admiral. In 1673, in the middle of the Third Dutch War, when York's unpopular conversion to Catholicism forced him to resign his office, Pepys was appointed secretary to the new commission of Admiralty and, as such, administrative head of the navy. In order to represent it in Parliament, he became member for two parishes (towns): first for Castle

Rising and, later, for Harwich. For the next six years he was engaged in stamping out the corruption that had paralyzed the activities of the navy. His greatest achievement was carrying through Parliament a program that, by beginning construction of 30 new warships, restored the balance of sea power, upset by the gigantic building programs of France and the Netherlands. In his work both at the Admiralty and in Parliament, Pepys's unbending passion for efficiency and honesty (combined with a certain childlike insistence on his own virtue and capacity for being always in the right) made for him powerful and bitter enemies.

One of these enemies was Lord Shaftesbury, who in 1678 endeavoured to strike at the succession and at the Catholic successor, the Duke of York, by implicating Pepys in the mysterious murder of the London magistrate Sir Edmund Berry Godfrey, the crime on which the full credulity of the populace in the Popish Plot (described in the previous section) depended. When Pepys produced an unanswerable alibi, his enemies endeavoured to fasten Godfrey's murder on him indirectly by accusing his confidential clerk, Samuel Atkins. Despite the interrogation methods employed against him, Pepys also proved an alibi for Atkins, who would otherwise almost certainly have perished. Six months later Pepys was flung into the Tower of London on a variety of false charges concocted by his enemies. Had not Charles II almost immediately dissolved Parliament and prevented a new one from meeting for a further year and a half, Pepys would have paid the penalty for his loyalty, efficiency, and incorruptibility with his life.

In 1683, when the king felt strong enough to ignore his opponents, Pepys was taken back into the public service, and in the spring of 1684, he was recalled by Charles II to his old post. As secretary of the affairs of the Admiralty of England, he combined the modern offices of first lord and secretary of the Admiralty, both administering the service and answering for it in Parliament. For the next four and a half years, Pepys was one of the greatest men in England, controlling the largest spending department of state. With his habitual courage and industry, he set himself to rebuild the naval edifice that the inefficiency and corruption of his enemies had shattered. When, at the beginning of 1689, after James II had been driven from the country, Pepys retired, he had created a navy strong enough to maintain a long ascendancy in the world's seas.

Pepys's last 14 years were spent in honourable retirement, amassing and arranging the library that he ultimately left to Magdalene College, Cambridge, corresponding with scholars and artists, and collecting material for a history of the navy that he never lived to complete. After his death, fellow diarist John Evelyn wrote of him: "He was universally belov'd, hospitable, generous, learned in many things, skilled in music, a very great cherisher of learned men of whom he had the conversation."

The Diary

The diary by which Pepys is chiefly known was kept between his 27th and 36th years. Written in shorthand, with the names in longhand, it extends to 1,250,000 words. It is far more than an ordinary record of its writer's thoughts and actions; it is a supreme work of art.

Pepys possessed the gift of summing up a scene or person in a few brilliant, arresting words. He makes us see what he sees in a flash: his Aunt James, "a poor, religious, well-meaning, good soul, talking of nothing but God Almighty, and that with so much innocence that mightily pleased me"; and his sister Pall, "a pretty, good-bodied woman and not over thick, as I thought she would have been, but full of freckles and not handsome in the face." He could describe with wonderful vividness a great scene, as when, for instance, the Great Fire of London threatened his home with destruction:

> *We saw the fire as only one entire arch of fire from this to the other side of the bridge, and in a bow up the hill for an arch of above a mile long: it made me weep to see it. The churches, houses, and all on fire and flaming at once; and a horrid noise the flames made, and the cracking of houses at their ruin.*

Pepys also possessed the artist's gift of being able to select the vital moment. He makes his readers share the very life of his time: "I staid up till the bell-man came by with his bell just under my window as I was writing of this very line, and cried, 'Past one of the clock, and a cold, and frosty, windy morning.'" He tells of the guttering candle, "which makes me write thus slobberingly," and of his new watch—"But Lord! to see how much of my old folly and childishness hangs on me still that I cannot forebear carrying my watch in my hand in the coach all the afternoon and seeing what o'clock it is one hundred times." He excluded nothing from his journal that seemed to him essential, however much it told against himself, for he possessed in a unique degree the quality of complete honesty. His diary paints not only his own infirmities but the frailty of all humankind.

NICOLAS BOILEAU

(b. November 1, 1636, Paris—d. March 13, 1711, Paris)

Nicolas Boileau-Despréaux was a French poet and a leading literary critic in his day. He was known for his influence in upholding classical standards in both French and English literature.

He was the son of a government official who had started his career as a clerk. Boileau made good progress at the Collège d'Harcourt and was encouraged to take up literary work by his brother Gilles Boileau, who was already established as a man of letters.

Boileau began by writing satires (*c.* 1658) attacking well-known public figures, which he read privately to his friends. After a printer who had managed to obtain the texts published them in 1666, Boileau brought out an authenticated version (March 1666) that he toned down considerably from the original. The following year he wrote one of the most successful of mock-heroic epics, *Le Lutrin* ("The Lectern"; Eng. trans. *Boileau's Lutrin: A Mock-Heroic Poem*), dealing with a quarrel of two ecclesiastical dignitaries over where to place a lectern in a chapel.

In 1674 he published *L'Art poétique* (*The Art of Poetry*), a didactic treatise in verse, setting out rules for the composition of poetry in the classical tradition. At the time, the work was considered of great importance, the definitive handbook of classical principles. It strongly influenced the English Augustan poets and critics Samuel Johnson, John Dryden, and Alexander Pope. It is now valued more for the insight it provides into the literary controversies of the period.

In 1677 Boileau was appointed historiographer royal and for 15 years avoided literary controversy; he was elected to the French Academy in 1684. Boileau resumed his disputatious role in 1692, when the literary world found itself divided between the so-called ancients—who believed that ancient Greece and Rome had supplied the only literature worthy of emulation—and moderns, who disagreed. Seeing women as supporters of the moderns, Boileau wrote his antifeminist satire *Contre les femmes*

("Against Women," published as *Satire x*, 1694), followed notably by *Sur l'amour de Dieu* ("On the Love of God," published as *Epitre xii*, 1698).

Boileau did not create the rules of classical drama and poetry, although it was long assumed that he had—a misunderstanding he did little to dispel. They had already been formulated by previous French writers, but Boileau expressed them in striking and vigorous terms. He also translated the classical treatise *On the Sublime*, attributed to Longinus. Ironically, it became one of the key sources of the aesthetics of Romanticism.

Jean Racine

(baptized December 22, 1639, La Ferté-Milon, France—d. April 21, 1699, Paris)

Jean-Baptiste Racine was a French dramatic poet and historiographer who was renowned for his mastery of French classical tragedy. His reputation rests on the plays he wrote between 1664 and 1677, notably *Andromaque* (1667), *Britannicus* (1669), *Bérénice* (1670), *Bajazet* (1672), and *Phèdre* (1677).

Life

Racine was born into a provincial family of minor administrators. His mother died 13 months after he was born, and his father died two years later. His paternal grandparents took him in, and when his grandmother, Marie des Moulins, became a widow, she brought Racine, then age nine, with her to the convent of Port-Royal des Champs near Paris. Since a group of devout scholars and teachers had founded a school there, Racine had the opportunity —rare for an orphan of modest social origins—to study the classics of Latin and Greek literature with distinguished masters. The school was steeped in the austere Roman Catholic reform movement known as Jansenism, which had recently been condemned by the church as heretical. Since the French monarchy suspected the Jansenists of being theologically and politically subversive, Racine's lifelong relationship with his former friends and teachers remained ambivalent, inasmuch as the ambitious artist sought admittance into the secular realm of court society.

Racine spent the years from 1649 to 1653 at Port-Royal, transferred to the College of Beauvais for almost two years, and then returned to Port-Royal in October 1655 to perfect his studies in rhetoric. The school at Port-Royal was closed by the authorities in 1656, but Racine was allowed to stay on there. When he was 18 he was sent to study law at the College of Harcourt in Paris. Racine had both the disposition and the talent to thrive in the cultural climate of Paris, where to conform and to please—in Racine's case, to please by his pen—were indispensable assets. One of the first manifestations of Racine's intentions was his composition of a sonnet in praise of Cardinal Mazarin, the prime minister of France, for successfully concluding a peace treaty with Spain (1659). This tribute reveals Racine's strategy of social conquest through literature.

There were three ways for a writer to survive in Racine's day: to attract a royal audience, to obtain an ecclesiastical benefice, or to compose for the theatre. The first was out of the question for the neophyte Racine, though he would eventually receive many gratuities in the course of his career. In 1661 Racine tried, through his mother's family, to acquire an ecclesiastical benefice from the diocese of Uzès in Languedoc, though without success after residing there for almost two years. He then returned to Paris to try his hand as a dramatist, even if it meant estrangement from his Jansenist mentors, who disapproved of his involvement with the theatre. A reaction from them was not long in coming. In the same month that Racine's play *Alexandre le grand* (1665) received its premiere, his former teacher Pierre Nicole published a public letter accusing novelists or playwrights of having no more redeeming virtues than a "public poisoner." Though Nicole avoided any direct reference to him, Racine believed that he was the object of Nicole's wrath and responded with a stinging open letter.

Racine's first play, *Amasie*, was never produced and has not survived. His career as a dramatist began with the production by Molière's troupe of his play *La Thébaïde; ou, Les Frères ennemis* ("The Thebaide; or, The Enemy Brothers") at the Palais-Royal Theatre on June 20, 1664. Molière's troupe also produced Racine's next play, *Alexandre le grand* (*Alexander the Great*), which premiered at the Palais Royal on December 4, 1665. This play was so well received that Racine secretly negotiated with the Hôtel de Bourgogne—a rival troupe that was more skilled in performing tragedy —to present a "second premiere" of *Alexandre* on December 15. The break with Molière was irrevocable—Racine even seduced Molière's leading actress, Thérèse du Parc, into joining him personally and professionally—and from this point onward all of Racine's secular tragedies would be presented by the actors of the Hôtel de Bourgogne.

Of the three audiences that a dramatist had to win over to succeed in the theatre—the court, the general public, and the scholar critics—Racine doggedly pursued all, though he had sharp clashes with the third group, who were mostly friends of his great rival, the older dramatist Pierre Corneille. Racine followed up his first masterpiece, *Andromaque* (1667), with the comedy *Les Plaideurs* (1668; *The Litigants*) before returning to tragedy with two plays set in imperial Rome, *Britannicus* (1669) and *Bérénice* (1670). He situated *Bajazet* (1672) in nearly contemporary Turkish history and depicted a famous enemy of Rome in *Mithridate* (1673) before returning to Greek mythology in *Iphigénie en Aulide* (1674; *Iphigenia in Aulis*) and the play that was his crowning achievement, *Phèdre* (1677). By this time Racine had achieved remarkable success both in the theatre and through it; his plays were ideally suited for dramatic expression and were also a useful vehicle for the social aspirations of their insecure and quietly driven author. Racine was the first French author to live principally on the income provided by his writings.

Within several months of the appearance of *Phèdre*, Racine married the pious and unintellectual Catherine de Romanet, with whom he would have two sons and five daughters. At about the same time, he retired from the commercial theatre and accepted the coveted post of royal historiographer with his friend Nicolas Boileau. Racine's withdrawal from the stage at the height of his prestige as a professional playwright probably sprang from a combination of factors. The preface he wrote for *Phèdre* leads one to believe that he was seeking a reconciliation with the Jansenists. He was, at the same time, leaving the socially disadvantageous situation of a playwright for the rarefied atmosphere of the court of King Louis XIV. Having to quit the theatre to assume his new duties near the king, Racine could now afford to effect a rapprochement with the Jansenists. He may also have found it difficult to continue to respect the cardinal principle of classical art—unity. In *Phèdre* there is fragmentation at significant levels: cosmic, social, psychological, and physical. Since fragmentation is a subversive notion in classical art, perhaps Racine abandoned a genre to whose classical tenets he no longer subscribed.

Jean Racine. DEA/G. Dagli Orti/De Agostini/Getty Images

As one of the royal historiographers, Racine chronicled Louis XIV's military campaigns in suitable prose. In 1679 he was accused by Catherine Monvoisin (called La Voisin) of having poisoned his mistress and star actress, the Marquise du Parc, but no formal charges were pressed and no consequences ensued. Racine's official duties culminated in the *Eloge historique du Roi sur ses conquêtes* (1682; "The Historical Panegyric for the King on His Conquests"). He also wrote the *Cantiques spirituels* (1694) and worked hard to establish his status and his fortune. In 1672 he was elected to the French Academy, and he came to exert almost dictatorial powers over it. In 1674 he acquired the noble title of treasurer of France, and he eventually obtained the higher distinctions of ordinary gentleman of the king (1690) and secretary of the king (1696).

In response to requests from Louis XIV's consort Madame de Maintenon, Racine returned to the theatre to write two religious plays for the convent girls at Saint-Cyr: *Esther* (1689) and *Athalie* (1691). His other undertakings during his last years were to reedit, in 1687 and finally in 1697, the edition of his complete works that he had first published in 1676, and to compose, probably as his last work, the *Abrégé de l'histoire de Port-Royal* ("Short History of Port-Royal"). Racine died in 1699 from cancer of the liver. In a codicil to his will, he expressed his wish to be buried at Port-Royal. When Louis XIV had Port-Royal razed in 1710, Racine's remains were transferred to a tomb in the Parisian church of Saint-Étienne-du-Mont.

Major Works

French classical tragedy pivots around two basic subjects: passion and politics. Since Racine's audience was intrigued by plots that dealt with the succession to a throne, he doubled their pleasure in his first successful play, *La Thébaïde*, by creating two legitimate pretenders who are also identical twins. The play centres on the twin sons of Oedipus who slay one another in mortal combat, one defending, the other attacking, their native city of Thebes. The deep hatred between the two brothers sounds the notes of separation, disunion, and alienation that would characterize all Racinian tragedy.

In *Andromaque* (1667) Racine replaced heroism with realism in a tragedy about the folly and blindness of unrequited love among a chain of four characters. The play is set in Epirus, Greece, after the Trojan War. Pyrrhus vainly loves his captive, the Trojan widow Andromache, and is in turn loved by the Greek princess Hermione, who in her turn is loved by Orestes. Power, intimidation, and emotional blackmail become the recourses by which these characters try to transmit the depths of their feelings to their beloved. But this form of communication is ultimately frustrated because the characters' deep-seated insecurity renders them self-absorbed and immune to empathy. Murder, suicide, and madness have destroyed all of them except Andromache by the play's end. *Andromaque*'s audience was fully aware that they were witnessing a new and powerful conception of the human condition in which passionate relationships are seen as basically political in their means and expression. *Andromaque* is more skillfully crafted than Racine's previous efforts: its exposition is a model of clarity and concision; the interplay of love, hate, and indifference are subtly yet compellingly arranged; and the rhetoric is forceful but close to normal speech. The play was the first of Racine's major tragedies and enjoyed public success.

With *Britannicus* (1669) Racine posed a direct challenge to Corneille's specialty: tragedy with a Roman setting. Racine portrays the events leading up to the moment when the teenage emperor Nero cunningly and ruthlessly frees himself from the tutelage of his domineering mother, Agrippina, and has Britannicus, a legitimate pretender to the throne, poisoned in the course of a fatal banquet of fraternal reconciliation. Despite its failure when it premiered in 1669, *Britannicus* has remained one of Racine's most frequently produced dramas.

Bérénice (1670) marks the decisive point in Racine's theatrical career, for with this play he found a felicitous combination of elements that he would use, without radical alteration, for the rest of his secular tragedies: a love interest, a relatively uncomplicated plot, striking rhetorical passages, and a highly poetic use of time. *Bérénice* is built around the unusual premise of three characters who are ultimately forced to live apart because of their virtuous sense of duty. In the play, Titus, who is to become the new Roman emperor, and his friend Antiochus are both in love with Berenice, the queen of Palestine. The play's "majestic sadness," as Racine put it in his preface to the play, flows from the tragic necessity of separation for individuals who yearn for union with their beloved and who express their sorrow in some of the most haunting passages of all of Racine's plays.

Racine followed the simplicity of *Bérénice* and its three main characters with a violent, relatively crowded production, *Bajazet* (1672). The play's themes of unrequited love and the struggle for power under the unrelenting pressure of time are recognizably Racinian, but its locale, the court of the Ottoman sultan in Constantinople, is the only contemporary setting used by Racine in any of his plays, and was sufficiently far removed in distance and in mores from 17th-century France to create an alluring exoticism for contemporary audiences. In the play, the main characters — the young prince Bajazet, his beloved Atalide, and the jealous sultana Roxane — are the mortal victims of the despotic cruelty of the absent sultan Amurat, whose reign is maintained by violence and secrecy.

Phèdre (1677) is Racine's supreme accomplishment because of the rigour and simplicity of its organization, the emotional power of its language, and the profusion of its images and meanings. Racine presents Phaedra as consumed by an incestuous passion for her stepson, Hippolytus. Receiving false information that her husband, King Theseus, is dead, Phaedra declares her love to Hippolytus, who is horrified. Theseus returns and is falsely informed that Hippolytus has been the aggressor toward Phaedra. Theseus invokes the aid of the god Neptune to destroy his son, after which Phaedra kills herself out of guilt and sorrow. A structural pattern of cycles and circles in *Phèdre* reflects a conception of human existence as essentially changeless, recurrent, and therefore asphyxiatingly tragic. Phaedra's own desire to flee the snares of passion repeatedly prompts her to contemplate a voluntary exile. References to ancient Greek mythological figures and to a wide range of geographical places lend a vast, cosmic dimension to the moral itinerary of Phaedra as she suffers bitterly from her incestuous propensities and a sense of her own degradation. *Phèdre* constitutes a daring representation of the contagion of sin and its catastrophic results.

Racine has been hailed by posterity as the foremost practitioner of tragedy in French history and the uncontested master of French classicism. He became the virtuoso of the poetic metre used in 17th-century French tragedy, the alexandrine line, and paid unwavering attention to the properly theatrical aspects of his plays, from actors' diction and gestures to space and decor. Ultimately, Racine's reputation derives from his unforgettable characters who, much like their creator, betray an inferiority complex in their noble yet frustrated attempts to transcend their limitations.

MARIANA ALCOFORADO

(baptized April 22, 1640, Beja, Portugal — d. July 28, 1723, Beja)

Mariana Alcoforado was a Portuguese nun long believed to have written *Lettres portugaise* (1669; "Portuguese Letters"), a widely read collection of five love letters. Most modern authorities reject her authorship in favour of Gabriel-Joseph de Lavergne, viscount of Guilleragues.

Alcoforado entered the convent of Nôtre Dame de la Conception in 1656 and became vice-abbess in 1709. The letters appeared in January 1669 in French, purportedly translated from lost originals. The publisher gave no information about his sources, nor the name of the translator. The letters were extremely popular, not least because of the intrigue to which they referred: a French officer had seduced a nun of good family in a convent in the province of Alentejo. Fearing the consequences, he had returned hurriedly to France. The letters vividly describe the nun's betrayed faith and disillusionment, and they were generally accepted as authentic at the time of their first publication.

In later editions the "man of quality" was identified as the "chevalier de C—" (taken to be the marquis de Chamilly) and the translator as "Guilleragues." During the 19th century, research proved that a nun called Maria Ana Alcoforado had been living at Beja in the 1660s. Despite certain inconsistencies, it was assumed that she was the author, until the scholar F.C. Green in 1926 found the original royal privilege (1668) that stated Guilleragues was the author, not the translator, of the *Lettres portugaises*.

Despite this evidence, however, debate over their author-ship continued into the 21st century.

The letters' effects were great. They were praised for sincerity and passion by many readers, and they influenced numerous writers, from French author and critic Stendhal to German poet Rainer Maria Rilke. Regardless of their authenticity, the *Lettres portugaises* remain a powerfully moving account of love and betrayal, and they were often republished throughout the 20th century, appearing in English translation under such titles as *The Love Letters of a Portuguese Nun* and *Letters from a Portuguese Nun*.

Aphra Behn

(b. 1640?, Harbledown?, Kent, England—d. April 16, 1689, London)

The English dramatist, fiction writer, and poet Aphra Behn was the first Englishwoman known to earn her living by writing.

Her origin remains a mystery, in part because Behn may have deliberately obscured her early life. One tradition identifies Behn as the child known only as Ayfara or Aphra who traveled in the 1650s with a couple named Amis to Suriname, which was then an English possession. She was more likely the daughter of a barber, Bartholomew Johnson, who may or may not have sailed with her and the rest of her family to Suriname in 1663. She returned to England in 1664 and married a merchant named Behn; he died (or the couple separated) soon after. Her wit and talent having brought her into high esteem, she was employed by King Charles II in secret service in the Netherlands in 1666. Unrewarded and

Aphra Behn. Hulton Archive/Getty Images

briefly imprisoned for debt, she began to write to support herself.

Behn's early works were tragicomedies in verse. In 1670 her first play, *The Forc'd Marriage*, was produced, and *The Amorous Prince* followed a year later. Her sole tragedy, *Abdelazer*, was staged in 1676. However, she turned increasingly to light comedy and farce over the course of the 1670s. Many of these witty and vivacious comedies, notably *The Rover* (two parts, produced 1677 and 1681), were commercially successful. *The Rover* depicts the adventures of a small group of English Cavaliers in Madrid and Naples during the exile of the future Charles II. *The Emperor of the Moon*, first performed in 1687, presaged the harlequinade, a form of comic theatre that evolved into the English pantomime.

Though Behn wrote many plays, her fiction today draws more interest. Her short novel *Oroonoko* (1688) tells the story of an enslaved African prince whom Behn claimed to have known in South America. Its engagement with the themes of slavery, race, and gender, as well as its influence on the development of the English novel, helped to make it, by the turn of the 21st century, her best-known work. Behn's other fiction includes the multipart epistolary novel *Love-Letters Between a Nobleman and His Sister* (1684–87) and *The Fair Jilt* (1688).

Behn's versatility, like her output, was immense; she wrote other popular works of fiction, and she often adapted works by older dramatists. She also wrote poetry, the bulk of which was collected in *Poems upon Several Occasions, with A Voyage to the Island of Love* (1684) and *Lycidus; or, The Lover in Fashion* (1688). Behn's charm and generosity won her a wide circle of friends, and her relative freedom as a professional writer, as well as the subject matter of her works, made her the object of some scandal.

WILLIAM WYCHERLEY

(b. 1641—d. January 1, 1716, London)

The English dramatist William Wycherley attempted to reconcile in his plays a personal conflict between deep-seated puritanism and an ardent physical nature. He perhaps succeeded best in *The Country-Wife* (1675), in which satiric comment on excessive jealousy and complacency was blended with a richly comic presentation, the characters unconsciously revealing themselves in laughter-provoking conversation. It was as a satirist that his own age most admired him: one contemporary, the dramatist William Congreve, regarded Wycherley as one appointed "to lash this crying age."

Wycherley's father was steward to the marquess of Winchester. Wycherley was sent to be educated in France at age 15. There he became a Roman Catholic. After returning to England to study law, in 1660 he entered Queen's College, Oxford. He soon left without a degree, though he had converted back to Protestantism. Little is known of his life in the 1660s; he may have traveled to Spain as a diplomat, and he probably fought in the naval war against the Dutch in 1665. In this period he drafted his first play, *Love in a Wood; or, St. James's Park*, and in the autumn of 1671 it was presented in London, bringing its author instant acclaim. Wycherley was taken up by Barbara Villiers, duchess of Cleveland, whose favours he shared with King Charles II, and he was admitted to the circle of wits at court. His next play, *The Gentleman Dancing-Master*, was presented in 1672 but proved unsuccessful. These early plays—both of which have some good farcical moments —followed tradition in "curing excess" by presenting a satiric portrait of variously pretentious characters. *The Plain-Dealer*, presented in 1676, satirizes rapacious greed. The satire is crude and brutal, but pointed and effective. In *The Country-Wife*, acted a year earlier, the criticism of manners and society remains severe, but there is no longer a sense of the author despising his characters.

Wycherley, who had led a fashionably dissolute life during these years, fell ill in 1678. In 1680 he secretly married the countess of Drogheda, a rigid puritan who kept him on such a short rein that he lost his favour at court. A year later the lady died, leaving her husband a considerable fortune. But the will was contested, and Wycherley ruined himself fighting the case. Cast into a debtor's prison, he was rescued seven years later by King James II, who paid off most of his debts and allowed him a small pension. This was lost when James was deposed in 1688. In the early 18th century, Wycherley befriended the young poet and critic Alexander Pope, who helped revise his poems. On his deathbed, Wycherley received the last rites of the Roman Catholic church, to which he had apparently reverted after being rescued from prison.

IHARA SAIKAKU

(b. 1642, Osaka, Japan—d. September 9, 1693, Osaka)

The poet and novelist Ihara Saikaku was one of the most brilliant figures of the 17th-century revival of Japanese literature. He enchanted readers with racy accounts of the amorous and financial affairs of the merchant class and the period's pleasure quarters.

Saikaku (whose original name was probably Hirayama Tōgo) first won fame for his amazing facility in composing haikai, humorous *renga* (linked-verse) poems from which the 17-syllable haiku was derived. In 1671 he turned out, in "a day and a night," 1,600 verses. Not satisfied with composing at the rate of one verse a minute, he steadily increased his prowess, reaching 4,000 in 24 hours in 1680 and the incredible figure of 23,500 in 1684. This was somewhat more than 16 haikai per minute, and the performance earned him the nickname of the "20,000 poet." Saikaku continued to write verse at more normal speeds, but his style was considered so bizarre that rival poets called it "Dutch" to indicate its outlandishness.

Saikaku is best known, however, for his novels, written in a swift, allusive, elliptic style that stems from his training as a haikai poet. Their content reflects, from many angles, Japanese society in a time when the merchant class had risen to such prominence that its tastes prevailed in the arts and the licensed pleasure quarters catered to its whims. *Kōshoku ichidai otoko* (1682; *The Life of an Amorous Man*), the first of Saikaku's many novels concerned with the pleasure quarters, relates the erotic adventures of its hero, Yonosuke, from his precocious experiences at the age of 6 to his departure at 60 for an island of women. Of other works in a similar vein, the best is thought to be *Kōshoku gonin onna* (1686; *Five Women Who Loved Love*).

Saikaku also wrote novels about the samurai (aristocratic warrior caste), but they were generally considered inferior to his erotic tales or to such accounts of tradesmen's lives as *Nihon Eitaigura* (1688; *The Japanese Family Storehouse*), a collection of stories on how to make (or lose) a fortune. Whatever the subject, Saikaku's satiric humour and his knack of being able to seize the one detail that best evokes a person's character or milieu are always conspicuous. Although most at home in dealing with the lively atmosphere of Osaka, he wrote about all Japan. His *Saikaku Shokoku Banashi* (1685; "Saikaku's Tales from the

Provinces") records many stories picked up on his travels. His popularity was enormous throughout Japan, and his influence on fiction continued after his death.

THOMAS SHADWELL

(b. 1642?, Norfolk, England—d. November 19, 1692, London)

The English dramatist and poet laureate Thomas Shadwell was known for his broad comedies of manners and for being the butt of the poet and playwright John Dryden's satire.

Educated at Caius College, Cambridge, and at the Middle Temple in London, Shadwell—after the restoration of Charles II as king in 1660—became one of the court wits and an acquaintance of the dramatist Sir Robert Howard and his brother, Edward. He satirized both Howards in *The Sullen Lovers* (1668), an adaptation of Molière's *Les Fâcheux*.

Shadwell wrote 18 plays, including a pastoral, *The Royal Shepherdess* (1669), an opera, *The Enchanted Island* (1674; adapted from William Shakespeare's *The Tempest*), a tragedy, *Psyche* (1674–75), and a blank verse tragedy, *The Libertine* (1675). In 1687 he translated the ancient Roman poet Juvenal's *The Tenth Satyr* and composed bitter attacks upon Dryden. He also instituted New Year and birthday odes when he became poet laureate.

Shadwell's friendship with Dryden ended with the political crisis of 1678–79, when Shadwell espoused the Whig cause, producing *The Lancashire Witches*, which caused offense with its anti-Catholic propaganda and attacks upon the Anglican clergy. Their feud produced three satires by each in the course of 1682, of which the best known are Dryden's *Absalom and Achitophel* and his mock-heroic verse satire, *MacFlecknoe*. The issue was partly political, partly a difference of opinion over dramatic technique, particularly Dryden's scorn for the wit of playwright Ben Jonson, who was one of Shakespeare's contemporaries, and Shadwell's uncritical reverence for Jonson.

When Dryden was removed from the laureateship and the position of historiographer royal during the Glorious Revolution (1688–89), Shadwell succeeded him. Shadwell continued in Jonson's style of the comedy of "humours" in many of his plays. They form a link between Jonson's art and the realistic fiction of the 18th century. *The Humourists* (1670) was a failure because he satirized the vices and follies of an age that did not care for generalized satire. His next play, *The Miser* (1671–72), was a rhymed adaptation of Molière that showed his gradual shift toward the wit of the comedy of manners. *Epsom-Wells* (1672) became his greatest success, being played for nearly half a century. *The Virtuoso* (1676) was an inventive satire of the Royal Society. In *The Squire of Alsatia* (1688) he presented middle-class people and villains, rascals and thieves. *Bury-Fair* (1689) showed the influence of the popular farce that was to put his fame in eclipse in his later years. His last play, *The Scowrers* (1690), was a precursor of sentimental comedy.

BASHŌ

(b. 1644, Ueno, Iga province, Japan—d. November 28, 1694, Osaka)

Matsuo Bashō was the supreme Japanese haiku poet. He greatly enriched the 17-syllable haiku form and made it an accepted medium of artistic expression.

Interested in haiku from an early age, Bashō (the pseudonym of Matsuo Munefusa) at first put his literary interests aside and entered the service of a local feudal lord. After his lord's death in 1666, however, Bashō abandoned his samurai (warrior) status to devote himself to poetry. Moving to the capital city of Edo (now Tokyo), he gradually acquired a reputation as a poet and critic. In 1679 he wrote his first verse in the "new style" for which he came to be known:

> *On a withered branch*
> *A crow has alighted:*
> *Nightfall in autumn.*

The simple descriptive mood evoked by this statement and the comparison and contrast of two independent phenomena became the hallmark of Bashō's style. He attempted to go beyond the stale dependence on form and ephemeral allusions to current gossip that had been characteristic of haiku, which in his day had amounted to little but a popular literary pastime. Instead he insisted that the haiku must be at once unhackneyed and eternal. Following the Zen philosophy he studied, Bashō attempted to compress the meaning of the world into the simple pattern of his poetry, disclosing hidden hopes in small things and showing the interdependence of all objects.

In 1684 Bashō made the first of many journeys that figure so importantly in his work. His accounts of his travels are prized not only for the haiku that record various sights along the way but also for the equally beautiful prose passages that furnish the backgrounds. *Oku no hosomichi* (1694; *The Narrow Road to the Deep North*), describing his visit to northern Japan, is one of the loveliest works of Japanese literature.

Bashō (standing), *woodblock print by Tsukioka Yoshitoshi, late 19th century.* Library of Congress Prints and Photographs Division

On his travels Bashō also met local poets and competed with them in composing the linked verse (*renga*), an art in which he so excelled that some critics believe his *renga* were his finest work. When Bashō began writing *renga* the link between successive verses had generally depended on a pun or play on words, but he insisted that poets must go beyond mere verbal dexterity and link their verses by "perfume," "echo," "harmony," and other delicately conceived criteria.

One term frequently used to describe Bashō's poetry is *sabi,* which means the love of the old, the faded, and the unobtrusive, a quality found in the verse

Scent of chrysanthemums...
And in Nara
All the ancient Buddhas.

Here the musty smell of the chrysanthemums blends with the visual image of the dusty, flaking statues in the old capital. Living a life that was in true accord with the gentle spirit of his poetry, Bashō maintained an austere, simple home that contrasted with the general flamboyance of his times. On occasion he withdrew from society altogether, retiring to Fukagawa, site of his Bashō-an ("Cottage of the Plantain Tree"), a simple hut from which the poet derived his pen name. Later admirers, honouring both the man and his poetry, revered him as the saint of the haiku.

The Narrow Road to Oku (1996), Donald Keene's translation of *Oku no hosomichi*, provides the original text and a modern-language version by Kawabata Yasunari. *The Monkey's Straw Raincoat and Other Poetry of the Basho School* (1981), a translation by Earl Miner and Hiroko Odagiri, presents a celebrated linked-verse sequence in which Bashō took part, along with a commentary.

JEAN DE LA BRUYÈRE

(b. August 1645, Paris, France—d. May 10/11, 1696, Versailles)

Jean de La Bruyère was a French satiric moralist who is best known for one work, *Les Caractères de Théophraste traduits du grec avec Les Caractères ou les moeurs de ce siècle* (1688; *The Characters, or the Manners of the Age, with The Characters of Theophrastus*), which is considered to be one of the masterpieces of French literature.

La Bruyère studied law at Orléans. Through the intervention of Jacques-Bénigne Bossuet, the eminent humanist and theologian, La Bruyère became one of the tutors to the Duke de Bourbon, grandson of the Prince de Condé, and remained in the Condé household as librarian at Chantilly. His years there were probably unhappy because, although he was proud of his middle-class origin, he was a constant butt of ridicule because of his ungainly figure, morose manner, and biting tongue; the bitterness of his book reflects the inferiority of his social position. His situation, however, afforded him the opportunity to make penetrating observations on the power of money in a demoralized society, the tyranny of social custom, and the perils of aristocratic idleness, fads, and fashions.

La Bruyère's masterpiece appeared as an appendage to his translation of the 4th-century BCE character writer Theophrastus in 1688. His method was that of Theophrastus: to define qualities such as dissimulation, flattery, or rusticity and then to give instances of them in actual people, making reflections on the "characters," or "characteristics," of the time, for the purpose of reforming manners. La Bruyère had an immense and richly varied vocabulary and a sure grasp of technique. His satire is constantly sharpened by variety of presentation, and he achieves vivid stylistic effects, which were admired by such eminent writers as the 19th-century novelists Gustave Flaubert and the Goncourt brothers.

Eight editions of the *Caractères* appeared during La Bruyère's lifetime. The portrait sketches were expanded because of their great popularity. Readers began putting real names to the personages and compiling keys to them, but La Bruyère denied that any was a portrait of a single person.

Topical allusions in his book made his election to the French Academy difficult, but he was eventually elected in 1693. The Duke de Saint-Simon, the diplomat and memoirist, described him as honourable, lovable, and unpretentious.

JOHN WILMOT, 2ND EARL OF ROCHESTER

(b. April 1, 1647, Ditchley Manor House, Oxfordshire, England—
d. July 26, 1680, Woodstock, England)

John Wilmot, 2nd earl of Rochester, was a court wit and a poet who helped establish English satiric poetry.

Wilmot succeeded his father to the earldom in 1658 and received an M.A. at Oxford in 1661. King Charles II, probably out of gratitude to the 1st earl, who had helped him to escape after the Battle of Worcester (1651), gave the young earl an annual pension and appointed Sir Andrew Balfour, a Scottish physician, as his tutor. They travelled on the Continent for three years until 1664.

On his return, as a leader of the court wits, Rochester became notorious at the Restoration court as the hero of numerous escapades and the lover of various mistresses. Among them was the actress Elizabeth Barry, whom he is said to have trained for the stage, and an heiress, Elizabeth

Malet. He volunteered for the navy and served with distinction in the war against the Dutch (1665–67). In 1667 he married Elizabeth Malet and was appointed a gentleman of the bedchamber to the king. In 1673 John Dryden dedicated to Rochester his comedy *Marriage A-la-Mode* in complimentary terms, acknowledging his help in writing it.

Rochester is generally thought to be the most considerable poet and the most learned among the Restoration wits. A few of his love songs have passionate intensity; many are bold and frankly erotic celebrations of the pleasures of the flesh. He is also one of the most original and powerful of English satirists. His "History of Insipids" (1676) is a devastating attack on the government of Charles II, and his "Maim'd Debauchee" has been described as "a masterpiece of heroic irony." *A Satyr Against Mankind* (1675) anticipates the satirist Jonathan Swift in its scathing denunciation of rationalism and optimism and in the contrast it draws between human perfidy and folly and the instinctive wisdom of the animal world.

In 1674 Rochester was appointed ranger of Woodstock Forest, where much of his later poetry was written. His health was declining, and his thoughts were turning to serious matters. His correspondence (dated 1679–80) with the Deist Charles Blount shows a keen interest in philosophy and religion, further stimulated by his friendship with Gilbert Burnet, later bishop of Salisbury. Burnet recorded their religious discussions in *Some Passages of the Life and Death of John, Earl of Rochester* (1680). In 1680 he became seriously ill and experienced a religious conversion, followed by a recantation of his past; he ordered "all his profane and lewd writings" burned.

His single dramatic work, the posthumous *Valentinian* (1685), an attempt to rehandle a tragedy by John Fletcher, contains two of his finest lyrics. His letters to his wife and to his friend Henry Savile are among the best of the period and show an admirable mastery of easy, colloquial prose.

SOR JUANA INÉS DE LA CRUZ

(b. November 12, 1651?, San Miguel Nepantla, Viceroyalty of New Spain [now in Mexico] — d. April 17, 1695, Mexico City)

Sor Juana Inés de la Cruz was a poet, dramatist, scholar, and nun who distinguished herself as an outstanding writer of the Latin American colonial period and of the Hispanic Baroque.

Juana Ramírez de Asbaje (Sor Juana Inés de la Cruz's original name) thirsted for knowledge from her earliest years and throughout her life. As a female, she had little access to formal education and would be almost entirely self-taught. Juana was born out of wedlock to a family of modest means in either 1651 or, according to a baptismal certificate, 1648 (there is no scholarly consensus on her birth date). Her mother was a Creole and her father Spanish. Juana's mother sent the gifted child to live with relatives in Mexico City. There her prodigious intelligence attracted the attention of the viceroy, Antonio Sebastián de Toledo, marquis de Mancera. He invited her to court as a lady-in-waiting in 1664 and later had her knowledge tested by some 40 noted scholars. In 1667, given what she called her "total disinclination to marriage" and her wish "to have no fixed occupation which might curtail my freedom to study," Sor (Spanish: "Sister") Juana began her life as a nun with a brief stay in the order of the Discalced Carmelites. She moved in 1669 to the more lenient Convent of Santa Paula of the Hieronymite order in Mexico City, and there she took her vows. Sor Juana remained cloistered in the Convent of Santa Paula for the rest of her life.

Sor Juana Inés de la Cruz. Album/Oronoz/Album/SuperStock

Convent life afforded Sor Juana her own apartment, time to study and write, and the opportunity to teach music and drama to the girls in Santa Paula's school. She also functioned as the convent's archivist and accountant. In her convent cell, Sor Juana amassed one of the largest private libraries in the New World, together with a collection of musical and scientific instruments. She was able to continue her contact with other scholars and powerful members of the court. The patronage of the viceroy and vicereine of New Spain, notably that of the marquis and marquise de la Laguna from 1680 to 1688, helped her maintain her exceptional freedom. They visited her, favoured her, and had her works published in Spain. For her part, Sor Juana, though cloistered, became the unofficial court poet in the 1680s. Her plays in verse, occasional poetry, commissioned religious services, and writings for state festivals all contributed magnificently to the world outside the convent.

Sor Juana's success during her lifetime in what is today Mexico and her enduring significance are due at least in part to her mastery of the full range of poetic forms and themes of the Spanish Golden Age. She was the last great writer of the Hispanic Baroque and the first great exemplar of colonial Mexican culture. Her writings display many of the qualities of the works of Spanish writers who preceded her: the boundless inventiveness of Lope de Vega, the wit and wordplay of Francisco de Quevedo, and the dense erudition and strained syntax of Luis de Góngora. The schematic abstraction of the playwright Pedro Calderón de la Barca, who succeeded Vega as Spain's greatest playwright, can also be found in her work. Sor Juana employed all of the poetic models then in fashion, including sonnets, romances (ballad form), and so on. She drew on a vast stock of Classical, biblical, philosophical, and mythological sources. She wrote moral, satiric, and religious lyrics, along with many poems of praise to court figures. Though it is impossible to date much of her poetry, it is clear that, even after she became a nun, Sor Juana wrote secular love lyrics. Her breadth of range—from the serious to the comical and the scholarly to the popular—is equally unusual for a nun. Sor Juana authored both allegorical religious dramas and entertaining cloak-and-dagger plays. Notable in the popular vein are the *villancicos* (carols) that she composed to be sung in the cathedrals of Mexico City, Puebla, and Oaxaca. Sor Juana was as prolific as she was encyclopaedic. The authoritative modern edition of her complete works, edited by Alfonso Méndez Plancarte and Alberto G. Salceda, runs to four lengthy volumes.

Sor Juana placed her own stamp on Spanish 17th-century literature. All of the nun's poetry, however densely Baroque, exhibits her characteristically tight logic. Her philosophical poems can carry the Baroque theme of the deceptiveness of appearances into a defense of empiricism that borders on Enlightenment reasoning. Sor Juana celebrated woman as the seat of reason and knowledge rather than passion. Her famous poem "Hombres necios" ("Foolish Men") accuses men of the illogical behaviour that they criticize in women. Her many love poems in the first person show a woman's *desengaño* (disillusionment) with love, given the strife, pain, jealousy, and loneliness that it occasions. Other first-person poems have an obvious autobiographical element, dealing with the burdens of fame and intellect. Sor Juana's most significant full-length plays involve the actions of daring, ingenious women. Sor Juana also occasionally wrote of her native Mexico. The short play that introduces her religious drama *El divino Narciso* (1689; *The Divine Narcissus*, in a bilingual edition) blends the Aztec and Christian religions. Her various carols contain an amusing mix of Nahuatl (a Mexican Indian language) and Hispano-African and Spanish dialects.

Sor Juana's most important and most difficult poem, known as the *Primero sueño* (1692; *First Dream,* published in *A Sor Juana Anthology*, 1988), is both personal and universal. The date of its writing is unknown. It employs the convoluted poetic forms of the Baroque to recount the torturous quest of the soul for knowledge. In the poem's opening, as night falls, the soul is unchained from the body to dream. Over the course of the night's dreaming, the soul attempts unsuccessfully to gain total knowledge by following the philosophical paths of Neoplatonism and Scholasticism. As the sun rises and routs the night, the dream fades and the body awakens, but the soul determines to persist in its efforts. The last lines of the poem refer to a female "I," which associates the foregoing quest with its author. In fact, the entire 975-line poem, thick with erudition, attests to the nun's lifelong pursuit of learning.

The prodigiously accomplished Sor Juana achieved considerable renown in Mexico and in Spain. But with that renown came disapproval from church officials. Sor Juana broke with her Jesuit confessor, Antonio Núñez de Miranda, in the early 1680s because he had publicly maligned her. The nun's privileged situation began definitively to collapse after the departure for Spain of her protectors, the marquis and marquise de la Laguna. In November 1690, Manuel Fernández de Santa Cruz, bishop of Puebla, published without Sor Juana's permission her critique of a 40-year-old sermon by the Portuguese Jesuit preacher António Vieira. Fernández de Santa Cruz entitled the critique *Carta atenagórica* ("Letter Worthy of Athena"). Using the female pseudonym of Sister Filotea, he also admonished Sor Juana to concentrate on religious rather than secular studies.

Sor Juana responded to the bishop of Puebla in March 1691 with her magnificent self-defense and defense of all women's right to knowledge, the *Respuesta a sor Filotea de la Cruz* ("Reply to Sister Filotea of the Cross"; translated in *A Sor Juana Anthology*, 1988). In the autobiographical section of the document, Sor Juana traces the many obstacles that her powerful "inclination to letters" had forced her to surmount throughout her life. Among the obstacles she discusses is having been temporarily forbidden by a prelate to read, which caused her to study instead "everything that God has created, all of it being my letters." Sor Juana famously remarks, quoting an Aragonese poet and also echoing St. Teresa of Ávila: "One can perfectly well philosophize while cooking supper." She justifies her study of "human arts and sciences" as necessary to understand sacred theology. In her defense of education for women in general, Sor Juana lists as models learned women of biblical, Classical, and contemporary times. She uses the words of Church Fathers such as St. Jerome and St. Paul, bending them to her purposes, to argue that women are entitled to private instruction. Throughout the *Respuesta*, Sor Juana concedes some personal failings but remains strong in supporting her larger cause. Similarly, in the same year of 1691, Sor Juana wrote for the cathedral of Oaxaca some exquisite carols to St. Catherine of Alexandria that sing the praises of this learned woman and martyr.

Yet by 1694 Sor Juana had succumbed in some measure to external or internal pressures. She curtailed her literary pursuits. Her library and collections were sold for alms. She returned to her previous confessor, renewed her religious vows, and signed various penitential documents. Sor Juana died while nursing her sister nuns during an epidemic.

Her story and accomplishments, however, have helped her live on. She now stands as a national icon of Mexico and Mexican identity; her former cloister is a centre for higher education, and her image adorns Mexican currency. Because of rising interest in feminism and women's writing, Sor Juana came to new prominence in the late 20th century as the first published feminist of the New World and as the most outstanding writer of the Spanish American colonial period.

THOMAS OTWAY

(b. March 3, 1652, Trotton, near Midhurst, Sussex, England— d. April 14, 1685, London)

The English dramatist and poet Thomas Otway was one of the forerunners of sentimental drama through his convincing presentation of human emotions in an age of heroic but artificial tragedies. His masterpiece, *Venice Preserved*, was one of the greatest theatrical successes of his period.

Otway studied at Winchester College and at the University of Oxford but left in 1671 without taking a degree. He went to London, where he was offered a part by Aphra Behn in one of her plays. He was overcome by stage fright, and his first performance was his last. His first play, a rhyming tragedy called *Alcibiades*, was produced at the Duke's Theatre at Dorset Garden in September 1675. The part of Draxilla in this play was created by the well-known actress Elizabeth Barry, and Otway fell deeply in love with her. Six unsigned love letters, said to be addressed to Barry, were published in a collection that appeared in 1697, 12 years after Otway's death. His second play, *Don Carlos*, produced in June 1676, had an immense success on the stage and is the best of his rhymed heroic plays. *Titus and Berenice*, adapted from Molière, and *The Cheats of Scapin*, adapted from Jean Racine, were published together in 1677.

In 1678 Otway obtained a commission in an English regiment serving in the Netherlands, and he was abroad when his first comedy, *Friendship in Fashion*, was staged. His next play, *Caius Marius*, a curious mixture of a story from the historian Plutarch of ancient Greece with an adaptation of *Romeo and Juliet*, was staged in 1679. He published his powerful, gloomy autobiographical poem, *The Poet's Complaint of His Muse*, in 1680.

Otway's most memorable dramatic work was done in the last years of his short life. In the spring of 1680 his fine blank-verse tragedy *The Orphan* had great success on the stage. On March 1 in the same year his best comedy, *The Soldier's Fortune*, probably drawn from his military experience, was produced. *Venice Preserved*, also written in blank verse, was first performed at the Duke's Theatre in 1682. Until the middle of the 19th century it was probably revived more often than any poetic play except those of Shakespeare. John Dryden, who wrote the prologue, praised it highly. Otway's tragedies, particularly *Venice Preserved*, are notable for their psychological credibility and their clear and powerful presentation of human passions.

CHIKAMATSU MONZAEMON

(b. 1653, Echizen [now in Fukui prefecture], Japan—
d. January 6, 1725, Amagasaki, Settsu province?)

Chikamatsu Monzaemon was a Japanese playwright who is widely regarded as among the greatest dramatists of that country. He is credited with more than 100 plays, most of which were written as *jōruri* dramas, performed by puppets. He was the first author of *jōruri* to write works that not only gave the puppet operator the opportunity to display his skill but also were of considerable literary merit.

Chikamatsu, whose original name was Sugimori Nobumori, was born into a samurai family, but his father apparently abandoned his feudal duties sometime between 1664 and 1670, moving the family to Kyoto. While there, Chikamatsu served a member of the court aristocracy. The origin of his connection to the theatre is unknown. *Yotsugi Soga* (1683; "The Soga Heir"), a *jōruri*, is the first play that can be definitely attributed to Chikamatsu. The following year he wrote a Kabuki play, and by 1693 he was writing exclusively for actors. In 1703 he reestablished an earlier connection with Takemoto Gidayū, and he moved in 1705 from Kyoto to Osaka to be nearer to Gidayū's puppet theatre, the Takemoto-za. Chikamatsu remained a staff playwright for this theatre until his death.

Chikamatsu's works fall into two main categories: *jidaimono* (historical romances) and *sewamono* (domestic tragedies). Modern Western critics generally prefer the latter plays because they are more realistic and closer to European conceptions of drama, but the historical romances are more exciting as puppet plays. Some of Chikamatsu's views on the art of the puppet theatre have been preserved in *Naniwa miyage*, a work written by a friend, Hozumi Ikan, in 1738. There Chikamatsu is reported to have said, "Art is something that lies in the slender margin between the real and the unreal," and in his own works he endeavoured accordingly to steer between the fantasy that had been the rule in the puppet theatre and the realism that was coming into vogue.

The characters who populate Chikamatsu's domestic tragedies are merchants, housewives, servants, criminals,

An early 20th-century woodcut by Japanese artist Kyūho Noda depicts one of Chikamatsu's characters, a man on a ship looking out to sea. Library of Congress Prints and Photographs Division

prostitutes, and all the other varieties of people who lived in the Osaka of his day. Most of his domestic tragedies were based on actual incidents, such as double suicides of lovers. *Sonezaki shinjū* (1703; *The Love Suicides at Sonezaki*), for example, was written within a fortnight of the actual double suicide on which it is based. The haste of composition is not at all apparent even in this first example of Chikamatsu's double-suicide plays, the archetype of his other domestic tragedies.

Chikamatsu's most popular work was *Kokusenya kassen* (1715; *The Battles of Coxinga*), a historical melodrama based loosely on events in the life of the Chinese-Japanese adventurer who attempted to restore the Ming dynasty in China. Another celebrated work is *Shinjū ten no Amijima* (1720; *Double Suicide at Amijima*), still frequently performed. Despite Chikamatsu's eminence, however, the decline in popularity of puppet plays has resulted in most members of the theatregoing public being unfamiliar with his work, except in the abridgments and considerably revised versions used in Kabuki theatre, on film, and elsewhere. Eleven of his best-known plays appear in *Major Plays of Chikamatsu* (1961, reissued 1990), translated by Donald Keene. Mainly historical plays are in *Chikamatsu: Five Late Plays* (2001), translated by C. Andrew Gerstle.

DANIEL DEFOE

(b. 1660, London, England—d. April 24, 1731, London)

Daniel Defoe was an English novelist, pamphleteer, and journalist. He is best known as the author of *Robinson Crusoe* (1719–22) and *Moll Flanders* (1722).

Early Life

Defoe's father, James Foe, was a hardworking and fairly prosperous tallow chandler (perhaps also, later, a butcher), of Flemish descent. By his middle 30s, Daniel was calling himself "Defoe," probably reviving a variant of what may have been the original family name. As a Nonconformist, or Dissenter, Foe could not send his son to the University of Oxford or to Cambridge; he sent him instead to the excellent academy at Newington Green kept by the Reverend Charles Morton. There Defoe received an education in many ways better, and certainly broader, than any he would have had at an English university. Morton was an admirable teacher, later becoming first vice president of Harvard College; and the clarity, simplicity, and ease of his style of writing—together with the Bible, the works of John Bunyan, and the pulpit oratory of the day—may have helped to form Defoe's own literary style.

Although intended for the Presbyterian ministry, Defoe decided against this and by 1683 had set up as a merchant. He called trade his "beloved subject," and it was one of the abiding interests of his life. He dealt in many commodities, traveled widely at home and abroad, and became an acute and intelligent economic theorist, in many respects ahead of his time; but misfortune, in one form or another, dogged him continually. He wrote of himself:

> *No man has tasted differing fortunes more,*
> *And thirteen times I have been rich and poor.*

It was true enough. In 1692, after prospering for a while, Defoe went bankrupt for £17,000. Opinions differ as to the cause of his collapse: on his own admission, Defoe was apt to indulge in rash speculations and projects; he may not always have been completely scrupulous, and he later characterized himself as one of those tradesmen who had "done things which their own principles condemned, which they are not ashamed to blush for." But undoubtedly the main reason for his bankruptcy was the loss that he sustained in insuring ships during the war with France—he was one of 19 "merchants insurers" ruined in 1692. In this matter Defoe may have been incautious, but he was not dishonourable, and he dealt fairly with his creditors (some of whom pursued him savagely), paying off all but £5,000 within 10 years. He suffered further severe losses in 1703, when his prosperous brick-and-tile works near Tilbury failed during his imprisonment for political offenses, and he did not actively engage in trade after this time.

Soon after setting up in business, in 1684 Defoe married Mary Tuffley, the daughter of a well-to-do Nonconformist (Dissenting) merchant. Not much is known about her, and he mentions her little in his writings, but she seems to have been a loyal, capable, and devoted wife. She bore eight children, of whom six lived to maturity, and when Defoe died the couple had been married for 47 years.

Mature Life and Works

With Defoe's interest in trade went an interest in politics. The first of many political pamphlets by him appeared in 1683. When the Roman Catholic James II ascended the throne in 1685, Defoe—as a staunch Dissenter and with characteristic impetuosity—joined the ill-fated rebellion of the Duke of Monmouth, managing to escape after the disastrous Battle of Sedgemoor. Three years later James had fled to France, and Defoe rode to welcome the army of William of Orange—"*William*, the Glorious, Great, and Good, and Kind," as Defoe was to call him. Throughout William III's reign, Defoe supported him loyally, becoming his leading pamphleteer. In 1701, in reply to attacks on the "foreign" king, Defoe published his vigorous and witty poem *The True-Born Englishman*, an enormously popular work that is still very readable and relevant in its exposure of the fallacies of racial prejudice. Defoe was clearly proud of this work, because he sometimes designated himself "Author of 'The True-Born Englishman'" in later works.

Foreign politics also engaged Defoe's attention. Since the Treaty of Rijswijk (1697) had brought an uneasy end to the War of the Grand Alliance, which had pitted Louis XIV of France against his rivals in Europe, it had become increasingly probable that what would, in effect, be a European war would break out as soon as the childless king of Spain died. In 1701 five gentlemen of Kent presented a petition, demanding greater defense preparations, to the House of Commons (then Tory-controlled) and were illegally imprisoned. Next morning Defoe, "guarded with about 16 gentlemen of quality," presented the speaker, Robert Harley, with his famous document "Legion's Memorial," which reminded the Commons in outspoken terms that "Englishmen are no more to be slaves to Parliaments than to a King." It was effective: the Kentishmen were released, and Defoe was feted by the citizens of London. It had been a courageous gesture and one of which Defoe was ever afterward proud, but it undoubtedly branded him in Tory eyes as a dangerous man who must be brought down.

What did bring him down, only a year or so later, and consequently led to a new phase in his career, was a religious question—though it is difficult to separate religion from politics in this period. Both Dissenters and "Low Churchmen" were mainly Whigs, and the "highfliers"—the High-Church Tories—were determined to undermine this working alliance by stopping the practice of "occasional conformity" (by which Dissenters of flexible conscience could qualify for public office by occasionally taking the sacraments according to the established church). Pressure on the Dissenters increased when the Tories came to power, and violent attacks were made on them by such rabble-rousing extremists as Dr. Henry Sacheverell. In reply, Defoe wrote perhaps the most famous and skillful of all his pamphlets, "The Shortest-Way With The Dissenters" (1702), published anonymously. His method was ironic: to discredit the highfliers by writing as if from their viewpoint but reducing their arguments to absurdity. The pamphlet had a huge sale, but the irony blew up in Defoe's face: Dissenters and High Churchmen alike took it seriously, and—though for different reasons—were furious when the hoax was exposed. Defoe was prosecuted for seditious libel and was arrested in May 1703. The advertisement offering a reward for his capture gives the only extant personal description of Defoe—an unflattering one, which annoyed him considerably: "a middle-size spare man, about 40 years old, of a brown complexion, and dark-brown coloured hair, but wears a wig, a hooked nose, a sharp chin, grey eyes, and a large mole near his mouth." Defoe was advised to plead guilty and rely on the court's mercy, but he received harsh treatment, and, in addition to being fined, was sentenced to stand three times in the pillory. It is likely that the prosecution was primarily political, an attempt to force him into betraying certain Whig leaders; but the attempt was evidently unsuccessful. Although miserably apprehensive of his punishment, Defoe had spirit enough, while awaiting his ordeal, to write the audacious "Hymn To The Pillory" (1703); and this helped to turn the occasion into something of a triumph, with the pillory garlanded, the mob drinking his health, and the poem on sale in the streets. In *An Appeal to Honour and Justice* (1715), he gave his own,

self-justifying account of these events and of other controversies in his life as a writer.

Triumph or not, Defoe was imprisoned again at
Newgate, and there he remained while his Tilbury business collapsed and he became ever more desperately
concerned for the welfare of his already numerous family. He appealed to Robert Harley, who, after many delays,
finally secured his release—Harley's part of the bargain
being to obtain Defoe's services as a pamphleteer and
intelligence agent.

Defoe certainly served his masters with zeal and
energy, traveling extensively, writing reports, minutes of
advice, and pamphlets. He paid several visits to Scotland,
especially at the time of the Act of Union in 1707, keeping Harley closely in touch with public opinion. Some of
Defoe's letters to Harley from this period have survived.
These trips bore fruit in a different way two decades later:
in 1724–26 the three volumes of Defoe's animated and
informative *Tour Through the Whole Island of Great Britain*
were published, in preparing which he drew on many of
his earlier observations.

Perhaps Defoe's most remarkable achievement during Queen Anne's reign, however, was his periodical, the
Review. He wrote this serious, forceful, and long-lived
paper practically single-handedly from 1704 to 1713. At
first a weekly, it became a thrice-weekly publication in
1705, and Defoe continued to produce it even when, for
short periods in 1713, his political enemies managed to
have him imprisoned again on various pretexts. It was,
effectively, the main government organ, its political line
corresponding with that of the moderate Tories (though
Defoe sometimes took an independent stand); but, in
addition to politics as such, Defoe discussed current
affairs in general, religion, trade, manners, morals, and so

on, and his work undoubtedly had a considerable influence on the development of later essay periodicals (such as Richard Steele and Joseph Addison's *The Tatler* and *The Spectator*) and of the newspaper press.

Later Life and Works

With George I's accession (1714), the Tories fell. The Whigs in their turn recognized Defoe's value, and he continued to write for the government of the day and to carry out intelligence work. At about this time, too (perhaps prompted by a severe illness), he

wrote the best known and most popular of his many didactic works, *The Family Instructor* (1715). The writings so far mentioned, however, would not necessarily have procured literary immortality for Defoe; this he achieved when in 1719 he turned his talents to an extended work of prose fiction and (drawing partly on the memoirs of voyagers and castaways such as Alexander Selkirk) produced *Robinson Crusoe*. A German critic has

Daniel Defoe's famous castaway, Robinson Crusoe, finding human footprints in the sand. **Hulton Archive/Getty Images**

called it a "world-book," a label justified not only by the enormous number of translations, imitations, and adaptations that have appeared but by the almost mythic power with which Defoe creates a hero and a situation with which every reader can in some sense identify.

Here (as in his works of the remarkable year 1722, which saw the publication of *Moll Flanders*, *A Journal of the Plague Year*, and *Colonel Jack*) Defoe displays his finest gift as a novelist—his insight into human nature. The men and women he writes about are all, it is true, placed in unusual circumstances; they are all, in one sense or another, solitaries; they all struggle, in their different ways, through a life that is a constant scene of jungle warfare; they all become, to some extent, obsessive. They are also ordinary human beings, however, and Defoe, writing always in the first person, enters into their minds and analyzes their motives. His novels are given verisimilitude by their matter-of-fact style and their vivid concreteness of detail; the latter may seem unselective, but it effectively helps to evoke a particular, circumscribed world. Defoe's range is narrow, but within that range he is a novelist of considerable power, and his plain, direct style, as in almost all of his writing, holds the reader's interest.

In 1724 he published his last major work of fiction, *Roxana*, though in the closing years of his life, despite failing health, he remained active and enterprising as a writer. Defoe's last years were clouded by legal controversies over allegedly unpaid bonds dating back a generation, and it is thought that he died in hiding from his creditors. His character Moll Flanders, born in Newgate Prison, speaks of poverty as "a frightful spectre," and it is a theme of many of his books.

JOHN ARBUTHNOT

(b. April 1667, Inverbervie, Kincardine, Scotland—
d. February 27, 1735, London, England)

The Scottish mathematician, physician, and occasional writer John Arbuthnot is best remembered as the close friend of the writers Jonathan Swift, Alexander Pope, and John Gay and as a founding member of their famous Scriblerus Club, which aimed to ridicule bad literature and false learning.

After taking a medical degree in 1696 at the University of St. Andrews, Arbuthnot became a fellow of the Royal Society in 1704 and was one of Queen Anne's physicians from 1705 until her death. Though he published mathematical and other scientific works, his fame rests on his reputation as a wit and on his satirical writings. The most important of the latter fall into two groups. The first consists of a political allegory dealing with the political jockeying of the British, French, Spanish, and Dutch that led up to the Treaty of Utrecht (1713). Published in five pamphlets, the earliest appearing in 1712, it was collected in 1727 under the composite title *Law is a Bottom-less Pit; or, The History of John Bull*, and it established and popularized for the first time the character who was to become the permanent symbol of England in cartoon and literature.

The other satire in which Arbuthnot had an important share was the *Memoirs of Martinus Scriblerus*, a mocking exposure of pedantry, first published in the 1741 edition of Pope's works but largely written as early as 1713–14 by the members of the Scriblerus Club. The other members of the club acknowledged Arbuthnot as the chief contributor and guiding spirit of the work. Arbuthnot was indifferent to literary fame, and many of his witticisms and ideas for satires were later developed by and credited to his more famous literary friends.

JONATHAN SWIFT

(b. November 30, 1667, Dublin, Ireland—d. October 19, 1745, Dublin)

The Anglo-Irish author Jonathan Swift remains among the foremost prose satirists in the English language. Besides the celebrated novel *Gulliver's Travels* (1726), he wrote such shorter works as *A Tale of a Tub* (1704) and *A Modest Proposal* (1729).

Early Life and Education

Swift's father, Jonathan Swift the elder, was an Englishman who had settled in Ireland after the Stuart Restoration (1660) and become steward of the King's Inns, Dublin. In 1664 he married Abigail Erick, who was the daughter of an English clergyman. In the spring of 1667 Jonathan the elder died suddenly, leaving his wife, baby daughter, and an unborn son to the care of his brothers. The younger Jonathan Swift thus grew up fatherless and dependent on the generosity of his uncles. His education was not neglected, however, and at the age of six he was sent to Kilkenny School, then the best in Ireland. In 1682 he entered Trinity College, Dublin, where he was granted his bachelor of arts degree in February 1686 *speciali gratia* ("by special favour"), his degree being a device often used when a student's record failed, in some minor respect, to conform to the regulations.

Swift continued in residence at Trinity College as a candidate for his master of arts degree until February 1689. But the Roman Catholic disorders that had begun to spread through Dublin after the Glorious Revolution

(1688–89) in Protestant England caused Swift to seek security in England, and he soon became a member of the household of a distant relative of his mother named Sir William Temple, at Moor Park, Surrey. Swift was to remain at Moor Park intermittently until Temple's death in 1699.

Years at Moor Park

Temple was engaged in writing his memoirs and preparing some of his essays for publication, and he had Swift act as a kind of secretary. During his residence at Moor Park, Swift twice returned to Ireland, and during the second of these visits, he took orders in the Anglican church, being ordained priest in January 1695. At the end of the same month he was appointed vicar of Kilroot, near Belfast. Swift came to intellectual maturity at Moor Park, with Temple's rich library at his disposal. Here, too, he met Esther Johnson (the future Stella), the daughter of Temple's widowed housekeeper. In 1692, through Temple's good offices, Swift received the degree of M.A. at the University of Oxford.

Between 1691 and 1694 Swift wrote a number of poems, notably six odes. But his true genius did not find expression until he turned from verse to prose satire and composed, mostly at Moor Park between 1696 and 1699, *A Tale of a Tub*, one of his major works. Published anonymously in 1704, this work was made up of three associated pieces: the *Tale* itself, a satire against "the numerous and gross corruptions in religion and learning"; the mock-heroic *Battle of the Books*; and the *Discourse Concerning the Mechanical Operation of the Spirit,* which ridiculed the manner of worship and preaching of religious enthusiasts at that period. In the *Battle of the Books,* Swift supports the ancients in the longstanding dispute about the relative merits of ancient versus modern literature and culture. But *A Tale of a Tub* is the most impressive of the three compositions. This work is outstanding for its exuberance of satiric wit and energy and is marked by an incomparable command of stylistic effects, largely in the nature of parody. Swift saw the realm of culture and literature threatened by zealous pedantry, while religion—which for him meant rational Anglicanism—suffered attack from both Roman Catholicism and the Nonconformist (Dissenting) churches. In the *Tale* he proceeded to trace all these dangers to a single source: the irrationalities that disturb man's highest faculties—reason and common sense.

Career as Satirist, Political Journalist, and Churchman

After Temple's death in 1699, Swift returned to Dublin as chaplain and secretary to the earl of Berkeley, who was then going to Ireland as a lord justice. During the ensuing years he was in England on some four occasions—in 1701, 1702, 1703, and 1707 to 1709—and won wide recognition in London for his intelligence and his wit as a writer. He had resigned his position as vicar of Kilroot, but early in 1700 he was preferred to several posts in the Irish church. His public writings of this period show that he kept in close touch with affairs in both Ireland and England. Among them is the essay *Discourse of the Contests and Dissensions between the Nobles and the Commons in Athens and Rome,* in which Swift defended the English constitutional balance of power between the monarchy and the two houses of Parliament as a bulwark against tyranny. In London he became increasingly well known through several works: his religious and political essays; *A Tale of a Tub*; and certain impish works, including the "Bickerstaff" pamphlets of 1708–09, which put an end to the career of John Partridge, a popular astrologer, by first prophesying his death and then describing it in circumstantial detail. Like all Swift's satirical works, these pamphlets were published anonymously and were exercises in impersonation. Their supposed author was "Isaac Bickerstaff." For many of the first readers, the very authorship of the satires was a matter for puzzle and speculation. Swift's works brought him to the attention of a circle of Whig writers led by Joseph Addison, but Swift was uneasy about many policies of the Whig administration. He was a Whig by birth, education, and political principle, but he was also passionately loyal to the Anglican church, and he came to view with apprehension the Whigs' growing determination to yield ground to the Nonconformists. He also frequently mimicked and mocked the proponents of "free thinking": intellectual skeptics who questioned Anglican orthodoxy. A brilliant and still-perplexing example of this is *Argument Against Abolishing Christianity* (1708).

A momentous period began for Swift when in 1710 he once again found himself in London. A Tory ministry headed by Robert Harley (later earl of Oxford) and Henry St. John (later Viscount Bolingbroke) was replacing that of the Whigs. The new administration, bent on bringing hostilities with France to a conclusion, was also assuming a more protective attitude toward the Church of England. Swift's reactions to such a rapidly changing world are vividly recorded in his *Journal to Stella*, a series of letters written between his arrival in England in 1710 and 1713, which he addressed to Esther Johnson and her companion, Rebecca Dingley, who were now living in Dublin. The astute Harley made overtures to Swift and won him over to the Tories. But Swift did not thereby renounce his essentially Whiggish convictions regarding the nature of government. The old Tory theory of the divine right of kings had no claim upon him. The ultimate power, he insisted, derived from the people as a whole and, in the English constitution, had come to be exercised jointly by king, lords, and commons.

Swift quickly became the Tories' chief pamphleteer and political writer and, by the end of October 1710, had taken over the Tory journal, *The Examiner*, which he continued to edit until June 14, 1711. He then began preparing a pamphlet in support of the Tory drive for peace with France. This, *The Conduct of the Allies*, appeared on November 27, 1711, some weeks before the motion in favour of a peace was finally carried in Parliament. Swift was rewarded for his services in April 1713 with his appointment as dean of St. Patrick's Cathedral in Dublin.

Withdrawal to Ireland

With the death of Queen Anne in August 1714 and the accession of George I, the Tories were a ruined party, and Swift's career in England was at an end. He withdrew to Ireland, where he was to pass most of the remainder of his life. After a period of seclusion in his deanery, Swift gradually regained his energy. He turned again to verse, which he continued to write throughout the 1720s and early '30s, producing the impressive poem *Verses on the Death of Doctor Swift,* among others. By 1720 he was also showing a renewed interest in public affairs. In his Irish pamphlets of this period he came to grips with many of the problems, social and economic, then confronting Ireland. His tone and manner varied from direct factual presentation to exhortation, humour, and bitter irony. Swift blamed Ireland's backward state chiefly on the blindness of the English government; but he also insistently called attention to the things that the Irish themselves might do in order to better their lot. Of his Irish writings, the *Drapier's Letters* (1724–25) and *A Modest Proposal* are the best known. The first is a series of letters attacking the English government for its scheme to supply Ireland with copper halfpence and farthings. *A Modest Proposal* is a grimly ironic letter of advice in which a public-spirited citizen suggests that Ireland's overpopulation and dire economic conditions could be alleviated if the babies of poor Irish parents were sold as edible delicacies to be eaten by the rich. Both were published anonymously.

Certain events in Swift's private life must also be mentioned. Stella (Esther Johnson) had continued to live with Rebecca Dingley after moving to Ireland in 1700 or 1701. It has sometimes been asserted that Stella and Swift were secretly married in 1716, but they did not live together, and there is no evidence to support this story. It was friendship that Swift always expressed in speaking of Stella, not romantic love. In addition to the letters that make up his *Journal to Stella*, he wrote verses to her, including a series of wry and touching poems titled *On Stella's Birthday*. The question may be asked, was this friendship strained as a result of the appearance in his life of another woman, Esther Vanhomrigh, whom he named Vanessa (and who also appeared in his poetry)? He had met Vanessa during his London visit of 1707–09, and in 1714 she had, despite all his admonitions, insisted on following him to Ireland. Her letters to Swift reveal her passion for him, though at the time of her death in 1723 she had apparently turned against him because he insisted on maintaining a distant attitude toward her. Stella herself died in 1728. Scholars are still much in the dark concerning the precise relationships between these three people, and the various melodramatic theories that have been suggested rest upon no solid ground.

Gulliver's Travels

Swift's greatest satire, *Gulliver's Travels*, was published in 1726. It is uncertain when he began this work, but it appears from his correspondence that he was writing in earnest by 1721 and had finished the whole by August 1725. Its success was immediate. Then, and since, it has succeeded in entertaining (and intriguing) all classes of readers. It was completed at a time when he was close to the poet Alexander Pope and the poet and dramatist John Gay. Through their correspondence, Pope continued to be one of Swift's most important connections to England.

Swift's masterpiece was originally published without its author's name under the title *Travels into Several Remote Nations of the World.* This work, which is told in Gulliver's "own words," is the most brilliant as well as the most bitter and controversial of his satires. In each of its four books the hero, Lemuel Gulliver, embarks on a voyage; but shipwreck or some other hazard usually casts him up on a

Gulliver in Lilliput, chatting with a Lilliputian nobleman. Hulton Archive/Getty Images

strange land. Book I takes him to Lilliput, where he wakes to find himself the giant prisoner of the six-inch-high Lilliputians. Man-Mountain, as Gulliver is called, ingratiates himself with the arrogant, self-important Lilliputians when he wades into the sea and captures an invasion fleet from neighbouring Blefescu; but he falls into disfavour when he puts out a fire in the empress's palace by urinating on it. Learning of a plot to charge him with treason, he escapes from the island.

Book II takes Gulliver to Brobdingnag, where the inhabitants are giants. He is cared for kindly by a nine-year-old girl, Glumdalclitch, but his tiny size exposes him to dangers and indignities, such as getting his head caught in a squalling baby's mouth. Also, the giants' small physical imperfections (such as large pores) are highly visible and disturbing to him. Picked up by an eagle and dropped into the sea, he manages to return home.

In Book III Gulliver visits the floating island of Laputa, whose absent-minded inhabitants are so preoccupied with higher speculations that they are in constant danger of accidental collisions. He visits the Academy of Lagado (a travesty of England's Royal Society), where he finds its lunatic savants engaged in such impractical studies as reducing human excrement to the original food. In Luggnagg he meets the Struldbruggs, a race of immortals, whose eternal senility is brutally described.

Book IV takes Gulliver to the Utopian land of the Houyhnhnms—grave, rational, and virtuous horses. There is also another race on the island, uneasily tolerated and used for menial services by the Houyhnhnms. These are the vicious and physically disgusting Yahoos. Although Gulliver pretends at first not to recognize them, he is forced at last to admit the Yahoos are human beings. He finds perfect happiness with the Houyhnhnms, but as he is only a more advanced Yahoo, he is rejected by them in general assembly and is returned to England, where he finds himself no longer able to tolerate the society of his fellow human beings.

Gulliver's Travels's matter-of-fact style and its air of sober reality confer on it an ironic depth that defeats oversimple explanations. Is it essentially comic, or is it a misanthropic depreciation of mankind? Swift certainly seems to use the various societies Gulliver encounters in his travels to satirize many of the errors, follies, and frailties that human beings are prone to. The warlike, disputatious, but essentially trivial Lilliputians in Book I and the deranged, impractical pedants and intellectuals in Book III are shown as imbalanced beings lacking common sense and even decency. The Houyhnhnms, by contrast, are the epitome of reason and virtuous simplicity, but Gulliver's own proud identification with these horses and his subsequent disdain for his fellow humans indicates that he too has become imbalanced, and that human beings are simply incapable of aspiring to the virtuous rationality that Gulliver has glimpsed.

Last Years

The closing years of Swift's life have been the subject of some misrepresentation, and stories have been told of his ungovernable temper and lack of self-control. It has been suggested that he was insane. From youth he had suffered from what is now known to have been Ménière's disease, an affliction of the semicircular canals of the ears, causing periods of dizziness and nausea. But his mental powers were in no way affected, and he remained active throughout most of the 1730s—Dublin's foremost citizen and Ireland's great patriot dean. In the autumn of 1739 a great celebration was held in his honour. He had, however, begun to fail physically and later suffered a paralytic stroke. In 1742 he was declared incapable of caring for himself, and guardians were appointed. After his death in 1745, he was buried in St. Patrick's Cathedral. On his memorial tablet is an epitaph of his own composition, which says that he lies "where savage indignation can no longer tear his heart."

WILLIAM CONGREVE

(b. January 24, 1670, Bardsey, near Leeds, Yorkshire, England—
d. January 19, 1729, London)

The English dramatist William Congreve shaped the English comedy of manners through his brilliant comic dialogue, his satirical portrayal of the war of the sexes, and his ironic scrutiny of the affectations of his age. His major plays were *The Old Bachelour* (1693), *The Double-Dealer* (1693), *Love for Love* (1695), and *The Way of the World* (1700).

Early Life

In 1674 Congreve's father was granted a commission in the army to join the garrison at Youghal, in Ireland. When he was transferred to Carrickfergus, Congreve, in 1681, was sent to school at Kilkenny, the Eton of Ireland. In April 1686 he entered Trinity College, Dublin (where he received an M.A. in 1696). He studied under the distinguished philosopher and mathematician St. George Ashe, who also tutored his elder schoolfellow and ultimate lifelong friend Jonathan Swift. It was probably during the Glorious Revolution (1688–89) that the family moved to the Congreve home at Stretton in Staffordshire, Congreve's father being made estate agent to the earl of

Cork in 1690. In 1691 he was entered as a law student at the Middle Temple. Never a serious reader in law, he published in 1692 under the pseudonym Cleophil a light but delightfully skillful near-parody of fashionable romance, possibly drafted when he was 17, *Incognita: or, Love and Duty reconcil'd*. He quickly became known among men of letters, had some verses printed in a miscellany of the same year, and became a protégé of John Dryden. In that year Dryden published his translation of the satires of Juvenal and Persius (dated 1693), in which Congreve collaborated, contributing the complimentary poem "To Mr. Dryden."

Literary Career

It was in March 1693 that Congreve achieved sudden fame with the production at the Theatre Royal, Drury Lane, of *The Old Bachelor*, written, he said, in 1690 to amuse himself during convalescence. Warmly heralded by Dryden, who declared that he had never read so brilliant a first play, though it needed to be given "the fashionable Cut of the Town," it was an enormous success, running for the then unprecedented length of a fortnight. His next play, *The Double-Dealer*, played in November or December at Drury Lane but did not meet with the same applause (it later became the more critically admired work, however). Its published form contained a panegyrical introduction by Dryden. *Love for Love* almost repeated the success of his first play. Performed in April 1695, it was the first production staged for the new theatre in Lincoln's Inn Fields, which was opened after protracted crises in the old Theatre Royal, complicated by quarrels among the actors. Congreve became one of the managers of the new theatre, promising to provide a new play every year.

In 1695 he began to write his more public occasional verse, such as his pastoral on the death of Queen Mary II

William Congreve, oil painting by Sir Godfrey Kneller. DEA Picture Library/De Agostini /Getty Images

and his "Pindarique Ode, Humbly Offer'd to the King on his taking Namure"; and John Dennis, then a young, unsoured critic, collecting his *Letters upon Several Occasions* (published 1696), extracted from Congreve his "Letter Concerning Humour in Comedy." By this time, Congreve's position among men of letters was so well established that he was considered worthy of one of those posts by which men of power in government rewarded literary merit: he was made one of the five commissioners for licensing hackney coaches, though at a reduced salary of £100 a year.

Though Congreve signally failed to carry out his promise of writing a play a year for the Lincoln's Inn theatre, he showed his good intentions by letting them stage *The Mourning Bride*. Although it is now his least regarded drama, this tragedy, produced early in 1697, swelled his reputation enormously and became his most popular play. No further dramatic work appeared until March 1700, when Congreve's masterpiece, *The Way of the World*, was produced—with a brilliant cast—at Lincoln's Inn Fields; though it is now his only frequently revived piece, it was a failure with the audience. This was Congreve's last attempt to write a play, though he did not entirely desert the theatre. He wrote librettos for two operas, and in 1704 he collaborated in translating Molière's *Monsieur de Pourceaugnac* for Lincoln's Inn Fields. In 1705 he associated himself for a short time with the playwright and architect Sir John Vanbrugh in the Queen's theatre, or Italian Opera house, writing an epilogue to its first production. It is likely that Congreve's retreat from the stage was partly a result of a campaign against the supposed immorality of contemporary comedies. This attack was led most notably by Jeremy Collier, author of the tract *A Short View of the Immorality and Profaneness of the English Stage* (1698), which specifically censured Congreve and Dryden, among others. In reply, Congreve wrote *Amendments of Mr. Collier's False and Imperfect Citations* (1698).

The rest of his life he passed quietly enough, being in easy circumstances thanks to his private income, the royalties on his plays, and his not very exacting posts in the civil service. In 1705 he was made a commissioner for wines, a post that he retained by virtue of Swift's good offices at the change of government in 1710 but which he relinquished in 1714 when he joined the customs service; his position was improved at the end of 1714 with the addition of the secretaryship of the island of Jamaica. He wrote a considerable number of poems, some of the light social variety, some soundly scholarly translations from ancient Greek and Roman writers—Homer, Juvenal, Ovid, and Horace—and some odes in the manner of Pindar. The volume containing these odes also comprised his timely *Discourse on the Pindarique Ode* (1706), which brought some order to a form that had become wildly unrestrained since the days of the poet Abraham Cowley, who died in the 1660s. Congreve's friendships were numerous, warm, and constant, as much with insignificant people, such as his early companions in Ireland, as with the literary figures of his time. No quarrels are attributed to him, except for a very brief one with Jacob Tonson, a publisher. Swift, whose friendship with him had begun in early days in Ireland, was unvarying in his affection; for John Gay, poet and author of *The Beggar's Opera*, he was the "unreproachful man"; Alexander Pope dedicated his *Iliad* to him; and Sir Richard Steele his edition of Joseph Addison's *The Drummer*. In his later years he was devotedly attached to the second duchess of Marlborough, and it is almost certain that he was the father of her second daughter, Lady Mary Godolphin, later duchess of Leeds. This would account for the large legacy, of almost all his fortune, which he left to the duchess of Marlborough. He died after a carriage accident.

Legacy

Congreve distinguished himself as the outstanding writer of the English comedy of manners, markedly different in many respects from others of this period of the drama. Taking as its main theme the manners and behaviour of the class to which it was addressed—that is, the antipuritanical theatre audience drawn largely from the court—it dealt with imitators of French customs, conceited wits, and fantastics of all kinds; but its main theme was the sexual life led by a large number of courtiers, with their philosophy of freedom and experimentation. Congreve rises above other dramatists of his time in both the delicacy of his feeling and the perfection of his phrasing.

Congreve's most successful work is his last play, *The Way of the World*. Here he is doing more than holding up to ridicule the assumptions that governed the society of his time. He could not regard love merely as the gratification of lust, a matter of appetite rather than of feeling, but he was equally averse to "rationalizing" love. Congreve goes deeper than any of his contemporaries, has more feeling for the individual, and is far subtler. He was a sensitive craftsman, and nothing came from his hand that was not thoughtfully conceived and expertly contrived. Though not the equal of Molière, he was the nearest English approach to him.

COLLEY CIBBER

(b. November 6, 1671, London, England—
d. December 11, 1757, London)

Colley Cibber was an English actor, theatre manager, playwright, and poet laureate of England whose play

Love's Last Shift; or, The Fool in Fashion (1696) is generally considered the first sentimental comedy, a form of drama that dominated the English stage for nearly a century. His autobiography, *An Apology for the Life of Mr. Colley Cibber* (1740), contains the best account of the theatre of his day and is an invaluable study of the art of acting as it was practiced by his contemporaries.

A well-educated son of the sculptor Caius Gabriel Cibber, he began his acting career in 1690 with Thomas Betterton's company at the Drury Lane Theatre, London. Marrying three years later and finding his earnings as an actor inadequate, he wrote *Love's Last Shift* to provide himself with a role; the play established his reputation both as actor and as playwright. The playwright Sir John Vanbrugh honoured it with a sequel, *The Relapse: or, Virtue in Danger* (1696), in which Cibber's character Sir Novelty Fashion has become Lord Foppington, a role created by Cibber. In 1700 Cibber produced his famous adaptation of William Shakespeare's *Richard III*, which held the stage as the preferred acting version of that play until the original version was restored by the actor Henry Irving in 1871. Cibber's adaptation was notable for such Shakespearean-sounding lines as "Off with his head—so much for Buckingham!" and "Conscience, avaunt, Richard's himself again!" Cibber also wrote other comedies of manners, including *She Wou'd, and She Wou'd Not* (1702) and *The Careless Husband* (1704).

At this time Cibber entered upon a series of complex intrigues to obtain a position in theatre management. By 1710 he was, with Robert Wilks and Thomas Doggett (the latter soon to be replaced by Barton Booth), one of a famous "triumvirate" of actor-managers under which Drury Lane Theatre conspicuously prospered.

After the death of Queen Anne, Cibber entered the political arena, writing and adapting plays (notably *The*

Non-Juror, in 1717, from Molière's *Tartuffe*) in support of the Whig cause, with a skill and energy that in 1730 led to his appointment as poet laureate. In 1728 he completed *The Provok'd Husband*, a play left unfinished by Vanbrugh at his death in 1726. Anne Oldfield, Cibber's leading actress, died in 1730; and Wilks, his first partner in management, died in 1733. The next year Cibber announced his retirement from management. Nevertheless, he did not make his final stage appearance until February 15, 1745, when he played in his own adaptation of Shakespeare's *King John*.

Tactless, rude, and supremely self-confident, Cibber was the target of many attacks, both personal and political. In the 1743 edition of Alexander Pope's satirical poem *The Dunciad*, Cibber was elevated to the doubtful eminence of hero. He responded with spirit, publishing three letters attacking Pope that, according to Samuel Johnson, caused the latter poet to writhe in anguish.

JOSEPH ADDISON

(b. May 1, 1672, Milston, Wiltshire, England—
d. June 17, 1719, London)

Joseph Addison was an English essayist, poet, and dramatist who, with Richard Steele, was a leading contributor to and guiding spirit of the periodicals *The Tatler* and *The Spectator*. During his lifetime, his writing skill led to his holding important posts in government while the political faction known as the Whigs were in power. Samuel Johnson's praise of *The Spectator* as a model of prose style, though, granted Addison the legacy of being one of the most admired and influential masters of prose in the English language.

Early Life

Addison was the eldest son of the Reverend Lancelot Addison, later archdeacon of Coventry and dean of Lichfield. After schooling in Amesbury and Salisbury and at Lichfield Grammar School, he was enrolled at age 14 in the Charterhouse in London. Here began his lifelong friendship with Richard Steele, who later became his literary collaborator. Both went on to the University of Oxford, where Addison matriculated at Queen's College in May 1687. Through distinction in Latin verse he won election as Demy (scholar) to Magdalen College in 1689 and took the degree of M.A. in 1693. He was a fellow from 1697 to 1711. At Magdalen he spent 10 years as tutor in preparation for a career as a scholar and man of letters. In 1695 *A Poem to his Majesty* (William III), with a dedication to Lord Keeper Somers, the influential Whig statesman, brought favourable notice not only from Somers but also Charles Montague (later earl of Halifax), who saw in Addison a writer whose services were of potential use to the crown. A treasury grant offered him opportunity for travel and preparation for government service. He also attained distinction by contributing the preface to Virgil's *Georgics*, in John Dryden's translation of 1697.

The European tour (1699–1704) enabled Addison not only to become acquainted with English diplomats abroad but also to meet contemporary European men of letters. After time in France, he spent the year 1701 in leisurely travel in Italy, during which he wrote the prose *Remarks on Several Parts of Italy* (1705; rev. ed. 1718) and the poetic epistle *A Letter from Italy* (1704). From Italy Addison crossed into Switzerland, where, in Geneva, he learned in March 1702 of the death of William III and the consequent loss of power of his two chief patrons, Somers and Halifax. He then toured through Austria, the German states, and the Netherlands before returning to England in 1704.

Government Service

In London Addison renewed his friendship with Somers and Halifax and other members of the Kit-Cat Club, which was an association of prominent Whig leaders and literary figures of the day—among them Steele, William Congreve, and Sir John Vanbrugh. In August 1704 London was electrified by the news of the duke of Marlborough's sweeping victory over the French at Blenheim, and Addison was approached by government leaders to write a poem worthy of the great occasion. Addison was meanwhile appointed commissioner of appeals in excise, a position left vacant by the death of John Locke. *The Campaign*, addressed to Marlborough, was published on December 14 (though dated 1705). By its rejection of conventional classical imagery and its effective portrayal of Marlborough's military genius, it was an immediate success that perfectly expressed the nation's great hour of victory.

The Whig success in the election of May 1705, which saw the return of Somers and Halifax to the Privy Council, brought Addison increased financial security in an appointment as undersecretary to the secretary of state, a busy and lucrative post. Addison's retention in a new, more powerful Whig administration in the autumn of 1706 reflected his further rise in government service. At this time he began to see much of Steele, helping him write the play *The Tender Husband* (1705). In practical ways Addison also assisted Steele with substantial loans and the appointment as editor of the official London *Gazette*. In 1708 Addison was elected to Parliament for Lostwithiel in Cornwall, and later in the same year he was made secretary to the earl of Wharton, the new lord lieutenant of Ireland. Addison's post was in effect that of secretary of state for Irish affairs, with a revenue of some £2,000 a year. He served as Irish secretary until August 1710.

Joseph Addison, engraving, early 19th century. © Photos.com/Thinkstock

The Tatler *and* The Spectator

It was during Addison's term in Ireland that his friend Steele began publishing *The Tatler*, which appeared three times a week under the pseudonym of Isaac Bickerstaff. Though at first issued as a newspaper presenting accounts of London's political, social, and cultural news, this periodical soon began investigating English manners and society, establishing principles of ideal behaviour and genteel conduct, and proposing standards of good taste for the general public. The first number of *The Tatler* appeared on April 12, 1709, while Addison was still in England; but while still in Ireland he began contributing to the new periodical. Back in London in September 1709, he supplied most of the essays during the winter of 1709–10 before returning to Ireland in May.

The year 1710 was marked by the overturn of the Whigs from power and a substantial Tory victory at the polls. Although Addison easily retained his seat in the Commons, his old and powerful patrons were again out of favour, and, for the first time since his appointment as undersecretary in 1705, Addison found himself without employment. He was thus able to devote even more time to literary activity and to cultivation of personal friendships not only with Steele and other Kit-Cats but, for a short period, with Jonathan Swift—until Swift's shift of allegiance to the rising Tory leaders resulted in estrangement. Addison continued contributing to the final numbers of *The Tatler*, which Steele finally brought to a close on January 2, 1711. Addison had written more than 40 of *The Tatler*'s total of 271 numbers and had collaborated with Steele on another 36 of them.

Thanks to Addison's help *The Tatler* was an undoubted success. By the end of 1710 Steele had enough material for a collected edition of *The Tatler*. Thereupon, he and Addison decided to make a fresh start with a new periodical. *The Spectator*, which appeared six days a week, from March 1, 1711, to December 6, 1712, offered a wide range of material to its readers, from discussion of the latest fashions to serious disquisitions on criticism and morality, including Addison's weekly papers on John Milton's *Paradise Lost* and the series on the "pleasures of the imagination." From the start, Addison was the leading spirit in *The Spectator*'s publication, contributing 274 numbers in all. In bringing learning "out of closets and libraries, schools and colleges, to dwell in clubs and assemblies, at tea-tables, and in coffee-houses," *The Spectator* was eminently successful. One feature of *The Spectator* that deserves particular mention is its critical essays, in which Addison sought to elevate public taste. He devoted a considerable proportion of his essays to literary criticism, which was to prove influential in the subsequent development of the English novel. His own gift for drawing realistic human characters found brilliant literary expression in the members of the Spectator Club, in which such figures as Roger de Coverley, Captain Sentry, Sir Andrew Freeport, and the Spectator himself represent important sections of contemporary society. More than 3,000 copies of *The Spectator* were published daily, and the 555 numbers were then collected into seven volumes. Two years later (from June 18 to December 20, 1714), Addison published 80 additional numbers, with the help of two assistants, and these were later reprinted as volume eight.

Addison's other notable literary production during this period was his tragedy *Cato*. Performed at Drury Lane on April 14, 1713, the play was a resounding success—largely, no doubt, because of the political overtones that both parties read into the play. To the Whigs Cato seemed the resolute defender of liberty against French tyranny, while the Tories were able to interpret the domineering Caesar as a kind of Roman Marlborough whose military victories were a threat to English liberties. The play enjoyed an unusual run of 20 performances in April and May 1713 and continued to be performed throughout the century.

Later Years

With the death of Queen Anne on August 1, 1714, and the accession of George I, Addison's political fortunes rose. He was appointed secretary to the regents (who governed until the arrival of the new monarch from Hanover) and in April 1717 was made secretary of state. Ill health, however, forced him to resign the following year. Meanwhile, he had married the widowed countess of Warwick and spent the remaining years of his life in comparative affluence at Holland House in Kensington. A series of political essays, *The Free-Holder, or Political Essays*, was published from December 23, 1715, to June 29, 1716, and his comedy *The Drummer* was produced at Drury Lane on March 10, 1716.

Meanwhile, Addison had a quarrel with the most gifted satirist of the age, Alexander Pope, who after Addison's death would make him the subject of one of the most celebrated satiric "characters" in the English language. In 1715 Pope had been angered by Addison's support of a rival translation of the *Iliad* by Thomas Tickell, and in 1735 Pope published "An Epistle to Dr. Arbuthnot," in which there appears a notable portrait of Addison as a narcissistic and envious man of letters. A second quarrel further embittered Addison; the dispute over a bill for restricting the peerage, in which he and Steele took opposing sides, estranged the two friends during the last year of Addison's life. Addison was buried in Westminster Abbey, near the grave of his old patron and friend Lord Halifax.

SIR RICHARD STEELE

(b. 1672, Dublin, Ireland—d. September 1, 1729, Carmarthen,
Carmarthenshire, Wales)

Sir Richard Steele was an English essayist, dramatist,
journalist, and politician best known as the principal
author (with Joseph Addison) of the periodicals *The Tatler*
and *The Spectator*.

Early Life and Works

Steele's father, an ailing and somewhat ineffectual attorney, died when the son was about five, and the boy was
taken under the protection of his uncle Henry Gascoigne,
confidential secretary to the Duke of Ormonde, to whose
bounty, as Steele later wrote, he owed "a liberal education." He was sent to study in England at Charterhouse
in 1684 and to Christ Church, Oxford, in 1689. At
Charterhouse he met Joseph Addison, and thus began
one of the most famous and fruitful of all literary friendships, which lasted until disagreements (mainly political)
brought about a cooling and a final estrangement shortly
before Addison's death in 1719. Steele moved to Merton
College in 1691 but, caught up with the excitement of
King William's campaigns against the French, left in 1692
without taking a degree to join the army. He was commissioned in 1697 and promoted to captain in 1699, but,
lacking the money and connections necessary for substantial advancement, he left the army in 1705.

Meanwhile, he had embarked on a second career, as a
writer. Perhaps partly because he gravely wounded a fellow officer in a duel in 1700 (an incident that inspired a

lifelong detestation of dueling), partly because of sincere feelings of disgust at the "irregularity" of army life and his own dissipated existence, he published in 1701 a moralistic tract, "The Christian Hero," of which 10 editions were sold in his lifetime. This tract led to Steele's being accused of hypocrisy and mocked for the contrast between his austere precepts and his genially convivial practice. For many of his contemporaries, however, its polite tone served as evidence of a significant cultural change from the Restoration (most notably, it advocated respectful behaviour toward women). The tract's moralistic tenor would be echoed in Steele's plays. In the same year (1701) Steele wrote his first comedy, *The Funeral.* Performed at Drury Lane "with more than expected success," this play made his reputation and helped to bring him to the notice of King William and the Whig leaders. Late in 1703 he followed this with his only stage failure, *The Lying Lover*, which ran for only six nights, being, as Steele said, "damned for its piety." Sententious and ill-constructed, with much moralizing, it is nevertheless of some historical importance as one of the first sentimental comedies.

A third play, *The Tender Husband*, with which Addison helped him (1705), had some success, but Steele continued to search for advancement and for money. In the next few years he secured various minor appointments, and in 1705, apparently actuated by mercenary motives, he married a widow, Margaret Stretch, who owned considerable property in Barbados. Almost immediately the estate was entangled in his debts (he lost two actions for debt, with damages, in 1706), but, when, late in 1706, Margaret conveniently died, she left her husband with a substantial income. Steele's second marriage, contracted within a year of Margaret's death, was to Mary Scurlock, who was completely adored by Steele, however much he might at times neglect her. His hundreds of letters and notes to her (she is often addressed as "Dear Prue") provide a vivid revelation of his personality during the 11 years of their marriage. Having borne him four children (of whom only the eldest, Elizabeth, long survived Richard), she died, during pregnancy, in 1718.

Mature Life and Works

Steele's most important appointment in the early part of Queen Anne's reign was that of gazetteer—writer of *The London Gazette,* the official government journal. Although this reinforced his connection with the Whig leaders, it gave little scope for his artistic talents, and, on April 12, 1709, he secured his place in literary history by launching the thrice-weekly essay periodical *The Tatler.* Writing under the name (already made famous by the satirist Jonathan Swift) of Isaac Bickerstaff, Steele created the mixture of entertainment and instruction in manners and morals that was to be perfected in *The Spectator.* "The general purpose of the whole," wrote Steele, "has been to recommend truth, innocence, honour, and virtue, as the chief ornaments of life"; and here, as in the later periodical, can be seen his strong ethical bent, his attachment to the simple virtues of friendship, frankness, and benevolence, his seriousness of approach tempered by the colloquial ease and lightness of his style. Addison contributed some 46 papers and collaborated in several others, but the great bulk of the 271 issues were by Steele himself, and, apart from bringing him fame, it brought a measure of prosperity. The exact cause of *The Tatler*'s demise is uncertain, but probably the reasons were mainly political: in 1710 power had shifted to the Tories and Steele, a Whig, had lost his gazetteership and had come near to losing his post of commissioner of stamps. *The Tatler* had contained a good deal of political innuendo, some of it aimed at Robert Harley, the Tory leader, himself, and Harley may well have put pressure on Steele to discontinue the paper.

The Tatler's greater successor, first appearing on March 1, 1711, was avowedly nonpolitical and was enormously successful. *The Spectator* was a joint venture; Steele's was probably the more original journalistic flair, and he evolved many of the most celebrated ideas and characters (such as Sir Roger de Coverley), although later Addison tended to develop them in his own way. Steele's attractive, often casual style formed a perfect foil for Addison's more measured, polished, and erudite writing. Of the 555 daily numbers, Steele contributed 251 (though about two-thirds made up from correspondents' letters).

Of Steele's many later ventures into periodical journalism, some, such as *The Englishman*, were mainly politically partisan. *The Guardian* (to which Addison contributed substantially) contains some of his most distinguished work, and *The Lover* comprises 40 of his most attractive essays. Other, short-lived, periodicals, such as *The Reader*, *Town-Talk*, and *The Plebeian*, contain matter of considerable political importance. Steele became, indeed, the chief journalist of the Whigs in opposition (1710–14), his writings being marked by an unusual degree of principle and integrity. His last extended literary work was *The Theatre*, a biweekly periodical.

Steele's political writings had stirred up enough storms to make his career far from smooth. He resigned as commissioner of stamps in 1713 and was elected to Parliament, but, as a consequence of his anti-Tory pamphlets "The Importance of Dunkirk Consider'd" and "The Crisis" (advocating the Hanoverian succession), he was expelled from the House of Commons for "seditious writings." Calmer weather, however, and rewards followed on George I's accession: Steele was appointed to the congenial and fairly lucrative post of governor of Drury

Lane Theatre in 1714, knighted in 1715, and reelected to Parliament in the same year.

Steele's health was gradually undermined by his cheerful intemperance, and he was long plagued by gout. Nevertheless, he busied himself conscientiously with parliamentary duties and, more erratically, with his part in the management of Drury Lane. One of his main contributions to that theatre's prosperity was his last and most successful comedy, *The Conscious Lovers* (1722)—one of the most popular plays of the century and perhaps the best example of English sentimental comedy.

In 1724 Steele retired to his late wife's estate in Wales and began to settle his debts. His closing years were quiet, but his health continued to deteriorate.

AHMED NEDIM

(b. 1681, Constantinople—d. 1730, Constantinople)

Ahmed Nedim was one of the greatest lyric poets of Ottoman Turkish literature.

The son of a judge, Nedim was brought up as a religious scholar and teacher and, winning the patronage of the grand vizier, Nevsheherli İbrahim Paşa, received an appointment as a librarian. Later, he became the Sultan's close friend—thus his name Nedim, meaning "Boon Companion." He lived during the Tulip Age (Lâle Devri) of Ottoman history, in the reign of Sultan Ahmed III (1703–30), so called because a fad of tulip growing was one manifestation of the court's passion for beauty and pleasure during this unusually peaceful interlude in Ottoman history.

Nedim's *qaṣīdah*s ("odes") and *ghazal*s ("lyrics") are bright and colourful, and he excelled especially in the writing of charming and lively *şarqıs* ("songs"), which are still sung today. Filled with grace and joy, they are the perfect accompaniment to the exuberance of the Tulip Period. Nedim was a poet of the old school who freed himself from its fetters sufficiently to be able to express his personality and charm in an original way. His divan (collection of poems) exhibits his masterly handling of the language and accounts for his popularity. Nedim was killed during the religious and civil revolts against the frivolity of the court, which brought the Tulip Period to its close.

Ludvig Holberg, Baron Holberg

(b. December 3, 1684, Bergen, Norway—
d. January 28, 1754, Copenhagen, Denmark)

Ludvig Holberg is the outstanding Scandinavian literary figure of the Enlightenment period. He is claimed by both Norway and Denmark as one of the founders of their literatures.

Orphaned as a child, Holberg lived with relatives in Bergen until the city was destroyed by fire in 1702, when he was sent to the University of Copenhagen. Longing to see the world, he set out for Holland (1704) after taking his degree, but he fell ill at Aachen and, having few resources, had to make his way back to Norway on foot. After working as a French tutor, he set out again in 1706 for London and Oxford, where he studied for two years, supporting himself by giving lessons on the flute and violin. While there, he must have begun his *Introduction til de fornemste europæiske rigers historie* ("Introduction to the History of Leading European Nations"), which was not

Ludvig Holberg. Library of Congress, Washington, D.C. (Digital file no. cph 3c30757)

published until 1711, when he was back in Denmark. It led to his receiving a royal grant that permitted him to study and travel.

Holberg accordingly set out in 1714 and visited, chiefly on foot, many of the great cities of Europe. In 1716 he returned to Denmark, where he published an unoriginal work on natural law and natural rights, *Introduction til natur- og folke-rettens kundskab* ("Introduction to Natural and International Law"). His pecuniary troubles ended at last in 1717, when he was appointed professor of metaphysics and logic at the University of Copenhagen. In 1720 he was promoted to the chair of Latin literature, and he was to obtain the chair of history in 1730.

Seized with a "poetic fit," Holberg began to create, under the pseudonym Hans Mikkelsen, an entirely new class of humorous literature. His seriocomic epic *Peder Paars* (1719), a parody of Virgil's *Aeneid*, was the earliest classic of the Danish language. In 1722 the first Danish-language theatre was opened in Copenhagen, and Holberg began to produce, with astonishing rapidity, the steady flow of comedies that resulted in his being called the "Molière of the North." Their freshness is such that many are still performed on the Danish and Norwegian stages. Among the best are *Den politiske kandestøber* (1722; *The Political Tinker*), *Den vægelsindede* (1723; *The Scatterbrain*), *Jean de France* (1723), *Jeppe på bjerget* (1723; *Jeppe of the Hill*), *Ulysses von Ithacia* (1725), *Den stundesløse* (1731; *The Fussy Man*), and *Erasmus Montanus* (1731). (Most of the above plays have been translated into English in *Jeppe of the Hill and Other Comedies* [1990].)

These plays' characters are often stock types, based on the Miles Gloriosus (braggart soldier) of Plautus or on the cuckold Sganarelle of Molière. But the manners are Danish with some Norwegian traits, and the targets of Holberg's satire are both contemporary and universal. A favourite target was the pretensions, jargon, and pedantry of the learned.

The shaky financial existence of the Danish-language theatre may have led the worried Holberg to write *Den danske comoedies liigbegiængelse* (1726; "The Burial of Danish Comedy"; Eng. trans. in *Jeppe of the Hill and Other Comedies*). In 1731 he published his performed comedies and five additional plays and closed the major chapter in his career as a dramatist. (The Danish theatre, having definitively ended a somewhat intermittent existence after the devastating Copenhagen fire of October 1728, reopened in 1747, and he resumed his playwriting, but these plays were never to be as successful as the earlier ones.)

Thereafter, Holberg turned to other forms of writing, notably a satirical novel about an imaginary voyage, *Nicolai Klimii Iter Subterraneum* (1741; *The Journey of Niels Klim to the World Underground*). *Niels Klim*, originally written in Latin and published in Germany (by its Danish publisher, who wished to avoid censorship), was translated into Danish in 1742. It was adapted for Danish television into a feature-length film in 1984. Still Holberg's most widely read work, it follows his comedies in attacking intolerance and other human follies.

Holberg was the rector of the University of Copenhagen from 1735 to 1736 and its bursar from 1737 to 1751. In 1747 he was made Baron Holberg. His fame and reputation rested in part on an international orientation, evinced by his continuing to write in Latin although he was widely feted for his works written in Danish. By making literary use of ideas from other European countries he enriched Danish literature immeasurably, lifting it from its provincial level to a cosmopolitanism equal to that of other west European countries. As the critic Sven Rossel indicated, Holberg added great flexibility and expressiveness to the Danish language while developing universal themes particularized in his portrayal of human idiosyncrasies. His witty satire, his sympathy for women, and his interest in social reform undoubtedly contributed to the admiration felt for him by Henrik Ibsen, who was perhaps the most important playwright in Europe during the late 19th century. *Niels Klim* has been referred to as "a Danish *Gulliver's Travels.*"

JOHN GAY

(b. June 30, 1685, Barnstaple, Devon, England— d. December 4, 1732, London)

The English poet and dramatist John Gay is chiefly remembered as the author of *The Beggar's Opera*, a work distinguished by good-humoured satire and technical assurance.

A member of an ancient but impoverished Devonshire family, Gay was educated at the free grammar school in Barnstaple. He was apprenticed to a silk dealer in London but was released early from his indentures and, after a further short period in Devonshire, returned to London, where he lived most of his life. Among his early literary friends were Aaron Hill and Eustace Budgell, whom he helped in the production of *The British Apollo*, a question-and-answer journal of the day. Gay's journalistic interests are clearly seen in a pamphlet, *The Present State of Wit* (1711), a survey of contemporary periodical publications.

From 1712 to 1714 he was steward in the household of the Duchess of Monmouth, which gave him leisure and security to write. He had produced a burlesque of the Miltonic style, *Wine*, in 1708, and in 1713 his first important poem, *Rural Sports*, appeared. This is a descriptive and didactic work in two short books dealing with hunting and fishing but containing also descriptions of the countryside and meditations on the Horatian theme of retirement. In it he strikes a characteristic note of delicately absurd artificiality, while a deliberate disproportion between language and subject pays comic dividends and sets a good-humoured and sympathetic tone. His finest poem, *Trivia: or, The Art of Walking the Streets of London* (1716), displays an assured and precise craftsmanship in which rhythm and diction underline whatever facet of experience he is describing. A sophisticated lady crossing the street, for example:

> *Her shoe disdains the street: the lady fair*
> *With narrow step affects a limping air.*

The couplet does not aim to startle the reader, yet the experience is perfectly conveyed. Another couplet, on the presence of spring felt throughout the whole of creation, states:

> *The seasons operate on every breast:*
> *'Tis hence that fawns are brisk,*
> *and ladies drest.*

Here the effect is at once satirical, sympathetic, and — in its correlation of the animal and human kingdoms — philosophical. It is in such delicate probing of the surface of social life that Gay excels. *The Shepherd's Week* (1714) is a series of mock classical poems in pastoral setting; the *Fables* (two series, 1727 and 1738) are brief, octosyllabic illustrations of moral themes, often satirical in tone.

Gay's poetry was much influenced by that of Alexander Pope, who was a contemporary and close friend. Gay was a member, together with Pope, Jonathan Swift, and John Arbuthnot, of the Scriblerus Club, a literary group that aimed to ridicule pedantry. These friends contributed to two of Gay's satirical plays: *The What D'ye Call It* (1715) and *Three Hours After Marriage* (1717).

His most successful play was *The Beggar's Opera*, produced in London on January 29, 1728, by the theatre manager John Rich at Lincoln's Inn Fields Theatre. It ran for 62 performances (not consecutive, but the longest run then known). A story of thieves and highwaymen, it was intended to mirror the moral degradation of society and, more particularly, to caricature the prime minister Sir Robert Walpole and his Whig administration. It also made fun of the prevailing fashion for Italian opera. The play was stageworthy, however, not so much because of its pungent satire but because of its effective situations and "singable" songs. The production of its sequel, *Polly*, was forbidden by the lord chamberlain (doubtless on Walpole's instructions); but the ban was an excellent advertisement for the piece, and subscriptions for copies of the printed edition made more than £1,000 profit for the author. (It was eventually produced in 1777, when it had a moderate success.) His *Beggar's Opera* was successfully transmitted into the 20th century by Bertolt Brecht and Kurt Weill as *Die Dreigroschenoper* (1928; *The Threepenny Opera*).

"Honest" John Gay lost most of his money through disastrous investment in South Sea stock, but he nonetheless left £6,000 when he died. He was buried in Westminster Abbey, next to the poet Geoffrey Chaucer, and his epitaph was written by Alexander Pope.

ALLAN RAMSAY

(b. October 15, 1686, Leadhills, Lanarkshire, Scotland—
d. January 7, 1758, Edinburgh)

Allan Ramsay was a Scottish poet and literary antiquary who maintained national poetic traditions by writing Scots poetry and by preserving the work of earlier Scottish poets at a time when most Scottish writers had been Anglicized. He was admired by the great Scottish poet Robert Burns as a pioneer in the use of Scots in contemporary poetry.

Ramsay settled in Edinburgh about 1700 and in 1701 became an apprentice wigmaker. Established in this respected craft, he married in 1712. In the same year, he helped found the Easy Club, a Jacobite literary society. His pen names, first Isaac Bickerstaff and later Gawin Douglas, suggest both Augustan English and medieval Scottish influences. He soon established a reputation as a prolific composer of verse in both English and Scots, much of it modeled on classical styles and traditional metrical patterns, sometimes uneasily adapted to suit contemporary Edinburgh Neoclassical taste. He made considerable use of Scots in humorous and satirical verse; and, by collecting and publishing poems by Robert Henryson, William Dunbar, and other late medieval Scottish writers, Ramsay, though no scholarly respecter of texts, made certain of their survival and indirectly gave impetus to more accurate editing of Scottish poetry and song later in the century.

In 1721 Ramsay published a subscriber's edition of his own poems, including renderings in Scots of Horace's *Odes*; a second volume appeared in 1728. An original pastoral comedy, *The Gentle Shepherd* (1725), gained much of its effect from the use of Scots. The appearance of John Gay's *Beggar's Opera* (1728) encouraged him to turn it into a ballad opera (1729). *The Tea-table Miscellany*, 3 vol. (1724–37), *The Ever Green*, 2 vol. (1724), and *Scots Proverbs* (1737) make up the bulk of his collection of old Scottish songs, poems, and wise sayings. *Fables and Tales* (1722–30) includes versions of the fables of Jean de La Fontaine and Antoine Houdar de La Motte in Scots.

After publication of the 1721 *Poems*, Ramsay changed from wigmaker to bookseller, and his shop became a meeting place for both townsmen and visitors. He founded Britain's first circulating library (1726); the Academy of St. Luke, for instruction in painting and drawing (1729); and a theatre (1736–39), eventually closed by extremists in the Church of Scotland presbytery, who found legal justification in the 1737 Licensing Act. He retired in 1740 but remained active until his death.

PIERRE MARIVAUX

(b. February 4, 1688, Paris, France—d. February 12, 1763, Paris)

Pierre Marivaux was a French dramatist, novelist, and journalist whose comedies are, among 18th-century French playwrights, second in popularity only to those of Molière.

Marivaux's wealthy aristocratic family moved to Limoges, where his father practiced law, the same profession for which the young Marivaux trained. Most interested in the drama of the courts, at 20 he wrote his first play, *Le Père prudent et équitable, ou Crispin l'heureux fourbe* ("The Prudent and Equitable Father"). Such early writings showed promise, and by 1710 he had joined Parisian salon society, whose atmosphere and conversational manners he absorbed for his occasional journalistic writings. He contributed *Réflexions...* on the various social classes to the *Nouveau Mercure* (1717–19) and modeled his own periodical, *Le Spectateur Français* (1720–24), after Joseph Addison's *The Spectator*.

The loss of his fortune in 1720, followed a few years later by the death of his young wife, caused Marivaux to take his literary career more seriously. He was drawn into several fashionable artistic salons and received a pension from Mme de Pompadour. He became a close associate of the *philosophes* Bernard de Fontenelle and Montesquieu and of the critic and playwright La Motte.

Marivaux's first plays were written for the Comédie-Française, among them the five-act verse tragedy *Annibal* (1727). But the Italian Theatre of Lelio, sponsored in Paris by the regent Philippe d'Orleans, attracted him far more. The major players Thomassin and Silvia of this commedia dell'arte troupe became Marivaux's stock lovers: Harlequin, or the valet, and the ingenue. (Commedia dell'arte ["comedy of the profession"] was an Italian theatrical form that flourished throughout Europe from the 16th through the 18th century.) *Arlequin poli par l'amour* (1723; "Harlequin Brightened by Love") and *Le Jeu de l'amour et du hasard* (1730; *The Game of Love and Chance*) display typical characteristics of his love comedies: romantic settings, an acute sense of nuance and the finer shades of feeling, and deft and witty wordplay. This verbal preciousness is still known as *marivaudage* and reflects the sensitivity and sophistication of the era. Marivaux also made notable advances in realism; his servants are given real feelings, and the social milieu is depicted precisely. Among his 30-odd plays are the satires *L'Île des esclaves* (1725; "Isle of Slaves") and *L'Île de la raison* (1727; "Isle of Reason"), which mock European society after the manner of *Gulliver's Travels*. *La Nouvelle colonie* (1729; "The New Colony") treats equality between the sexes, while *L'École des mères* (1724; "School for Mothers") studies mother-daughter rapport.

Marivaux's human psychology is best revealed in his romance novels, both unfinished. *La Vie de Marianne* (1731–41; *The Life of Marianne*), which preceded English novelist Samuel Richardson's *Pamela* (1740), anticipates the novel of sensibility in its glorification of a woman's feelings and intuition. *Le Paysan parvenu* (1734–35; Eng. trans. *Up from the Country*) is the story of a handsome, opportunistic young peasant who uses his attractiveness to older women to advance in the world. Both works concern struggles to arrive in society and reflect the author's rejection of authority and religious orthodoxy in favour of simple morality and naturalness. His attitude won him the wholehearted admiration of the philosopher and political theorist Jean-Jacques Rousseau, whose works were foundational to the French Revolution.

Though Marivaux was elected to the French Academy in 1743 and became its director in 1759, he was not fully appreciated during his lifetime. He died quite impoverished and remained without real fame until his work was reappraised by the critic Charles-Augustin Sainte-Beuve in the 19th century. Marivaux has since been regarded as an important link between the Age of Reason and the Age of Romanticism.

ALEXANDER POPE

(b. May 21, 1688, London, England—
d. May 30, 1744, Twickenham, near London)

Alexander Pope, who was among the finest poets and satirists of the English Augustan period, is best known for his poems *An Essay on Criticism* (1711), *The Rape of the Lock* (1712–14), *The Dunciad* (1728), and *An Essay on Man* (1733–34). He was the first English poet to enjoy contemporary fame in France and Italy and throughout the European continent and to see translations of his poems into modern as well as ancient languages.

Early Life and Works

Pope's father, a wholesale linen merchant, retired from business in the year of his son's birth and in 1700 went to live at Binfield in Windsor Forest. The Popes were Roman Catholics, and at Binfield they came to know several neighbouring Catholic families who were to play an important part in the poet's life. Pope's religion procured him some lifelong friends, notably the wealthy squire John Caryll (who persuaded him to write *The Rape of the Lock*, on an incident involving Caryll's relatives) and Martha Blount, to whom Pope addressed some of the most memorable of his poems and to whom he bequeathed most of his property. But his religion also precluded him from a formal course of education, since Catholics were not admitted to the universities.

He was trained at home by Catholic priests for a short time and attended Catholic schools at Twyford, near Winchester, and at Hyde Park Corner, London, but he was mainly self-educated. He was a precocious boy, eagerly reading Latin, Greek, French, and Italian, which he managed to teach himself, and an incessant scribbler, turning out verse upon verse in imitation of the poets he read. The best of these early writings are the *Ode on Solitude* and a paraphrase of St. Thomas à Kempis, both of which he claimed to have written at age 12.

Windsor Forest was near enough to London to permit Pope's frequent visits there. He early on grew acquainted with former members of the poet and playwright John Dryden's circle, notably William Wycherley, William Walsh, and Henry Cromwell. By 1705 his *Pastorals* were in draft and were circulating among the best literary judges of the day. In 1706 Jacob Tonson, the leading publisher of poetry, had solicited their publication, and they took the place of honour in his *Poetical Miscellanies* in 1709.

This early emergence of a man of letters may have been assisted by Pope's poor physique. As a result of too much study, so he thought, he acquired a curvature of the spine and some tubercular infection, probably Pott disease, that limited his growth and seriously impaired his health. His full-grown height was 4 feet 6 inches (1.4 metres), but the grace of his profile and fullness of his eye gave him an attractive appearance. He was a lifelong sufferer from headaches, and his deformity made him abnormally sensitive to physical and mental pain. Though he was able to ride a horse and delighted in travel, he was inevitably precluded from much normal physical activity, and his energetic, fastidious mind was largely directed to reading and writing.

When the *Pastorals* were published, Pope was already at work on a poem on the art of writing. This was *An Essay on Criticism*, published in 1711. Its brilliantly polished epigrams (e.g., "A little learning is a dangerous thing," "To err is human, to forgive, divine," and "For fools rush in where angels fear to tread"), which have become part of the proverbial heritage of the language, are readily traced to their sources in Horace, Quintilian, Nicolas Boileau, and other critics, ancient and modern, in verse and prose; but the charge that the poem is derivative, so often made in the past, takes insufficient account of Pope's success in harmonizing a century of conflict in critical thinking and in showing how nature may best be mirrored in art.

The well-deserved success of *An Essay on Criticism* brought Pope a wider circle of friends, notably Richard Steele and Joseph Addison, who were then collaborating on the periodical *The Spectator*. To this journal Pope contributed the most original of his pastorals, *The Messiah* (1712), and perhaps other papers in prose. He was clearly influenced by *The Spectator*'s policy of correcting public morals by witty admonishment, and in this vein he wrote the first version of his mock epic, *The Rape of the Lock*, to reconcile two Catholic families. (The first version, in two cantos, or divisions, was published in 1712; a second version, in five cantos, was published in 1714.) A young man in one family had stolen a lock of hair from a young lady in the other. Pope treated the dispute that followed as though it were comparable to the mighty quarrel between Greeks and Trojans, which had been Homer's theme. Telling the story with all the pomp and circumstance of epic made not only the participants in the quarrel but also the society in which they lived seem ridiculous. Though it was a society where

> *...Britain's statesmen oft the fall foredoom*
> *Of foreign tyrants, and of nymphs at home;*

as if one occupation concerned them as much as the other, and though in such a society a young lady might do equally ill to

> *...Stain her honour, or her new brocade;*
> *Forget her pray'rs, or miss a masquerade;*

Pope managed also to suggest what genuine attractions existed amid the ridiculousness. It is a glittering poem about a glittering world. He acknowledged how false the sense of values was that paid so much attention to external appearance, but ridicule and rebuke slide imperceptibly into admiration and tender affection as the heroine, Belinda, is conveyed along the Thames to Hampton Court, the scene of the theft of the young lady's hair:

> *But now secure the painted vessel glides,*
> *The sunbeams trembling on the floating tides:*
> *While melting music steals upon the sky,*
> *And soften'd sounds along the waters die;*

Smooth flow the waves, the zephyrs gently play,
Belinda smil'd, and all the world was gay.

A comparable blend of seemingly incompatible responses—love and hate, bawdiness and decorum, admiration and ridicule—is to be found in all Pope's later satires. The poem is thick with witty allusions to classical verse and, notably, to Milton's *Paradise Lost*. The art of allusion is an element of much of Pope's poetry.

Pope had also been at work for several years on *Windsor-Forest*. In this poem, completed and published in 1713, he proceeded, as Virgil had done, from the pastoral vein to the georgic (a poem dealing with practical aspects of agriculture) and celebrated the rule of Queen Anne as the Latin poet had celebrated the rule of Augustus. In another early poem, *Eloisa to Abelard,* Pope borrowed the form of Ovid's "heroic epistle" (in which an abandoned lady addresses her lover) and showed imaginative skill in conveying the struggle between sexual passion and dedication to a life of celibacy.

Homer and The Dunciad

These poems and other works were collected in the first volume of Pope's *Works* in 1717. When it was published, he was already far advanced with the greatest labour of his life, his verse translation of Homer. He had announced his intentions in October 1713 and had published the first volume, containing the *Iliad*, Books I–IV, in 1715. The *Iliad* was completed in six volumes in 1720. The work of translating the *Odyssey* (vol. i–iii, 1725; vol. iv and v, 1726) was shared with William Broome, who had contributed notes to the *Iliad*, and Elijah Fenton. The labour had been great, but so were the rewards. By the two translations Pope cleared about £10,000 and was able to claim that, thanks to Homer, he could "...live and thrive / Indebted to no Prince or Peer alive."

The merits of Pope's Homer lie less in the accuracy of translation and in correct representation of the spirit of the original than in the achievement of a heroic poem as his contemporaries understood it: a poem Virgilian in its dignity, moral purpose, and pictorial splendour, yet one that consistently kept Homer in view and alluded to him throughout. Pope offered his readers the *Iliad* and the *Odyssey* as he felt sure Homer would have written them had he lived in early 18th-century England.

Political considerations had affected the success of the translation. As a Roman Catholic, he had Tory affiliations rather than Whig; and though he retained the friendship of such Whigs as the literary figures William Congreve and Nicholas Rowe and the painter Charles Jervas, Pope's ties with Steele and Addison grew strained as a result of the political animosity that occurred at the end of Queen Anne's reign. He found new and lasting friends in Tory circles —the writers Jonathan Swift, John Gay, John Arbuthnot, and Thomas Parnell; and Robert Harley, earl of Oxford, and Henry Saint John, Viscount Bolingbroke, both prominent Tory politicians. He was associated with the first five in the Scriblerus Club (1713–14), which met to write joint satires on pedantry, later to mature as *Peri Bathouse; or, The Art of Sinking in Poetry* (1728) and the *Memoirs of Martinus Scriblerus* (1741); and these were the men who encouraged his translation of Homer. The Whigs, who associated with Addison at Button's Coffee-House, put up a rival translator in Thomas Tickell, who published his version of the *Iliad*, Book I, two days after Pope's. Addison preferred Tickell's manifestly inferior version; his praise increased the resentment Pope already felt because of a series of slights and misunderstandings; and when Pope heard gossip of further malice on Addison's part, he sent him a satiric view of his character, published later as the character of Atticus, the insincere arbiter of literary taste in *An Epistle to Dr. Arbuthnot* (1735).

Alexander Pope, portrait by Thomas Hudson; in the National Portrait Gallery, London. Courtesy of the National Portrait Gallery, London

Even before the Homer quarrel, Pope had found that the life of a wit was one of perpetual warfare. There were few years when either his person or his poems were not objects of attacks from the critic John Dennis, the bookseller Edmund Curll, the historian John Oldmixon, and other writers of lesser fame. The climax was reached over his edition of William Shakespeare's works. He had altered the plays, in the spirit of a literary editor, to accord with contemporary taste (1725), but his practice was exposed by the scholar Lewis Theobald in *Shakespeare Restored* (1726). Though Pope had ignored some of these attacks, he had replied to others with squibs in prose and verse. But he now attempted to make an end of the opposition and to defend his standards, which he aligned with the standards of civilized society, in the mock epic *The Dunciad* (1728). Theobald was represented in it as the Goddess of Dullness's favourite son, a suitable hero for those leaden times, and others who had given offense were preserved like flies in amber. Pope reissued the poem in 1729 with an elaborate mock commentary of prefaces, notes, appendixes, indexes, and errata; this burlesque of pedantry whimsically suggested that *The Dunciad* had fallen a victim to the spirit of the times and been edited by a dunce.

Life at Twickenham

Pope and his parents had moved from Binfield to Chiswick in 1716. There his father died (1717), and two years later he and his mother rented a villa on the Thames at Twickenham, then a small country town where several Londoners had retired to live in rustic seclusion. This was to be Pope's home for the remainder of his life. There he entertained such friends as Swift, Bolingbroke, Oxford, and the painter Jonathan Richardson. These friends were all enthusiastic gardeners, and it was Pope's pleasure to advise and superintend their landscaping according to the best contemporary principles, formulated in his *Epistle to the Right Honourable Richard Earl of Burlington* (1731). This poem, one of the most characteristic works of his maturity, is a rambling discussion in the manner of Horace on false taste in architecture and design, with some suggestions for the worthier employment of a nobleman's wealth.

Pope now began to contemplate a new work on the relations of man, nature, and society that would be a grand organization of human experience and intuition, but he was destined never to complete it. *An Essay on Man* (1733–34) was intended as an introductory book discussing the overall design of this work. The poem has often been charged with shallowness and philosophical inconsistency, and there is indeed little that is original in its thought, almost all of which can be traced in the work of the great thinkers of Western civilization. Subordinate themes were treated in greater detail in *Of the Use of Riches, an Epistle to Bathurst* (1732), *An Epistle to Cobham, of the Knowledge and Characters of Men* (1733), and *Of the Characters of Women: An Epistle to a Lady* (1735).

Pope was deflected from this "system of ethics in the Horatian way" by the renewed need for self-defense. Critical attacks drove him to consider his position as satirist. He chose to adapt for his own defense the first satire of Horace's second book, where the ethics of satire are propounded, and, after discussing the question in correspondence with John Arbuthnot, he addressed to him an epistle in verse (1735), one of the finest of his later poems, in which were incorporated fragments written over several years. His case in *An Epistle to Dr. Arbuthnot* was a traditional one: that depravity in public morals had roused him to stigmatize outstanding offenders beyond the reach of the law, concealing the names of some and representing others as types, and that he was innocent of personal ran-cour and habitually forbearing under attack.

The success of his *First Satire of the Second Book of Horace, Imitated* (1733) led to the publication (1734–38) of 10 more of these paraphrases of Horatian themes adapted to the contemporary social and political scene. Pope's poems fol-lowed Horace's satires and epistles sufficiently closely for him to print the Latin on facing pages with the English, but whoever chose to make the comparison would notice a continuous enrichment of the original by parenthetic thrusts and compliments, as well as by the freshness of the imagery. The series was concluded with two dialogues in verse, republished as the *Epilogue to the Satires* (1738), where, as in *An Epistle to Dr. Arbuthnot,* Pope ingeniously combined a defense of his own career and character with a restatement of the satirist's traditional apology. In these imitations and dialogues, Pope directed his attack upon the materialistic standards of the commercially minded Whigs in power and upon the corrupting effect of money, while restating and illustrating the old Horatian standards of serene and temperate living. His anxiety about prevail-ing standards was shown once more in his last completed work, *The New Dunciad* (1742), reprinted as the fourth book of a revised *Dunciad* (1743), in which Theobald was replaced as hero by Colley Cibber, the poet laureate and actor-manager, who not only had given more recent cause of offense but seemed a more appropriate representative of the degenerate standards of the age. In *Dunciad*, Book IV, the Philistine culture of the city of London was seen to overtake the court and seat of government at Westminster, and the poem ends in a magnificent but baleful prophecy of anarchy. Pope had begun work on *Brutus*, an epic poem in blank verse, and on a revision of his poems for a new edition, but neither was complete at his death.

LADY MARY WORTLEY MONTAGU

(baptized May 26, 1689, London, England—
d. August 21, 1762, London)

Lady Mary Wortley Montagu (née Pierrepont) was a versatile writer whose literary reputation chiefly rests on her so-called Turkish embassy letters. But her literary genius, like her personality, had many facets. She is principally remembered as a prolific letter writer in almost every epistolary style; she was also a distinguished minor poet, always competent, sometimes glittering and genuinely eloquent. She is further remembered as an essayist, feminist, and traveler. Her beauty was marred by a severe attack of smallpox while she was still a young woman, and she later pioneered in England the practice of inoculation against the disease, having noticed the effectiveness of this precaution during a stay in Turkey.

The daughter of the 5th earl of Kingston and

Lady Mary Wortley Montagu. **Edward Gooch/Hulton Archive/ Getty Images**

Lady Mary Fielding (a cousin of the novelist Henry Fielding), she eloped with Edward Wortley Montagu, a Whig member of Parliament, rather than accept a marriage that had been arranged by her father. In 1714 the Whigs came to power, and Edward Wortley Montagu was in 1716 appointed ambassador to Turkey, taking up residence with his wife in Constantinople (now Istanbul). After his recall in 1718, they bought a house in Twickenham, west of London. For reasons not wholly clear, Lady Mary's relationship with her husband was by this time merely formal and impersonal.

At Twickenham Lady Mary embarked upon a period of intense literary activity. She had earlier written a set of six "town eclogues" that were witty adaptations of the Roman poet Virgil. (An eclogue is a short poem which traditionally focuses on rural subjects.) In these, she was helped by her friends John Gay and Alexander Pope (who later turned against her, satirizing her in *The Dunciad* and elsewhere, to which attacks Lady Mary replied with spirit, though she quickly abandoned poetic warfare). Among the works that she then composed was an anonymous and lively attack on the satirist Jonathan Swift (1734), a play, *Simplicity* (written C. 1735), adapted from the French of Pierre Marivaux, and a series of crisp essays dealing obliquely with politics and directly with feminism and the moral cynicism of her time.

In 1736 Lady Mary became infatuated with Francesco Algarotti, an Italian writer on the arts and sciences who had come to London to further his career, and she proposed that they live together in Italy. She set out in 1739, pretending to her husband and friends that she was traveling to the continent for reasons of health. Algarotti, however, did not join her, for he had been summoned to Berlin by Frederick II the Great, from whom he could expect greater rewards; and, when at length they met in Turin (1741), it proved a disagreeable experience. In 1742 she settled in the papal state of Avignon, France, where she lived until 1746. She then returned to Italy with the young Count Ugo Palazzi, with whom she lived for the next 10 years in the Venetian province of Brescia. Her letters from there to her daughter Mary, the Countess of Bute, contain descriptions of her essentially simple life. In 1756 she moved to Venice and, after her husband's death in 1761, began planning her return to England. She set out in September of that year and was reunited with her daughter. Discontented in London, she would have returned to Italy; but she was seriously ill with cancer and died only seven months after her homecoming.

The 52 Turkish embassy letters for which she is known were written after she departed for England from Constantinople in 1718; she used her actual letters and journals as source material. The letters were published in 1763 from an unauthorized copy and were acclaimed throughout Europe. Later editions of her letters, sanctioned by her family, added selections from her personal letters together with most of her poetry. *The Complete Letters of Lady Mary Wortley Montagu*, 3 vol. (ed. Robert Halsband, 1965–67), was the first full edition of Lady Mary's letters.

SAMUEL RICHARDSON

(baptized August 19, 1689, Mackworth, near Derby, Derbyshire, England—d. July 4, 1761, Parson's Green, near London)

Samuel Richardson was an English writer who expanded the dramatic possibilities of the novel by developing what came to be known as the epistolary novel, which used letters written by its characters to structure its action. His major novels were *Pamela* (1740) and *Clarissa* (1747–48).

Richardson was 50 years old when he wrote *Pamela*, but of his first 50 years little is known. His ancestors were of yeoman stock. His father, also Samuel, and his mother's father, Stephen Hall, became London tradesmen, and his father, after the death of his first wife, married Stephen's daughter, Elizabeth, in 1682. A temporary move of the Richardsons to Derbyshire accounts for the fact that the novelist was born in Mackworth. They returned to London when Richardson was 10. He had at best what he called "only Common School-Learning." The perceived inadequacy of his education was later to preoccupy him and some of his critics.

Richardson was bound apprentice to a London printer, John Wilde. Sometime after completing his apprenticeship he became associated with the Leakes, a printing family whose presses he eventually took over when he set up in business for himself in 1721 and married Martha Wilde, the daughter of his master. Elizabeth Leake, the sister of a prosperous bookseller of Bath, became his second wife in 1733, two years after Martha's death. His domestic life was marked by tragedy. All six of the children from his first marriage died in infancy or childhood. By his second wife he had four daughters who survived him, but two other children died in infancy. These and other bereavements contributed to the nervous ailments of his later life.

In his professional life Richardson was hardworking and successful. With the growth in prominence of his press went his steady increase in prestige as a member, an officer, and later master, of the Stationers' Company (the guild for those in the book trade). During the 1730s his press became known as one of the three best in London, and with prosperity he moved to a more spacious London house and leased the first of three country houses in which he entertained a circle of friends that included Samuel Johnson, the painter William Hogarth, the actors Colley Cibber and David Garrick, Edward Young, and Arthur Onslow, speaker of the House of Commons, whose influence in 1733 helped to secure for Richardson lucrative contracts for government printing that later included the journals of the House.

In this same decade he began writing in a modest way. At some point, he was commissioned to write a collection of letters that might serve as models for "country readers," a volume that has become known as *Familiar Letters on Important Occasions.* Occasionally he hit upon continuing the same subject from one letter to another, and, after a letter from "a father to a daughter in service, on hearing of her master's attempting her virtue," he supplied the daughter's answer. This was the germ of his novel *Pamela.* With a method supplied by the letter writer and a plot by a story that he remembered of an actual serving maid who preserved her virtue and was rewarded by marriage, he began writing the work in November 1739 and published it as *Pamela: or, Virtue Rewarded* a year later.

Most of the story is told by the heroine herself. On the death of Pamela's mistress, her son, Mr. B, begins a series of stratagems designed to end in Pamela's seduction. These failing, he abducts her and renews his siege in earnest. Pamela preserves her virtue, and halfway through the novel Mr. B offers marriage. In the second half Richardson shows Pamela winning over those who had disapproved of the misalliance. Though the novel was immensely popular, Richardson was criticized by those who thought his heroine a calculating minx or his own morality dubious. Actually his heroine is a vividly imagined blend of the artful and the artless. She is a sadly perplexed girl of 15, with a divided mind, who faces a real dilemma because she wants to preserve her virtue without losing the man with whom she has fallen in love. Since Richardson wrote the novel from Pamela's point of view, it is less clear that Mr. B's problem arises from his having fallen in love with a servant, who, traditionally, would have been merely a target for seduction. In a clever twist, he is converted by her letters, which he has been intercepting and reading. The author resolved the conflicts of both characters too facilely, perhaps, because he was firmly committed to the plot of the true story he had remembered. When the instantaneous popularity of *Pamela* led to a spurious continuation of her story, he wrote his own sequel, *Pamela in her Exalted Condition* (1742), a two-volume work that did little to enhance his reputation.

By 1744 Richardson seems to have completed a first draft of his second novel, *Clarissa: or, The History of a Young Lady*, but he spent three years trying to bring it within the compass of the seven volumes in which it was published. He first presents the heroine, Clarissa Harlowe, when she is discovering the barely masked motives of her family, who would force her into a loveless marriage to improve their fortunes. Outside the orbit of the Harlowes stands Lovelace, nephew of Lord M and a romantic who held the code of the Harlowes in contempt. In her desperate straits, Clarissa appraises too highly the qualities that set Lovelace beyond the world of her family, and, when he offers protection, she runs off with him. She is physically attracted by if not actually in love with Lovelace and is responsive to the wider horizons of his world, but she is to discover that he wants her only on his own terms. In Lovelace's letters to his friend Belford, Richardson shows that what is driving him to conquest and finally to rape is really her superiority. In the correspondence of Clarissa and her friend Anna Howe, Richardson shows the distance that separates her from her confidant, who thinks her quixotic in not accepting a marriage; but marriage as a way out would have been a sacrifice to that same consciousness of human dignity that had led her to defy her family. As the novel comes to its long-drawn-out close, she is removed from the world of both the Harlowes and the Lovelaces, and dies, a child of heaven. In providing confidants for his central characters and in refusing to find a place in the social structure into which to fit his sorely beset heroine, Richardson made his greatest advances over *Pamela*. He was determined, as his postscript indicates, to write a novel that was also a tragedy.

Richardson's third novel was his bow to requests for the hero as a good man, a counter-attraction to the errant hero of Henry Fielding's *Tom Jones* (1749). Fielding had been among those who thought Pamela a scheming minx, as he had shown in his parody *An Apology for the Life of Mrs. Shamela Andrews* (1741). In spite of Fielding's critical praise of *Clarissa* and the friendship that later developed between Richardson and Fielding's sister, Sarah, Richardson never forgave the author of what he stigmatized as "that vile Pamphlet Shamela." In *The History of Sir Charles Grandison* (1753–54), he provides a hero who is a model of benevolence. He faces little that a good heart cannot remedy and extricates himself from the nearest thing to a dilemma that he has to encounter: a "divided love" between an English woman, Harriet Byron, and an Italian, Signora Clementina. He is saved for Harriet by the last-minute refusal of the Roman Catholic Clementina to marry a firmly committed English churchman. The uneasy minds of Clementina and Harriet are explored with some penetration, but Sir Charles faces nothing in his society or within himself that requires much of a struggle. Furthermore, his dilemma is not so central to the novel as were those of Pamela and Clarissa.

He is surrounded with a large cast of characters who have their parts to play in social comedy that anticipates the novel of manners of the late 18th century.

Richardson was an indefatigable reviser of his own work, and the various editions of his novels differ greatly. Much of his revision was undertaken in anxious, self-censoring response to criticism; the earliest versions of his novels are generally the freshest and most daring.

Richardson's *Pamela* is often credited with being the first English novel. Although the validity of this claim depends on the definition of the term *novel*, it is not disputed that Richardson was innovative in his concentration on a single action, in this case a courtship. By telling the story in the form of letters, he provided if not the "stream" at least the flow of consciousness of his characters, and he pioneered in showing how his characters' sense of class differences and their awareness of the conflict between sexual instincts and the moral code created dilemmas that could not always be resolved. These characteristics reappear regularly in the subsequent history of the novel. Above all, Richardson was the writer who made the novel a respectable genre.

Richardson had disciples when he died. Some of them show the influence of *Clarissa*, which seems to have been most responsible for the cult of Richardson that arose on the European continent. It was *Grandison*, however, that set the tone of most of Richardson's English followers and for Jane Austen, who was said to have remembered "every circumstance" in this novel, everything "that was ever said or done." By the end of the 18th century, Richardson's reputation was on the wane both in England and abroad. It was reborn in the late 20th century, however, and *Clarissa* is now widely admired as one of the great psychological novels of European literature.

PHILIP DORMER STANHOPE, 4TH EARL OF CHESTERFIELD

(b. September 22, 1694, London, England—
d. March 24, 1773, London)

Philip Dormer Stanhope, 4th earl of Chesterfield, was an English statesman, diplomat, and wit who was chiefly remembered as the author of *Letters to His Son* and *Letters to His Godson*—guides to manners, the art of pleasing, and the art of worldly success.

After a short period of study at Trinity Hall, Cambridge, he spent some time abroad, mainly in Paris. He was a great admirer of French manners, culture, and taste. He succeeded to the earldom in 1726 and became ambassador to Holland in 1728. Philip Stanhope, the son who was the recipient of the letters, was born there in 1732. Returning to England in the same year, Chesterfield took up a parliamentary career for the next decade as a strong opponent of Sir Robert Walpole. In spite of his connection by marriage to the king, he lost favour at court until he demonstrated his abilities as a statesman in his short term (August 1745–April 1746) as lord lieutenant of Ireland. After a term as secretary of state (1746–48), he gradually retired from public life because of increasing deafness, though he was largely responsible for Britain's decision to adopt the Gregorian calendar in 1752.

Chesterfield's winning manners, urbanity, and wit were praised by many of his leading contemporaries, and he was on familiar terms with such major literary figures of his day as Alexander Pope, John Gay, and Voltaire. He was the patron of many struggling authors but had unfortunate relations with one of them, Samuel Johnson, who condemned him in a famous letter (1755) attacking patrons. Johnson further damaged Chesterfield's reputation when he described the *Letters* as teaching "the morals of a whore, and the manners of a dancing master." The novelist Charles Dickens later caricatured him as Sir John Chester in *Barnaby Rudge* (1841). The opinion of these two more popular writers—both of whom epitomized middle-class morality—has contributed to Chesterfield's image as a cynical man of the world and a courtier. Careful readers of Chesterfield's letters, which were not written for publication, consider this an injustice. The strongest charge against his philosophy is that it leads to concentration on worldly ends. But within this limitation his advice is shrewd and presented with wit and elegance. Ironically, Chesterfield's painstaking advice seems to have fallen on deaf ears: his son was described by contemporaries as "loutish," and his godson was described by Fanny Burney as having "as little good breeding as any man I ever met."

Chesterfield left many other letters that are models of wit and charm, especially those written to the diplomat Solomon Dayrolles, a lifelong friend who was with him at his deathbed.

VOLTAIRE

(b. November 21, 1694, Paris, France—d. May 30, 1778, Paris)

Voltaire is one of the greatest of all French writers. Although only a few of his works are still read, he continues to be held in worldwide repute as a courageous crusader against tyranny, bigotry, and cruelty. Through its critical capacity, wit, and satire, Voltaire's work vigorously propagates an ideal of progress to which people of all nations have remained responsive, and his activities throughout his life have influenced the direction taken by European civilization.

Heritage and Youth

Voltaire—the pseudonym of François-Marie Arouet—grew up in a middle-class environment. According to his birth certificate he was born on November 21, 1694, but the hypothesis that his birth was kept secret cannot be dismissed, for he stated on several occasions that in fact it took place on February 20. He believed that he was the son of an officer named Rochebrune, who was also a songwriter. He had no love for either his putative father, François Arouet, a onetime notary who later became receiver in the Cour des Comptes (audit office), or his elder brother Armand. Almost nothing is known about his mother of whom he hardly said anything. Having lost her when he was seven, he seems to have become an early rebel against family authority.

He decided against the study of law after he left the Jesuit college of Louis-le-Grand in Paris. Employed as secretary at the French embassy in The Hague, he became infatuated with the daughter of an adventurer. Fearing scandal, the French ambassador sent him back to Paris, where he aimed to devote himself wholly to literature. After the death of King Louis XIV, under the morally relaxed Regency, Voltaire became the wit of that city's society, and his epigrams were widely quoted. But when he dared to mock the dissolute regent, the Duc d'Orléans, he was banished from Paris and then imprisoned in the Bastille for nearly a year (1717).

Mid-18th-century portrait of Voltaire. Apic/Hulton Fine Art Collection/Getty Images

Behind his cheerful facade, he was fundamentally serious and set himself to learn the accepted literary forms. In 1718, after the success of *Oedipe*, the first of his tragedies, he was acclaimed as the successor of the great classical dramatist Jean Racine and thenceforward adopted the name of Voltaire. The origin of this pen name remains doubtful. It is not certain that it is the anagram of Arouet le jeune ("Arouet the younger"). Above all he desired to be the Virgil that France had never known. He worked at an epic poem whose hero was Henry IV, the king beloved by the French people for having put an end to the wars of religion. In this poem, the *Henriade*, his contemporaries saw the generous ideal of tolerance that inspired it. These literary triumphs earned him a pension from the regent and the warm approval of the young queen, Marie. He thus began his career of court poet.

United with other thinkers of his day—literary men and scientists—in the belief in the efficacy of reason, Voltaire was a philosophe, as the 18th century termed it. He became interested in England, the country that tolerated freedom of thought; he visited the Tory leader Henry Saint John, Viscount Bolingbroke, exiled in France—a politician, an orator, and a philosopher whom Voltaire admired to the point of comparing him to the ancient Roman statesman Cicero. On Bolingbroke's advice he learned English in order to read the philosophical works of John Locke. His intellectual development was furthered by an accident: as the result of a quarrel with a member of one of the leading French families, the Chevalier de Rohan, who had made fun of his adopted name, he was beaten, taken to the Bastille, and then conducted to Calais on May 5, 1726, from where he set out for London. His destiny was now exile and opposition.

Exile to England and Return to France

During a stay that lasted more than two years he succeeded in learning the English language, and he met such English men of letters as Alexander Pope, Jonathan Swift, and William Congreve, the philosopher George Berkeley, and Samuel Clarke, the theologian. He was presented at court, and he dedicated his *Henriade* to Queen Caroline. Though at first Bolingbroke, who had returned from exile, acted as his patron, it appears that Voltaire quarrelled with the Tory leader and turned to Sir Robert Walpole and his fellow liberal Whigs. He admired the liberalism of English institutions, though he was shocked by the partisan violence. He envied English intrepidity in the discussion of religious and philosophic questions, was seduced by English notions of personal liberty, and believed that France could learn from England even in literature.

Voltaire returned to France at the end of 1728 or the beginning of 1729 and decided to present England as a model to his compatriots. By judicious monetary speculation he also began to build up the vast fortune that guaranteed his independence. In addition, he attempted to revive tragedy by discreetly imitating William Shakespeare. After several attempts that achieved middling to no success, *Zaïre* found an appreciative public. The play, in which the sultan Orosmane, deceived by an ambiguous letter, stabs his prisoner, the devoted Christian-born Zaïre, in a fit of jealousy, captivated audiences with its exotic subject.

At the same time, Voltaire had turned to a new literary genre: history. His time in London spurred his interest in the Swedish king Charles XII, which resulted in *Histoire de Charles XII* (1731; Eng. trans. *Lion of the North, Charles XII of Sweden*), a carefully documented historical narrative that reads like a novel. Philosophic ideas began to impose themselves as he wrote: the king of Sweden's exploits brought desolation, whereas his rival Peter the Great brought Russia into being, bequeathing a vast, civilized empire. Great men are not warmongers, he concluded; they further civilization—a stance that tallied with the example of England. It was this line of thought that Voltaire brought to fruition, after prolonged meditation, in a work of incisive brevity: the *Lettres philosophiques* (1734; Eng. trans. *Letters on England*). These fictitious letters are primarily a demonstration of the benign effects of religious toleration. After elucidating the English political system, its commerce, and its literature, Voltaire concludes with an attack on the French mathematician and religious philosopher Blaise Pascal: the purpose of life is not to reach heaven through penitence but to assure happiness to all individuals by progress in the sciences and the arts, a fulfillment for which their nature is destined. This small, brilliant book is a landmark in the history of thought: not only does it embody the philosophy of the 18th century, but it also defines the essential direction of the modern mind.

Life with Mme du Châtelet

Scandal followed publication of this work that spoke out so frankly against the religious and political establishment. When a warrant of arrest was issued in May of 1734, Voltaire took refuge in the château of Mme du Châtelet at Cirey in Champagne and thus began his liaison with this young, extremely intelligent woman.

The life these two lived together was both luxurious and studious. During this time he brought *Alzire* to the stage in 1736 with great success. The action of *Alzire*—in Lima, Peru, at the time of the Spanish conquest—brings out the moral superiority of a humanitarian civilization over methods of brute force. Despite its conventional portrayal of "noble savages," the tragedy kept its place in the repertory of the Comédie-Française for almost a century. Mme du Châtelet was passionately drawn to the sciences and metaphysics and influenced Voltaire's work in that direction. While she was learning English in order to translate Newton, Voltaire popularized, in his *Éléments de la philosophie de Newton* (1738; *The Elements of Sir Isaac Newton's Philosophy*), those discoveries of English science that were familiar only to a few advanced minds in France. At the same time, he continued to pursue his historical studies. He began *Le Siècle de Louis XIV* (*The Age of Louis XIV*), sketched out a universal history that became the *Essai sur les moeurs* (1756; Eng. trans. *An Essay on Universal History, the Manners and Spirit of Nations from the Reign of Charlemaign to the Age of Lewis XIV*), and plunged into biblical exegesis.

Because of a lawsuit, he followed Mme du Châtelet to Brussels in May 1739, and thereafter they were constantly on the move between Belgium, Cirey, and Paris. Voltaire corresponded with the crown prince of Prussia, who, rebelling against his father's rigid system of military training and education, had taken refuge in French culture. When the prince acceded to the throne as Frederick II (the Great), Voltaire visited his disciple first at Cleves (Kleve, Germany), then at Berlin. When the War of the Austrian Succession broke out, Voltaire was sent to Berlin (1742–43) on a secret mission to rally the king of Prussia —who was proving himself a faithless ally—to the assistance of the French Army. Such services brought him into favour again at Versailles. After his poem celebrating the victory of Fontenoy (1745), he was appointed historiographer, gentleman of the king's chamber, and academician. His tragedy *Mérope*, about the mythical Greek queen, won public acclaim on the first night (1743). He amassed a vast fortune through the manipulations of Joseph Pâris

Duverney, the financier in charge of military supplies, who was favoured by Mme de Pompadour, the mistress of Louis XV.

Yet he was not spared disappointments. King Louis XV disliked him, and the pious Catholic faction at court remained acutely hostile. He was guilty of indiscretions that forced him into hiding. Ill and exhausted by his restless existence, he at last discovered the literary form that ideally fitted his lively and disillusioned temper: he wrote his first *contes* (stories), which would appear in such books as *Micromégas* (1752), a work which uses the form to measure the littleness of humankind in the cosmic scale.

The great crisis of his life was drawing near. In 1748 at Commercy, where he had joined the court of Stanisław (the former king of Poland), he detected the love affair of Mme du Châtelet and the poet Jean-Françoise de Saint-Lambert, a slightly ludicrous passion that resulted in Châtelet's becoming pregnant. On September 10, 1749, he witnessed the death in childbirth of the woman who for 15 years had been his guide and counsellor.

Later Travels

The failure of some of his plays aggravated his sense of defeat. He had attempted the *comédie larmoyante*, or "sentimental comedy," that was then fashionable, but various plays in this manner met with no success. He found that Parisian audiences preferred the tragedies of Prosper Jolyot, sieur de Crébillon, to his own. Exasperated and disappointed, he yielded to the invitation of Frederick II and set out for Berlin on June 28, 1750.

At first he was enchanted by his sojourn in Berlin and Potsdam, but soon difficulties arose, and Voltaire provoked a controversy with the president of Frederick's academy of science, the Berlin Academy, that left Frederick enraged.

Voltaire left Prussia on March 26, 1753, further aggravating Frederick; on the journey Voltaire was held under house arrest at an inn at Frankfurt. Louis XV forbade him to approach Paris. Not knowing where to turn, he stayed at Colmar for more than a year. At length he found asylum at Geneva, where he purchased a house called Les Délices.

He now completed his two major historical studies. *Le Siècle de Louis XIV* (1751), a book on the century of Louis XIV, had been prepared after an exhaustive 20-year interrogation of the survivors of *le grand siècle*. The *Essai sur les moeurs*, the study on customs and morals that he had begun in 1740 (first complete edition, 1756), traced the course of world history since the end of the Roman Empire. He supplemented these two works with several others on world history.

At Geneva, he had at first been welcomed and honoured as the champion of tolerance. Attracted by his volatile intelligence, Calvinist pastors as well as women and young people thronged to his salon. But soon he made those around him feel uneasy, and he provoked the hostility of important Swiss intellectuals. The storm broke in November 1757, when volume seven of Denis Diderot's *Encyclopédie* was published. Voltaire had inspired the article on Geneva that his fellow philosopher Jean d'Alembert had written after a visit to Les Délices; not only was the city of Calvin asked to build a theatre within its walls but also certain of its pastors were praised for their doubts of Christ's divinity. The scandal sparked a quick response: the *Encyclopédie* was forced to interrupt publication, and Jean-Jacques Rousseau attacked the rational philosophy of the philosophes in general in a polemical treatise on the question of the morality of theatrical performances. Rousseau's view that drama might well be abolished marked a final break between the two writers.

Voltaire no longer felt safe in Geneva, and he longed to retire from these quarrels. In 1758 he wrote what was to be his most famous work, *Candide*. In this philosophical fantasy, the youth Candide, disciple of Doctor Pangloss, saw and suffered such misfortune that he was unable to believe that this was "the best of all possible worlds." Having retired with his companions to the shores of the Propontis, he discovered that the secret of happiness was "to cultivate one's garden," a practical philosophy excluding excessive idealism and nebulous metaphysics. Voltaire's own garden became Ferney, a property he bought at the end of 1758, together with Tourney in France, on the Swiss border. By crossing the frontier he could thus safeguard himself against police incursion from either country.

Achievements at Ferney

At Ferney, Voltaire entered on one of the most active periods of his life. Both patriarch and lord of the manor, he developed a modern estate, sharing in the movement of agricultural reform in which the aristocracy was interested at the time. He could not be true to himself, however, without stirring up village feuds. He meddled in Genevan politics, taking the side of the workers (or *natifs*, those without civil rights), and installed a stocking factory and watchworks on his estate in order to help them. He called for the liberation of serfs in the Jura, but without success. Such generous interventions in local politics earned him enormous popularity, and his fame became worldwide. "Innkeeper of Europe"—as he was called—he welcomed such literary figures as James Boswell, Giovanni Casanova, and Edward Gibbon as well as the fashionable philosophers of Paris. He kept up an enormous correspondence on all subjects, renewed contact with Frederick II, and exchanged letters with Catherine II of Russia.

His main interest at this time, however, was his opposition to *l'infâme*, a word he used to designate the church, especially when it was identified with intolerance. He also produced a prodigious number of polemical writings, often engaging in personal attacks delivered from a thicket of pseudonyms. As a part-time scholar he constructed a personal *Encyclopédie*, the *Dictionnaire philosophique* (1764; *Philosophical Dictionary*).

Throughout the mass of writings he produced during this period, Voltaire again and again returned to his chosen themes: the establishment of religious tolerance, the growth of material prosperity, and respect for the rights of the individual by the abolition of torture and useless punishments. His intervention in some of the notorious public scandals of these years allowed him to retain leadership of the philosophic movement. As a writer, though, he also wanted to halt a development he deplored—that which led to Romanticism. He made concessions to a public that adored scenes of violence and exoticism in an attempt that he believed would save theatrical tragedy. For instance, in *L'Orphelin de la Chine* (1755; *The Orphan of China*), Lekain (Henri-Louis Cain), who played the part of Genghis Khan, was clad in a sensational Mongol costume. Lekain, whom Voltaire considered the greatest tragedian of his time, also played the title role of *Tancrède*, which was produced with a sumptuous decor (1760) and which proved to be Voltaire's last triumph. Subsequent tragedies, arid and ill-constructed and overweighted with philosophic propaganda, were either booed off the stage or not produced at all. Romanticism would ultimately triumph.

But it was the theatre that brought him back to Paris in 1778. Wishing to direct the rehearsals of his *Irène*, he made his triumphal return to the city he had not seen for 28 years on February 10. More than 300 persons called on him the day after his arrival. When *Irène* was played before a delirious audience, he was crowned in his box. His health was profoundly impaired by all this excitement, and on

May 30 he died. His body was swiftly transported to the Abbey of Scellières, where it was given Christian burial by the local clergy; the prohibition of such burial arrived after the ceremony. His remains were transferred to the Panthéon during the French Revolution in July 1791.

RICHARD SAVAGE

(b. *c.* 1697, England—d. August 1, 1743, Bristol)

Richard Savage was an English poet and satirist and the subject of one of the best short biographies in English, Samuel Johnson's *An Account of the Life of Mr. Richard Savage* (1744).

By his own account in the preface to the second edition of his *Miscellaneous Poems* (1728; 1st ed., 1726), Savage was born out of wedlock to Anne, countess of Macclesfield, and Richard Savage, the 4th earl of Rivers. His exact date of birth is uncertain. In any event, in November 1715 a young man taken into custody for having written treasonable poetry identified himself as "Mr. Savage, natural son to the late Earl Rivers" and continued so to describe himself for the rest of his life. This was the poet Savage whose life Johnson chronicled. In 1727 Savage was tried for the murder of one James Sinclair in a tavern brawl but was acquitted.

In 1717 he published *The Convocation*, a poem about a religious dispute known as the Bangorian controversy, and in 1718 *Love in a Veil* (published 1719), a comedy adapted from the Spanish of the 17th-century playwright Pedro Calderón de la Barca, was produced at Drury Lane. There, in 1723, his Neoclassical tragedy *Sir Thomas Overbury* was also produced. His most considerable poem, *The Wanderer*, a discursive work, appeared in 1729, as did his prose satire on Grub Street, *An Author to Be Let*. In 1737–38 he met Samuel Johnson, then newly arrived in London, and to Johnson's perceptive and compassionate biography he owes his continuing fame. Savage was a quarrelsome and an impecunious man. His friends, the poet Alexander Pope prominent among them, eventually provided him money to convey him out of London. After a year in Wales, he died miserably in debtor's prison.

JAMES THOMSON

(b. September 11, 1700, Ednam, Roxburgh, Scotland—
d. August 27, 1748, Richmond, England)

The best verse of the Scottish poet James Thomson foreshadowed some of the attitudes of the Romantic movement. His poetry also gave expression to the achievements of Newtonian science and to a Great Britain that was reaching toward great political power based on commercial and maritime expansion.

Educated at Jedburgh Grammar School and the University of Edinburgh, Thomson went to London in 1725. While earning his living there as a tutor, he published his masterpiece, a long, blank verse poem in four parts, called *The Seasons*: *Winter* in 1726, *Summer* in 1727, *Spring* in 1728, and the whole poem, including *Autumn*, in 1730.

The Seasons was the first sustained nature poem in English and concludes with a "Hymn to Nature." The work was a revolutionary departure; its novelty lay not only in subject matter but in structure. What was most striking to Thomson's earliest readers was his audacity in unifying his poem without a "plot" or other narrative device, thereby defying the Aristotelian criteria revered by the Neoclassicist critics.

Thomson's belief that the scientist and poet must collaborate in the service of God, as revealed through nature, found its best expression in *To the Memory of Sir Isaac Newton* (1727).

The poet also is remembered as the author of the famous ode "Rule, Britannia," from *Alfred, a Masque* (1740, with music by T.A. Arne); for his ambitious poem in five parts, *Liberty* (1735–36); and for *The Castle of Indolence* (1748), an allegory of what may occur when Indolence overcomes Industry.

HENRY BROOKE

(b. *c.* 1703, County Cavan, Ireland—d. October 10, 1783, Dublin)

The Irish novelist and dramatist Henry Brooke is best known for *The Fool of Quality*, one of the outstanding English examples of the novel of sensibility—a novel in which the characters demonstrate a heightened emotional response to events around them.

After attending Trinity College, Dublin, Brooke went to London in 1724 to study law. There he became friendly with the poet Alexander Pope; he had already met the writer Jonathan Swift in Ireland. In 1739 Brooke wrote a celebrated drama, *Gustavus Vasa, the Deliverer of His Country*, performance of which was forbidden because of the supposition that Sir Robert Walpole, the prime minister, was depicted in the part of the villain. Brooke returned to Ireland, and the play was printed and later performed in Dublin as *The Patriot*. Brooke's own patriotic sentiments led to his involvement in the establishment of the influential newspaper *The Freeman's Journal* in 1763.

Brooke's novel, *The Fool of Quality* (1765–70), is a rambling and digressive narrative centred on the education of an ideal nobleman. Its moral message recommended it to John Wesley, a founder of Methodism, who edited an abridged version in 1780, and, later, to the clergyman–author Charles Kingsley, who published it with an enthusiastic biographical preface in 1859.

ANTÔNIO JOSÉ DA SILVA

(b. May 8, 1705, Rio de Janeiro, Brazil—
d. October 18, 1739, Lisbon, Portugal)

Antônio José da Silva was a Portuguese writer whose comedies, farces, and operettas briefly revitalized the Portuguese theatre in a period of dramatic decadence.

Silva was born in Brazil, the son of Jews. Though his parents professed Christianity, his mother was accused by the Inquisition of relapsing into Judaism, and in 1712, when Antônio was seven years old, the family was forced to leave Brazil for Portugal for her trial. Silva studied canon law at Coimbra, but at 21 he was imprisoned with his mother and brothers and forced under torture to renounce his Jewish faith. On his release, he completed his studies (1728), joined his father's legal practice in Lisbon, and married a cousin who had also suffered religious persecution.

During a brief period (1729–37) when he was unmolested by the authorities, Silva wrote eight plays, all for the *ópera dos bonecos* (puppet theatre), performed at the Bairro Alto Theatre in Lisbon. Prose dialogue is interspersed with arias, minuets, and *modinhas* (popular, light songs). His best plays are generally considered to be *A Vida do grande D. Quixote de la Mancha* (1733; "The Life of

Don Quixote of La Mancha") and *As Guerras do Alecrim e da Mangerona* (1737; "The Wars of the Rosemary and the Marjoram"). Altogether they constitute a skilled and witty satire against the pretensions of a society based on caste and privilege.

In 1739 Silva and his wife were both charged by the Inquisition with the heresy of Judaizing and imprisoned on October 5. Thirteen days later, Silva was garrotted and burned at an *auto-da-fé* (public burning at the stake), witnessed by his wife, who died soon thereafter.

BENJAMIN FRANKLIN

(b. January 17 [January 6, Old Style], 1706, Boston, Massachusetts
[U.S.]—d. April 17, 1790, Philadelphia, Pennsylvania, U.S.)

Benjamin Franklin was an American printer and publisher, author, inventor and scientist, and diplomat. Best known as one of the foremost of the Founding Fathers—he helped draft the Declaration of Independence and was one of its signers—Franklin also made important contributions to science, especially in the understanding of electricity, and is remembered for the wit, wisdom, and elegance of his writing.

Early Life

Franklin was born the 10th son of the 17 children of a man who made soap and candles, one of the lowliest of the artisan crafts. His formal education ended at age 10, and at 12 he was apprenticed to his brother James, a printer. His mastery of the printer's trade, of which he was proud to the end of his life, was achieved between 1718 and 1723. In the same period he read tirelessly and taught himself to write effectively.

His first enthusiasm was for poetry, but, discouraged with the quality of his own, he gave it up. Prose was another matter. Young Franklin discovered a volume of *The Spectator*—featuring Joseph Addison and Sir Richard Steele's famous periodical essays, which had appeared in England in 1711–12—and saw in it a means for improving his writing. He read these *Spectator* papers over and over, copied and recopied them, and then tried to recall them from memory. Franklin realized, as all the Founders did, that writing competently was such a rare talent in the 18th century that anyone who could do it well immediately attracted attention.

Youthful Adventures

After leaving home following a bitter quarrel and failing to find work in New York City, Franklin at age 17 went on to Quaker-dominated Philadelphia, a much more open and religiously tolerant place than Puritan Boston. Soon after his arrival he was employed as a printer, and by the spring of 1724 he was being urged to set up in business for himself by the governor of Pennsylvania, Sir William Keith. After failing to secure money from his father, Franklin won backing from Keith, who arranged Franklin's passage to England so that he could choose his type and make connections with London stationers and booksellers. Franklin sailed for London in November 1724. Not until his ship was well out at sea did he realize that Keith had not delivered the letters of credit and introduction he had promised.

Nonetheless, in London Franklin quickly found employment in his trade and was able to lend money to

James Ralph, who was travelling with Franklin as his companion and was trying to establish himself as a writer. The two young men enjoyed the theatre and the other pleasures of the city, but by 1726 Franklin was tiring of London. He considered becoming an itinerant teacher of swimming, but, when Thomas Denham, a Quaker merchant, offered him a clerkship in his store in Philadelphia with a prospect of fat commissions in the West Indian trade, he decided to return home.

Achievement of Security and Fame

Denham died, however, a few months after Franklin entered his store. The young man, now 20, returned to the printing trade and in 1728 was able to set up a partnership with a friend. Two years later he borrowed money to become sole proprietor.

Franklin's private life during this period was complicated, involving as it did a child born out of wedlock, two children born to a common-law marriage to Deborah Reade, who had been abandoned by a previous husband, and other difficulties. But these failed to hinder Franklin's pursuit of business. Franklin and his partner's first coup was securing the printing of Pennsylvania's paper currency. Franklin helped get this business by writing *A Modest Enquiry into the Nature and Necessity of a Paper Currency* (1729), and later he also became public printer of New Jersey, Delaware, and Maryland. Other moneymaking ventures included the *Pennsylvania Gazette*, published by Franklin from 1729 and generally acknowledged as among the best of the colonial newspapers, and *Poor Richard's* almanac, printed annually from 1732 to 1757. Despite some failures, Franklin prospered. By the late 1740s he had become one of the wealthiest colonists in the northern part of the North American continent, which enabled him to concoct a variety of projects for social improvement. He was also picking up some political offices: he became clerk of the Pennsylvania legislature in 1736 and postmaster of Philadelphia in 1737.

In 1748 Franklin, at age 42, had become wealthy enough to retire from active business. He became a gentleman, a distinctive status in the 18th century. Franklin never again worked as a printer; instead, he became a silent partner in the comfortably profitable printing firm of Franklin and Hall. He announced his new status as a gentleman through the acquisition of a coat of arms and several slaves, and he moved to a new and more spacious house. Most important, as a gentleman, he decided to do what other gentlemen did—engage in what he termed "Philosophical Studies and Amusements." In the

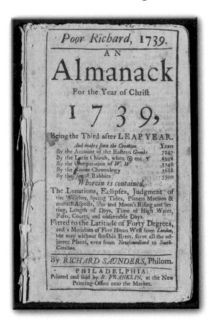

1740s electricity was one of these curious amusements. Investigations into electrical phenomena by Franklin and three of his friends culminated in an 86-page book consisting of Franklin's reports on their activities. Titled *Experiments and Observations on Electricity* (1751), the book went through multiple English editions and was translated into French, Italian, and German. Its many original findings made Franklin famous.

Title page for Poor Richard's almanac for 1739, written, printed, and sold by Benjamin Franklin. **Rare Book and Special Collections Division, Library of Congress, Washington, D.C.**

Public Service

Franklin, however, never thought science was as important as public service. As a leisured gentleman, he soon became involved in more high-powered public offices. He became a member of the Philadelphia City Council in 1748, justice of the peace in 1749, and in 1751 a city alderman and a member of the Pennsylvania Assembly. But he had his sights on being part of a larger arena, the British Empire. In 1753 Franklin became a royal officeholder, deputy postmaster general, in charge of mail in all the northern colonies. Thereafter he began to think in intercolonial terms. Through his participation in 1754 in the Albany Congress, which adopted his plan of union for the British colonies in North America, Franklin had become acquainted with important imperial officials. Even though that plan failed, his ambition to succeed within the imperial hierarchy had been whetted.

In 1757 he went to England as the agent of the Pennsylvania Assembly in order to get the family of William Penn, the proprietors under the colony's charter, to allow the colonial legislature to tax their ungranted lands. But Franklin and some of his allies in the assembly had a larger goal of persuading the British government to oust the Penn family as the proprietors of Pennsylvania and make that colony a royal province. Except for a two-year return to Philadelphia in 1762–64, Franklin spent the next 18 years living in London.

Before he left for London, Franklin decided to bring his *Poor Richard's* almanac to an end. While at sea in 1757, he completed a 12-page preface for the final 1758 edition of the almanac titled "Father Abraham's Speech" and later known as the *The Way to Wealth*. In this preface Father Abraham cites only those proverbs that concern hard work, thrift, and financial prudence. *The Way to*

Wealth eventually became the most widely reprinted of all Franklin's works, including the *Autobiography*.

This time Franklin's experience in London was very different from his sojourn in 1724–26. London was the largest city in Europe, and Franklin was famous; consequently, he met everyone else who was famous, including the philosopher David Hume, Captain James Cook, and John Pringle, who was physician to Lord Bute, the king's chief minister. Franklin received honorary degrees from the University of Saint Andrews in Scotland (1759) and the University of Oxford (1762). He fell in love with the sophistication of London and England and disparaged the provinciality and vulgarity of America.

Reluctantly, Franklin had to go back to Pennsylvania in 1762 in order to look after his post office, but he promised his friends in London that he would soon return. After losing an election to the Pennsylvania Assembly in 1764, Franklin could hardly wait to get back to London. His wife, Deborah, stayed in Philadelphia and would die in 1774; Franklin never saw her again.

He soon had to face the problems arising from the Stamp Act of 1765, which created a firestorm of opposition in America. Like other colonial agents, Franklin opposed Parliament's stamp tax, asserting that taxation ought to be the prerogative of the colonial legislatures. But once he saw that passage of the tax was inevitable, he sought to make the best of the situation. He ordered stamps for his printing firm in Philadelphia and procured for his friend John Hughes the stamp agency for Pennsylvania. But he and Hughes were faced with the mobs that effectively prevented enforcement of the Stamp Act everywhere in North America. Only Franklin's four-hour testimony before Parliament denouncing the act in 1766 saved his reputation in America. The experience shook Franklin, and his earlier confidence in the wisdom of British officials became punctuated by doubts and resentments. He began to feel what he called his "Americanness" as never before.

During the next four or five years Franklin sought to bridge the growing gulf between the colonies and the British government. Between 1765 and 1775 he wrote 126 newspaper pieces, most of which tried to explain each side to the other. But, as he said, the English thought him too American, while the Americans thought him too English. He had not, however, given up his ambition of acquiring a position in the imperial hierarchy. But in 1771 opposition by Lord Hillsborough, who had just been appointed head of the new American Department, left Franklin depressed and dispirited; in a mood of frustration, nostalgia, and defiance, he began writing his *Autobiography*.

When the signals from the British government shifted and Hillsborough was dismissed from the cabinet, Franklin dropped the writing of the *Autobiography*, which he would not resume until 1784 in France following the successful negotiation of the treaty establishing American independence. Franklin still thought he might be able to acquire an imperial office and work to hold the empire together. But he became involved in the affair of the Hutchinson letters—an affair that ultimately destroyed his position in England. In 1772 Franklin had sent back to Boston some letters written in the 1760s by Thomas Hutchinson, then lieutenant governor of Massachusetts, in which Hutchinson had made some indiscreet remarks about the need to abridge American liberties. Franklin naively thought that these letters would somehow throw blame for the imperial crisis on native officials such as Hutchinson and thus absolve the ministry in London of responsibility. This, Franklin believed, would allow his friends in the ministry, such as

Lord Dartmouth, to settle the differences between the mother country and her colonies, with Franklin's help. The move backfired completely, however, and on January 29, 1774, Franklin stood silent in an amphitheatre near Whitehall while being viciously attacked by the British solicitor-general before the Privy Council and the court. Two days later he was fired as deputy postmaster. After some futile efforts at reconciliation, he sailed for America in March 1775.

Although upon his arrival in Philadelphia Franklin was immediately elected to the Second Continental Congress, some Americans remained suspicious of his real loyalties. He was delighted that the Congress in 1776 sent him back to Europe as the premier agent in a commission seeking military aid and diplomatic recognition from France. He played on the French aristocracy's liberal sympathies for the oppressed Americans and extracted not only diplomatic recognition of the new republic but also loan after loan from an increasingly impoverished French government. His image as the democratic folk genius from the wilderness of America preceded him, and he exploited it brilliantly for the American cause.

Benjamin Franklin at the court of France, 1778, engraving after a painting by Hobens. National Archives, Washington, D.C.

Franklin first secured military and diplomatic alliances with France in 1778 and then played a crucial role in bringing about the final peace treaty with Britain in 1783. In violation of their instructions and the French alliance, Franklin and his fellow American peace commissioners signed a separate peace with Britain. It was left to Franklin to apologize to the comte de Vergennes, Louis XVI's chief minister, which he did in a beautifully wrought diplomatic letter.

Last Years

In 1785, after what he considered the happiest years of his life, Franklin reluctantly had to come to America to die. Although he feared he would be "a stranger in my own country," he now knew that his destiny was linked to America.

His reception was not entirely welcoming. The family and friends of his fellow commissioners in France spread stories of his overweening love of that country and his dissolute ways. The Congress treated him shabbily, ignoring his requests. Upon his death the Senate refused to go along with the House in declaring a month of mourning for Franklin. In contrast to the many expressions of French affection for Franklin, his fellow Americans gave him one public eulogy—and that was delivered by his inveterate enemy the Rev. William Smith.

But in the succeeding decades, particularly after the publication of his hugely popular *Autobiography* in 1794, he became the hero of countless early 19th-century artisans and self-made businessmen who were seeking a justification of their rise and their moneymaking. They were the creators of the modern folksy image of Franklin, the man who came to personify the American dream.

CARLO GOLDONI

(b. February 25, 1707, Venice—d. February 6, 1793, Paris)

Carlo Goldoni was a prolific dramatist who renovated the well-established Italian commedia dell'arte dramatic form by replacing its masked stock figures with more realistic characters, its loosely structured and often repetitive action with tightly constructed plots, and its predictable farce with a new spirit of gaiety and spontaneity. For these innovations Goldoni is considered the founder of Italian realistic comedy.

The precocious son of a physician, Goldoni read comedies from his father's library when young and ran away from school at Rimini in 1721 with a company of strolling players. Back in school at the papal college in Pavia, Goldoni read comedies by the ancient Greek and Roman playwrights Plautus, Terence, and Aristophanes. Later he studied French in order to read the greatest French writer of comedies, Molière.

For writing a satire on the ladies of the town, Goldoni was expelled from the Ghislieri College in Pavia, and he reluctantly began law studies at the University of Pavia. Although he practiced law in Venice (1731–33) and Pisa (1744–48) and held diplomatic appointments, his real interest was the dramatic works he wrote for the Teatro San Samuele in Venice.

In 1748 Goldoni agreed to write for the Teatro Sant'Angelo company of the Venetian actor-manager Girolamo Medebac. Although Goldoni's early plays veer between the old style and the new, he dispensed with masked characters altogether in such plays as *La*

Pamela (performed 1750; Eng. trans., *Pamela, a Comedy*), a serious drama based on Samuel Richardson's novel of the same name.

During the 1750–51 season Goldoni promised defecting patrons 16 new comedies and produced some of his best, notably *I pettegolezzi delle donne* ("Women's Gossip"), a play in Venetian dialect; *Il bugiardo* (*The Liar*), written in commedia dell'arte style; and *Il vero amico* ("The True Friend"), an Italian comedy of manners.

From 1753 to 1762 Goldoni wrote for the Teatro San Luca (now Teatro Goldoni). There he increasingly left commedia dell'arte behind him. Important plays from this period are the Italian comedy of manners *La locandiera* (performed 1753; Eng. trans., *Mine Hostess*) and two fine plays in Venetian dialect, *I rusteghi* (performed 1760; "The Tyrants") and *Le baruffe chiozzote* (performed 1762; "Quarrels at Chioggia").

Already engaged in rivalry with the playwright Pietro Chiari, whom he satirized in *I malcontenti* (performed 1755; "The Malcontent"), Goldoni was assailed by Carlo Gozzi, an adherent of the commedia dell'arte, who denounced Goldoni in a satirical poem (1757), then ridiculed both Goldoni and Chiari in a commedia dell'arte classic, *L'amore delle tre melarance* (performed 1761; "The Love of the Three Oranges").

In 1762 Goldoni left Venice for Paris to direct the Comédie-Italienne. Subsequently, he rewrote all of his French plays for Venetian audiences; his French *L'Éventail* (performed 1763) became in Italian one of his finest plays, *Il ventaglio* (performed 1764; *The Fan*).

Goldoni retired in 1764 to teach Italian to the princesses at Versailles. In 1783 he began his celebrated *Mémoires* in French (1787). After the French Revolution his pension was cancelled, and he died in dire poverty.

HENRY FIELDING

(b. April 22, 1707, Sharpham Park, Somerset, England—
d. October 8, 1754, Lisbon, Portugal)

The novelist and playwright Henry Fielding is, with Samuel Richardson, considered a founder of the English novel. Among his major novels are *Joseph Andrews* (1742) and *Tom Jones* (1749).

Early Life

Fielding was born of a family that by tradition traced its descent to a branch of the Habsburgs. The 1st earl of Denbigh, William Fielding, was a direct ancestor, while Henry's father, Col. Edmund Fielding, had served under John Churchill, duke of Marlborough, an early 18th-century general, "with much bravery and reputation." His mother was a daughter of Sir Henry Gould, a judge of the Queen's Bench, from whom she inherited property at East Stour, in Dorset, where the family moved when Fielding was three years old. His mother died just before his 11th birthday. His father having married again, Fielding was sent to Eton College, where he laid the foundations of his love of literature and his considerable knowledge of the classics. There he befriended George Lyttelton, who was later to be a statesman and an important patron to him.

Leaving school at 17, a strikingly handsome youth, he settled down to the life of a young gentleman of leisure; but four years later, after an abortive elopement with an heiress and the production of a play at the Drury Lane Theatre in London, he resumed his classical studies at the

University of Leiden in Holland. After 18 months he had to return home because his father was no longer able to pay him an allowance. "Having," as he said, "no choice but to be a hackney-writer or a hackney-coachman," he chose the former and set up as playwright. In all, he wrote some 25 plays. Although his dramatic works have not held the stage, their wit cannot be denied. He was essentially a satirist; for instance, *The Author's Farce* (1730) displays the absurdities of writers and publishers, while *Rape upon Rape* (1730) satirizes the injustices of the law and lawyers. His target was often the political corruption of the times. In 1737 he produced at the Little Theatre in the Hay (later the Haymarket Theatre), London, his *Historical Register, For the Year 1736,* in which the prime minister, Sir Robert Walpole, was represented practically undisguised and mercilessly ridiculed. It was not the first time Walpole had suffered from Fielding's pen, and his answer was to push through Parliament the Licensing Act, by which all new plays had to be approved and licensed by the lord chamberlain before production.

The passing of this act marked the end of Fielding's career as a playwright. The 30-year-old writer had a wife and two children to support but no source of income. He had married Charlotte Cradock in 1734, this time after a successful elopement, the culmination of a four-year courtship. How much he adored her can be seen from the two characters based on her, Sophia Western in *Tom Jones* and Amelia in the novel of that name: one the likeness of her as a beautiful, high-spirited, generous-minded girl, the other of her as a faithful, much-troubled, hard-working wife and mother. To restore his fortunes, Fielding began to read for the bar, completing in less than three years a course normally taking six or seven. Even while studying, however, he was editing, and very largely writing, a thrice-weekly newspaper, the *Champion; or, British Mercury,* which ran from November 1739 to June 1741.

Maturity

As a barrister, Fielding, who rode the Western Circuit (a judicial subdivision of England) twice a year, had little success. In 1740, however, Samuel Richardson published his novel *Pamela: or, Virtue Rewarded*, which tells how a servant girl so impressed her master by resistance to his every effort at seduction that in the end "he thought fit to make her his wife." Something new in literature, its success was unparalleled. A crop of imitations followed. In April 1741 there appeared a parody entitled *An Apology for the Life of Mrs. Shamela Andrews*, satirizing Richardson's sentimentality and prudish morality. It was published anonymously and, though Fielding never claimed it, *Shamela* was generally accepted as his work in his lifetime, and stylistic evidence supports the attribution.

Fielding's *Joseph Andrews* was published anonymously in 1742. Described on the title page as "Written in Imitation of the Manner of Cervantes, author of *Don Quixote*," it begins as a burlesque of *Pamela*, with Joseph, Pamela's virtuous footman brother, resisting the attempts of a highborn lady to seduce him. The parodic intention soon becomes secondary, and the novel develops into a masterpiece of sustained irony and social criticism, with, at its centre, Parson Adams, one of the great comic figures of literature and a striking confirmation of the contention of the 19th-century Russian novelist Fyodor Dostoyevsky that the positively good man can be made convincing in fiction only if rendered to some extent ridiculous. Fielding explains in his preface that he is writing "a comic Epic-Poem in Prose." He was certainly inaugurating a new genre in fiction.

Joseph Andrews was written in the most unpropitious circumstances: Fielding was crippled with gout, his six-year-old daughter was dying, and his wife was "in a condition very little better." He was also in financial trouble, from which he was at least temporarily rescued by the generosity of his friend the philanthropist Ralph Allen, who appears in *Tom Jones* as Mr. Allworthy.

In 1743 Fielding published three volumes of *Miscellanies*, works old and new, of which by far the most important is *The Life of Mr. Jonathan Wild the Great.* Here, narrating the life of a notorious criminal of the day, Fielding satirizes human greatness, or rather human greatness confused with power over others. Permanently topical, *Jonathan Wild*, with the exception of some passages by his older contemporary, the Anglo-Irish satirist Jonathan Swift, is perhaps the grimmest satire in English and an exercise in unremitting irony.

After the *Miscellanies* Fielding gave up writing for more than two years, partly, perhaps, out of disappointment with the rewards of authorship, partly in order to devote himself to law. His health was bad; his practice at the bar did not flourish; worst of all, his wife was still ill. In the autumn of 1744 he took her to Bath for the medicinal waters; she "caught a fever, and died in his arms." According to Lady Mary Wortley Montagu, the 18th-century letter writer and Fielding's cousin, his grief "approached to frenzy," and it was almost a year before he recovered his fortitude. By then he had taken a house in London in the Strand (on the site of the present law courts), and there he lived with his daughter, his sister Sarah, also a novelist, and Mary Daniel, who had been his wife's maid. In 1747, to the derision of London, he married Mary, who was pregnant by him. According to Fielding himself, writing shortly before his death, she discharged "excellently well her own, and all the tender offices becoming the female character... besides being a faithful friend, an amiable companion, and a tender nurse."

In 1745 came the Jacobite Rebellion (an attempt to restore the descendants of the deposed Stuart king James II), which led Fielding to write the pamphlet "A Serious Address to the People of Great Britain. In Which the Certain Consequences of the Present Rebellion, Are Fully Demonstrated. Necessary To Be Perused by Every Lover of his Country at This Juncture." An upholder of the Church of England, he warned of the implications of this rising led by the Roman Catholic pretender to the throne, Prince Charles Edward. A month later, he became editor of a new weekly paper, *The True Patriot: And the History of Our Own Times*, which he wrote almost single-handedly until it ceased publication on the defeat of the Pretender at the Battle of Culloden (April 16, 1746). A year later, Fielding edited another one-man weekly called *The Jacobite's Journal*, the title reflecting its ironical approach to current affairs. Its propaganda value was deemed so great that the government purchased 2,000 copies of each issue for free distribution among the inns and alehouses of the kingdom.

Fielding was now a trusted supporter of the government. His reward came in 1748, when he was appointed justice of the peace (or magistrate) for Westminster and Middlesex, with his own courthouse, which was also his residence, in Bow Street in central London. The office carried no salary; former Bow Street magistrates had made what they could out of the fees paid by persons brought before them and, often, out of bribes. Fielding was a magistrate of a different order. Together with his blind half brother, John Fielding, also a magistrate, he turned an office without honour into one of great dignity and importance and established a new tradition of justice and the suppression of crime in London. Among other things, Fielding strengthened the police force at his disposal by recruiting a small body of able and energetic "thieftakers"—the Bow Street Runners. To improve relations between the law and the public, he started a newspaper, *The Covent Garden Journal*, in which the following appeared regularly:

All persons who shall for the future suffer by robbers, burglars, etc., are desired immediately to bring or send the best description they can of such robbers, etc., with the time, and place, and circumstances of the fact, to Henry Fielding, Esq., at his house in Bow Street.

Last Years

The History of Tom Jones, a Foundling was published on February 28, 1749. With its great comic gusto, vast gallery of characters, and contrasted scenes of high and low life in London and the provinces, it has always constituted the most popular of his works. Like its predecessor, *Joseph Andrews*, it is constructed around a romance plot. The hero, whose true identity remains unknown until the novel's conclusion, loves the beautiful Sophia Western, and at the end of the book he wins her hand. Numerous obstacles have to be overcome before he achieves this, however, and in the course of the action the various sets of characters pursue each other from one part of the country to another, giving Fielding an opportunity to paint an incomparably vivid picture of England in the mid-18th century. The introductory chapters at the beginning of each Book make it clear how carefully Fielding had considered the problem of planning the novel. No novelist up until then had so clear an idea of what a novel should be, so that it is not surprising that *Tom Jones* is a masterpiece of literary engineering. The characters fall into several distinct groups—romance characters, villainous characters, Jonsonian "humours," "low" comic characters, and the virtuous Squire Allworthy, who remains in the background and emerges to ensure the conventional happy ending. The novel is further marked by deft alternations between humour and romance, occasional tricks straight from the theatre, and above all the speed and ease of the dialogue. The reading of this work is essential both for an understanding of 18th-century England and for its revelation of the generosity and charity of Fielding's view of humanity.

Two years later *Amelia* was published. Being a much more sombre work, it has always been less popular than *Tom Jones* and *Joseph Andrews*. Fielding's mind must have been darkened by his experiences as a magistrate, as it certainly had been by his wife's death, and *Amelia* is no attempt at the comic epic poem in prose. Rather, it anticipates the Victorian domestic novel, being a study of the relationship between a man and his wife and, in the character of Amelia, a celebration of womanly virtues. It is also Fielding's most intransigent representation of the evils of the society in which he lived, and he clearly finds the spectacle no longer comic.

His health was deteriorating. By 1752 his gout was so bad that his legs were swathed in bandages, and he often had to use crutches or a wheelchair. In August of 1753 he decided to go to Bath for rest and the waters. That year was a particularly bad one for crime in London, however, and on the eve of his leaving he was invited by Thomas Pelham-Holles, duke of Newcastle (then secretary of war), to prepare a plan for the Privy Council for the suppression of "those murders and robberies which were every day committed in the streets." His plan, undertaking "to demolish the then reigning gangs" and to establish means of preventing their recurrence, was accepted, and despite the state of his health—to gout had been added asthma and edema—he stayed in London for the rest of the year, waging war against criminal gangs with such success that "there was, in the remaining month of November, and in all December, not only no such thing as a murder, but not even a street-robbery committed."

In the following June, Fielding set out for Portugal to seek the sun, writing an account of his journey, *The Journal*

Created C. *1780, this drawing depicts a scene from Fielding's* The History of Tom Jones, a Foundling; *one man is seen standing in a doorway with a candle, the other on the ground with a dead game bird.* Hulton Archive /Getty Images

of a Voyage to Lisbon. This work presents an extraordinarily vivid picture of the tortuous slowness of 18th-century sea travel, the horrors of contemporary medicine, the caprices of arbitrary power as seen in the conduct of customs officers and other petty officials, and, above all, his indomitable courage and cheerfulness when almost completely helpless, for he could scarcely walk and had to be carried on and off ship. Fielding landed at Lisbon on August 7, 1754. He died in October and was buried in the British cemetery at Lisbon.

ANTIOKH DMITRIYEVICH KANTEMIR

(b. September 21 [September 10, Old Style], 1708, Constantinople [now Istanbul], Turkey—d. April 11 [March 31], 1744, Paris, France)

A ntiokh Dmitriyevich Kantemir was a distinguished Russian statesman who was his country's first secular poet and one of its leading writers of the classical school.

The son of the statesman and scientist Dmitry Kantemir, who was an adviser to Peter the Great, he was tutored at home and attended (1724–25) the St. Petersburg Academy. Between 1729 and 1731 he wrote several poems, the most important probably being two satires, "To His Own Mind: On Those Who Blame Education" and "On the Envy and Pride of Evil-Minded Courtiers." These poems denounced the opposition to the reforms of the emperor Peter the Great and enjoyed great success when circulated in manuscript (they were not printed until 1762). As ambassador to England (1732–36), he took to London the manuscript of his father's history of the Ottoman Empire, furnishing a biography of his father that appeared with the English translation of the history.

From 1736 until his death, Kantemir was minister plenipotentiary in Paris, where he formed friendships with Voltaire and Montesquieu and continued to write satires and fables. His Russian translations of several classical and contemporary authors include his 1740 translation of the French man of letters Bernard Le Bovier de Fontenelle's *Entretiens sur la pluralité des mondes* (1686; "Interviews on the Pluralitism of the World"), which was suppressed as heretical. He also wrote a philosophical work, *O prirode i cheloveke* (1742; "Letters on Nature and Man"), and a tract on the old syllabic system of Russian verse composition (1744).

Jean-Baptiste-Louis Gresset

(b. August 29, 1709, Amiens, France—d. June 16, 1777, Amiens)

The French poet and dramatist Jean-Baptiste-Louis Gresset received immediate and lasting acclaim for his irreverently comic narrative poem *Ver-Vert* (1734; *Ver-Vert, or the Nunnery Parrot*), describing with wit tinged with malice the adventures of a parrot who attempts to maintain his decorous convent background while on a visit to another convent.

Brought up by Jesuits, Gresset was a brilliant pupil and, after entering the Jesuit order in 1726, continued his education in Paris before returning to teach in Amiens and Tours. *Ver-Vert*, which was circulated privately and printed without the author's permission, brought him instant success in Parisian circles, where the literati were astounded that such a refined wit could come from within the Roman Catholic church.

In spite of the objections of some of his superiors, Gresset continued to write light occasional verse, within a year publishing *La Carême impromptu* ("The Lenten Impromptu") and *Le Lutrin vivant* ("The Living Lectern"). Returning to Paris in 1735 for a year's study of theology, he wrote *La Chartreuse* ("The Carthusian") and *Les Ombres* ("The Shadows"). These lively accounts of life in a Jesuit college, precise and pointed in detail, led first to his banishment to the provinces and then to his expulsion from the order; his keen eye for absurdity and his natural frivolity were seen as anticlerical and impious. Supported by an official pension, he turned to drama; his first plays, the tragedy *Édouard III* (performed 1740), which included the first murder ever enacted on the French stage, and a verse comedy, *Sidney* (1745), were not especially successful, but *Le Méchant* (1747; "The Sorry Man"), a witty exposé of salon life, was highly praised for its pithy, polished dialogue. Admitted to the French Academy in 1748, he caused a stir with his criticism of nonresident bishops (1754). In 1759 Gresset wrote *Lettre sur la comédie* ("Letter on Comedy"), in which he renounced all his previous poetic and dramatic works as irreligious. He retired to Amiens in the same year, where he remained (except for trips to Paris for meetings of the French Academy) until his death.

SAMUEL JOHNSON

(b. September 18, 1709, Lichfield, Staffordshire, England—
d. December 13, 1784, London)

Samuel Johnson was an English critic, biographer, essayist, poet, and lexicographer who is regarded as one of the greatest figures of 18th-century life and letters. His career can be seen as a literary success story of the sickly boy from the provinces who by talent, tenacity, and intelligence became the foremost literary figure and the most formidable conversationalist of his time.

Early Life

Samuel Johnson was the son of Michael Johnson, a bookseller, and his wife, Sarah. From childhood he suffered from a number of physical afflictions. By his own account, he was born "almost dead," and he early contracted scrofula (tuberculosis of the lymphatic glands). Various medical treatments left him with disfiguring scars on his face and neck. He was nearly blind in his left eye and suffered from highly noticeable tics that may have been indications of Tourette syndrome. Despite his many physical afflictions, Johnson was strong, vigorous, and, after a fashion, athletic. He liked to ride, walk, and swim, even in later life. He was tall and became huge.

In 1717 Johnson entered grammar school in Lichfield, and in 1728 he entered Pembroke College, Oxford. He stayed only 13 months, until December 1729, because he lacked the funds to continue. Yet it proved an important year. While an undergraduate, Johnson, who claimed to have been irreligious in adolescence, read a new book, William Law's *A Serious Call to a Devout and Holy Life*, which led him to make concern for his soul the primary focus of his life. Despite the poverty that caused him to leave, he retained great affection for Oxford, and his first publication—a translation into Latin of *Messiah* by Alexander Pope, the leading poet of the age—appeared in 1731 in *A Miscellany of Poems* along with the poetry of other Oxford students.

For a short time Johnson was undermaster at a grammar school before he made his way to Birmingham, where he published some essays in *The Birmingham Journal* in 1732 or 1733, none of which have survived. In 1735 he married Elizabeth Porter, a widow 20 years his senior. (She would die in 1752, just as Johnson was achieving widespread recognition.) His wife's marriage settlement enabled him to open a school in Edial, near Lichfield, the following year, and one of his students, David Garrick, would become the greatest English actor of the age and a lifelong friend. The school soon proved a failure, however, and he and Garrick left for London in 1737.

The Gentleman's Magazine
and Early Publications

In 1738 Johnson began his long association with *The Gentleman's Magazine*, often considered the first modern magazine. He soon contributed poetry and, later, prose, including a number of biographies of European scholars, physicians, and British admirals. In 1738 and 1739 he also published a series of satiric works that attacked the government of Sir Robert Walpole and the Hanoverian monarchy: *London* (his first major poem), *Marmor Norfolciense*, and *A Compleat Vindication of the Licensers of the Stage*. The latter two works show the literary influence of the Irish writer Jonathan Swift, while *London* is an "imitation" of the Roman satirist Juvenal's third satire. (A loose translation, an imitation applies the manner and topics of an earlier poet to contemporary conditions.) Before he leaves the corrupt metropolis for Wales, Thales (the poem's main speaker) rails against the pervasive deterioration of life in London and thus in England as a whole, evident in such ills as masquerades, atheism, the excise tax, and the ability of foreign nations to offend against "English honour" with impunity. The most famous line in the poem (and the only one in capitals) is: "SLOW RISES WORTH, BY POVERTY DEPRESSED," which may be taken as Johnson's motto at this time. Since his translations and magazine writings barely supported him, he was about this time trying again to obtain a position as a schoolteacher.

From 1741 to 1744 Johnson's most substantial contribution to *The Gentleman's Magazine* was a series of speeches purporting to represent the actual debates in the House of Commons. This undertaking was not without risk because reporting the proceedings of Parliament, which had long been prohibited, was actually punished since the spring of 1738. The speeches' status was complicated by the fact that Johnson, who had visited the House of Commons only once, wrote the debates on the basis of scant information about the speakers' positions. Hence they were political fictions. During this time Johnson also collaborated with William Oldys, antiquary and editor, on a catalog of the great Harleian Library; helped Robert James, a lifelong friend and his schoolfellow at Lichfield, with *A Medicinal Dictionary*; and issued proposals for an edition of William Shakespeare's works. His *Miscellaneous Observations on the Tragedy of Macbeth* (1745), intended as a preliminary sample of his work, was his first significant Shakespeare criticism. In 1746 he wrote *The Plan of a Dictionary of the English Language* and signed a contract for *A Dictionary of the English Language*. His major publication of this period was *An Account of the Life of Mr. Richard Savage, Son of the Earl Rivers* (1744). It was widely admired, and it was even reviewed in translation by the French philosopher Denis Diderot. Johnson's biography, in its mixture of pathos and satire, at once commemorates and criticizes Savage.

Maturity and Recognition

In 1749 Johnson published *The Vanity of Human Wishes*, his most impressive poem as well as the first work published with his name. It is a panoramic survey of the futility of human pursuit of greatness and happiness. Like *London*, the poem is an imitation of one of Juvenal's satires, but it emphasizes the moral over the social and political themes of Juvenal. It is imbued with the Hebrew Bible message of Ecclesiastes that "all is vanity" and replaces Juvenal's Stoic virtues with the Christian virtue of "patience." The poem surpasses any of Johnson's other poems in its richness of imagery and powerful conciseness.

Johnson's connections to the theatre in these years included writing several prologues, one for Garrick's farce *Lethe* in 1740 and one for the opening of the Drury Lane theatre. Garrick, now its manager, returned the favours. Early in 1749 Johnson's play *Irene*—which dramatizes a sultan's love for Irene, a Christian slave captured in Constantinople—was performed. Thanks to Garrick's production, which included expensive costumes and highly popular afterpieces for the last three performances, the tragedy ran a respectable nine nights.

The Rambler *and the* Dictionary

With *The Rambler* (1750–52), a twice-weekly periodical, Johnson entered upon the most successful decade of his career. He wrote over 200 essays that cover a wide range of subjects. Whatever their topic, Johnson intended his pieces to "inculcate wisdom or piety" in conformity with Christianity. In tone these works are far more serious than those of his most important predecessor, Joseph Addison, whose writings had been published four decades earlier in *The Spectator*.

A

DICTIONARY

OF THE

ENGLISH LANGUAGE:

IN WHICH

The WORDS are deduced from their ORIGINALS,

AND

ILLUSTRATED in their DIFFERENT SIGNIFICATIONS

BY

EXAMPLES from the beſt WRITERS.

TO WHICH ARE PREFIXED,

A HISTORY of the LANGUAGE,

AND

An ENGLISH GRAMMAR.

By SAMUEL JOHNSON, A.M.

IN TWO VOLUMES.

VOL. I.

THE SECOND EDITION.

Cum tabulis animum cenſoris ſumet honeſti :
Audebit quæcunque parum ſplendoris habebunt,
Et ſine pondere erunt, et honore indigna ferentur.
Verba movere loco ; quamvis invita recedant,
Et verſentur adhuc intra penetralia Veſtæ :
Obſcurata diu populo bonus eruet, atque
Proferet in lucem ſpecioſa vocabula rerum,
Quæ priſcis memorata Catonibus atque Cethegis,
Nunc ſitus informis premit et deſerta vetuſtas.   Hor.

LONDON,

Printed by W. STRAHAN,

For J. and P. KNAPTON; T. and T. LONGMAN; C. HITCH and L. HAWES;
A. MILLAR; and R. and J. DODSLEY.

MDCCLV.

Title page from Samuel Johnson's Dictionary of the English Language. British Library/Robana/Hulton Fine Art Collection/ Getty Images

A Dictionary of the English Language was published in two volumes in 1755, six years later than planned but remarkably quickly for so extensive an undertaking. The degree of Master of Arts, conferred on him by the University of Oxford for his *Rambler* essays and the *Dictionary*, was proudly noted on the title page. Johnson henceforth would be known in familiar 18th-century style as "Dictionary Johnson" or "The Rambler."

There had been earlier English dictionaries, but none on the scale of Johnson's. In addition to giving etymologies, not the strong point of Johnson and his contemporaries, and definitions, in which he excelled, Johnson illustrated usage with quotations drawn almost entirely from writing from the Elizabethan period to his own time, though few living authors were quoted (the novelists Samuel Richardson and Charlotte Lennox, Garrick, Reynolds, and Johnson himself among them). He was pleased that what took the French Academy 40 years to perform for their language was accomplished by one Englishman in 9 years. Johnson did not work systematically from a word list but marked up the books he read for copying. Thus it should be no surprise that some dictionaries previous to Johnson's contain more words and that Johnson's has striking omissions ("literary" for one). Yet his definitions were a great improvement over those of his predecessors. In its choice of authors and of illustrative selections, the *Dictionary* also reveals itself to be a personal work. These give the whole the aspect of both an encyclopaedia and a conduct book. Even though Johnson defined "lexicographer" as "a writer of dictionaries; a harmless drudge," the drudgery of the *Dictionary* fell into the decade of Johnson's most important writing and must be seen in part as enabling it.

The payment for the *Dictionary* amounted to relatively little after deductions were made for his six amanuenses and his own expenses. He took up smaller lodgings in 1759, ending the major decade of his literary activity famous and poor.

The Literary Magazine *and* The Idler

From 1756 onward Johnson wrote harsh criticism and satire of England's policy in the Seven Years' War (1756–63) fought against France (and others) in North America, Europe, and India. This work appeared initially in a new journal he was editing, *The Literary Magazine*. He also contributed important book reviews when reviewing was still in its infancy.

He also wrote yet another series of essays, called *The Idler*. Lighter in tone and style than those of *The Rambler*, its 104 essays appeared from 1758 to 1760 in a weekly newspaper, *The Universal Chronicle*. While not admired as greatly as *The Rambler*, Johnson's last essay series contained many impressive numbers, such as No. 84, in which he praised autobiography over biography and drew his self-portrait as "Mr. Sober," a consummate idler.

Rasselas

Johnson's essays included numerous short fictions, but his only long fiction is *Rasselas* (originally published as *The Prince of Abissinia: A Tale*), which he wrote in 1759, during the evenings of a single week, in order to be able to pay for the funeral of his mother. This story explores and exposes the futility of the pursuit of happiness, a theme that links it to *The Vanity of Human Wishes*. Prince Rasselas, weary of life in the Happy Valley, where ironically all are dissatisfied, escapes with his sister and the widely traveled poet Imlac to experience the world and make a thoughtful "choice of life." Yet their journey is filled with disappointment and disillusionment. They examine the lives of men in a wide range of occupations and modes of life in both urban and rural settings, and they discover that all occupations fail to bring satisfaction. Johnson's major characters resolve to substitute the "choice of eternity" for the "choice of life," and to return to Abyssinia (but not the Happy Valley) on their circular journey.

Johnson never again had to write in order to raise funds. In 1762 he was awarded a pension of £300 a year, "not," as Lord Bute, the British prime minister, told him, "given you for anything you are to do, but for what you have done." This in all likelihood meant not only his literary accomplishments but also his opposition to the Seven Years' War, which the new king, George III, and his prime minister had also opposed. Although in his *Dictionary* Johnson had added to his definition of "pension," "In England it is generally understood to mean pay given to a state hireling for treason to his country," he believed that he could accept his with a clear conscience.

Friendships and Social Life

In 1763 Johnson met the 22-year-old James Boswell, who would go on to make him the subject of the best-known and most highly regarded biography in English. The first meeting with this libertine son of a Scottish laird and judge was not auspicious, but Johnson quickly came to appreciate the ingratiating and impulsive young man.

Johnson participated actively in clubs in London, which kept him in contact with some of the leading figures of his era. In 1764 he and his close friend the painter Sir Joshua Reynolds founded the Club (later known as The Literary Club), which became famous for the distinction of its members. The original nine members included the politician Edmund Burke and the playwright Oliver Goldsmith. Boswell, whose 1768 account of the Corsican struggle against Genoese rule earned him a reputation throughout

Europe, was admitted in 1773. Other members elected later included Garrick, the historian Edward Gibbon, the dramatist Richard Brinsley Sheridan, and the economist and moral philosopher Adam Smith. This club and others provided the conversation and society he desired and kept him from the loneliness and insomnia that he faced at home.

In 1765 Johnson established a friendship that soon enabled him to call another place "home." Henry Thrale, a wealthy brewer and member of Parliament for Southwark, and his lively and intelligent wife, Hester, opened their country house at Streatham to him and invited him on trips to Wales and, in 1775, to France, his only tour outside Great Britain. Their friendship and hospitality gave the 56-year-old Johnson a renewed interest in life. Following her husband's death in 1781 and her marriage to her children's music master, Gabriel Piozzi, Hester Thrale's and Johnson's close friendship came to an end. His letters to Mrs. Thrale, remarkable for their range and intimacy, helped make him one of the great English letter writers.

The Edition of Shakespeare

The pension Johnson had received in 1762 freed him from the necessity of writing for a living, but it had not released him from his obligation to complete the Shakespeare edition, for which he had taken money from subscribers. The edition finally appeared in eight volumes in 1765. Johnson edited and annotated the text and wrote a preface, which is his greatest work of literary criticism. In that preface, Johnson exerts considerable energy defending Shakespeare against various criticisms, including those directed at his failure to adhere to tenets of Neoclassical doctrine popular during Johnson's time, including the requirement that a play's action occur in a single place on a single day. Johnson argues that Shakespeare merits praise, above all, as "the poet of nature; the poet that holds up to his readers a faithful mirror of manners and of life."

In 1765 Johnson also received an honorary Doctor of Laws degree from Trinity College, Dublin, and 10 years later he was awarded the Doctor of Civil Laws from the University of Oxford. He never referred to himself as Dr. Johnson, though a number of his contemporaries did, and Boswell's consistent use of the title in *The Life of Samuel Johnson, LL.D.* made it popular.

Journey to the Hebrides and The Lives of the Poets

In 1773 Johnson set forth on a journey to the Hebrides islands off the west coast of Scotland. Given his age, ailments, and purported opinion of the Scots, Johnson may have seemed a highly unlikely traveler to this distant region, but in the opening pages of his *A Journey to the Western Islands of Scotland* (1775) he confessed to a long-standing desire to make the trip and the inducement of having Boswell as his companion. His book, a superb contribution to 18th-century travel literature, combines historical information with what would now be considered sociological and anthropological observations about the lives of common people.

Johnson's last great work, *Prefaces, Biographical and Critical, to the Works of the English Poets* (conventionally known as *The Lives of the Poets*), was conceived modestly as short prefatory notices to an edition of English poetry. When Johnson was approached by some London booksellers in 1777 to write what he thought of as "little Lives, and little Prefaces, to a little edition of the English Poets," he readily agreed. He loved anecdote and "the biographical part" of literature best of all. The project, however, expanded in scope; Johnson's prefaces alone filled the first 10 volumes (1779–81), and the poetry grew to 56 volumes.

The lives are ordered chronologically by date of death, not birth, and range in length from a few pages to an entire volume. Among the major lives are those of Abraham Cowley, John Milton, John Dryden, Joseph Addison, and Alexander Pope; some of the minor ones, such as those of William Collins and William Shenstone, are striking. Johnson's personal dislike of some of the poets whose lives he wrote, such as John Milton and Thomas Gray, has been used as a basis for arguing that he was prejudiced against their poetry, but it may well be that too much has been made of this. *The Life of Pope* is at once the longest and the best of these works. Pope's life and career were fresh enough and public enough to provide ample biographical material. His moving, unsentimental account of Pope's life is sensitive to his physical sufferings and yet unwilling to accept them as an excuse.

Last Years

Throughout much of his adult life Johnson suffered from physical ailments as well as depression ("melancholy"). After the loss of two friends, Henry Thrale in 1781 and Robert Levett in 1782, and the conclusion of *The Lives of the Poets*, his health deteriorated. Above all, his chronic bronchitis and "dropsy" (edema), a swelling of his legs and feet, caused great discomfort. In 1783 he suffered a stroke. His last year was made still bleaker by his break with Mrs. Thrale over her remarriage. Yet he insisted on fighting: "I will be conquered; I will not capitulate." A profoundly devout Anglican, Johnson was in dread at the prospect of death and judgment, for he feared damnation. Yet in the winter of 1784, following a day of prayer after which his edema spontaneously disappeared, he entered into a pre-viously unknown state of serenity. He accepted this release from illness as a sign that he might be saved after all and referred to it as a "late conversion." He died on December 13 and was buried in Westminster Abbey.

SARAH FIELDING

(b. November 8, 1710, East Stour, Dorset, England—
d. April 9, 1768, Bath, Somerset)

Sarah Fielding was an English author and translator whose novels were among the earliest in the English language and the first to examine the interior lives of women and children.

Fielding was the younger sister of the novelist Henry Fielding, whom many readers believed to be the author of novels she published anonymously, although he denied these speculations in print. She lived with her brother following the death of his wife in 1744. That year she published her first book, *The Adventures of David Simple*, a novel whose comic prose style imitated that of both her brother and his chief literary rival, Samuel Richardson, who was also one of her close friends. With the sequel, *The Adventures of David Simple, Volume the Last: In Which His History Is Concluded* (1753), she developed a style more distinctly her own, which shows greater intricacy of feeling, fuller development of character, and a reduced reliance on plot.

The Governess (1749) is didactic and portrays with comic sensibility the hazards of British social life for the moral development of women. Considered the first novel for girls in the English language, it was an immediate success and went through five editions in Fielding's lifetime while inspiring numerous imitations.

She published only one book under her own name, a translation from the ancient Greek of *Xenophon's Memoirs of Socrates* (1762), a significant achievement in that few women of Fielding's time acquired a scholarly command of Classical languages. Other works include a collaboration with her friend Jane Collier titled *The Cry: A New Dramatic Fable* (1754). Although didacticism frequently overshadows the narrative drive of Fielding's prose, critics credit her as an innovator with a shrewd sense of human motive and keen ironic humour.

Laurence Sterne

(b. November 24, 1713, Clonmel, County Tipperary, Ireland —
d. March 18, 1768, London, England)

The Irish-born English novelist and humorist Laurence Sterne is best known as the author of *Tristram Shandy* (1759–67), a freewheeling comic novel in which the free associations and digressions of its narrator often threaten to hijack the novel's plot. He is also known for the novel *A Sentimental Journey* (1768).

Life

Sterne's father, Roger, though grandson of an archbishop of York, was an infantry officer of the lowest rank who fought in many battles during the War of the Spanish Succession (1701–14). In Flanders, Roger married Agnes, the widow of an officer, but of a social class much below Roger's. The regiment retired to Ireland, and there Laurence was born. Most of his early childhood was spent in poverty, following the troops about Ireland. Later, Sterne expressed his affection for soldiers through his portraits in *Tristram Shandy* of the gentle uncle Toby and Corporal Trim.

At age 10, Sterne was sent to school in England, at Hipperholme, near Halifax, where his uncle, Richard Sterne, whose estate was nearby, could look out for him. He grew into a tall, thin man, with a long nose but a likable face. Sterne attended Jesus College, Cambridge, on a scholarship. At college he met his great friend John Hall-Stevenson (Eugenius in his fiction) and also suffered his first severe hemorrhage of the lungs. He had incurable tuberculosis.

After graduating he remained in England and took holy orders, becoming vicar of Sutton-on-the-Forest, north of York. He soon became a prebendary (or canon) of York Minster and acquired the vicarage of Stillington. At first he was helped by another uncle, Jaques Sterne, precentor of York and archdeacon of Cleveland, a powerful clergyman but a mean-tempered man and a rabid politician. In 1741–42 Sterne wrote political articles supporting the administration of the prime minister Sir Robert Walpole for a newspaper founded by his uncle but soon withdrew from politics in disgust. His uncle became his archenemy, thwarting his advancement whenever possible.

In 1741 Sterne married Elizabeth Lumley. As a clergyman Sterne worked hard but erratically. In two ecclesiastical courts he served as commissary (judge), and his frequent sermons at York Minster were popular. Externally, his life was typical of the moderately successful clergy. But Elizabeth, who had several stillborn children, was unhappy. (According to the account of an acquaintance, Sterne's infidelities were a cause of discord in the marriage.) Only one child, Lydia, lived.

In 1759, to support his dean in a church squabble, Sterne wrote *A Political Romance* (later called *The History of a Good Warm Watch-Coat*), a satire in the spirit of Irish writer Jonathan Swift that skewered dignitaries of the spiritual courts. At the demands of embarrassed churchmen, the book was burned. Thus, Sterne lost his chances for clerical advancement but discovered his real talents. Turning over his parishes to a curate, he began *Tristram Shandy*. An initial, sharply satiric version was rejected by Robert Dodsley, the London printer, just when Sterne's personal life was upset. His mother and uncle both died. His wife had a nervous breakdown and threatened suicide. Sterne continued his comic novel, but every sentence, he said, was "written under the greatest heaviness of heart." In this mood, he softened the satire and told about Tristram's opinions, his eccentric family, and ill-fated childhood with a sympathetic humour, sometimes hilarious, sometimes sweetly melancholic—a comedy skirting tragedy.

At his own expense, Sterne published the first two volumes of *The Life and Opinions of Tristram Shandy, Gentleman* at York late in 1759, but he sent half of the imprint to Dodsley to sell in London. By March 1760, when he went to London, *Tristram Shandy* was the rage, and he was famous. Dodsley's brother James, the new proprietor, brought out a second edition of the novel, and two volumes of sermons followed. The witty, naughty "Tristram Shandy," or "Parson Yorick," as Sterne was called after characters in his novel, was the most sought-after man in town. Although the timing was coincidental, Lord Fauconberg, a Yorkshire neighbour, presented him with a third parish, Coxwold. Sterne returned north joyfully to settle at Coxwold in his beloved "Shandy Hall," a charming old house that subsequently became a museum. He began to write at Shandy Hall during the summers, going to London in the winter to publish what he had written. James Dodsley brought out two more volumes of *Tristram Shandy*; thereafter, Sterne became his own publisher. In London he enjoyed the company of many great people, but his nights were sometimes wild. In 1762, after almost dying from lung hemorrhages, he fled the damp air of

England into France, a journey he described as Tristram's flight from death. This and an ensuin trip abroad gave him much material for his later *Sentimental Journey*. Elizabeth, now recovered, followed him to France, where she and their daughter settled permanently. Sterne returned to England virtually a single man.

In 1767 he published the final volume of *Tristram Shandy*. Soon thereafter he fell in love with Eliza Draper, who was half his age and unhappily married to an official of the East India Company. They carried on an open, sentimental flirtation, but Eliza was under a promise to return to her husband in India. After she sailed, Sterne finished *A Sentimental Journey Through France and Italy, by Mr. Yorick*, published it to acclaim early in 1768, and collapsed.

Lying in his London lodgings, he put up his arm as though to ward off a blow, saying, "Now it is come," and died. Soon after burial at London, Sterne's body was stolen by grave robbers, taken to Cambridge, and used for an anatomy lecture. Someone recognized the body, and it was quietly returned to the grave. The story, only whispered at the time, was confirmed in 1969: Sterne's remains were exhumed and now rest in the churchyard at Coxwold, close to Shandy Hall.

Tristram Shandy *and* A Sentimental Journey

Sterne's *Tristram Shandy* was published in nine slim volumes (released in five installments) from 1759 to 1767. In it the narrator, Tristram, sets out to do the impossible—to tell the story of his life. He begins with the story of his conception—an innocent remark of his mother upsetting his father's concentration and causing poor Tristram to be conceived a weakling. To understand that, Tristram must then explain John Locke's principle of the association of ideas. This, in turn, embroils him in a discussion of his parents' marriage contract, his Uncle Toby, Parson Yorick, the midwife, and Dr. Slop. He has so much to tell that he does not get himself born until the third volume. Finally reality dawns upon Tristram: it takes more time to tell the story of his life than it does to live it; he can never catch himself.

At one level *Tristram Shandy* is a satire upon intellectual pride. Walter Shandy thinks he can beget and rear the perfect child, yet Tristram is misconceived, misbaptized, miseducated, and circumcised by a falling window sash. He grows to manhood an impotent weakling whose only hope of transcending death is to tell the story of himself and his family. Finally, Tristram turns to the sweet, funny story of his Uncle Toby's amours with the Widow Wadman, concluding the novel at a point in time years before Tristram was born. A hilarious, often ribald novel, *Tristram Shandy* nevertheless makes a serious comment on the isolation of people from each other caused by the inadequacies of language and describes the breaking-through of isolation by impulsive gestures of sympathy and love. A second great theme of the novel is that of time—the discrepancy between clock time and time as sensed, the impinging of the past upon the present, the awareness that a joyous life inexorably leads to death.

Sterne's second and last novel, *A Sentimental Journey,* is the story of Yorick's travels through France; Sterne did not live to complete the part on Italy. He called it a "sentimental" journey because the point of travel was not to see sights or visit art collections, but to make meaningful contact with people. Yorick succeeds, but in every adventure, his ego or inappropriate desires and impulses get in the way of "sentimental commerce." The result is a light-hearted comedy of moral sentiments. *A Sentimental Journey* was translated into many languages, but the translations tended to lose the comedy and emphasize the sentiments. Abroad Sterne became the "high priest of sentimentalism," and as such had a profound impact upon continental letters in the second half of the 18th century.

THOMAS GRAY

(b. December 26, 1716, London, England—
d. July 30, 1771, Cambridge)

Thomas Gray was an English poet whose "An Elegy Written in a Country Church Yard" is one of the best known of English lyric poems. Although his literary output was slight, he was the dominant poetic figure in the mid-18th century and a precursor of the Romantic movement.

Born into a prosperous but unhappy home, Gray was the sole survivor of 12 children of a harsh and violent father and a long-suffering mother, who operated a millinery business to educate him. A delicate and studious boy, he was sent to Eton in 1725 at the age of eight. There he formed a "Quadruple Alliance" with three other boys who liked poetry and classics and disliked rowdy sports and the Hogarthian manners of the period. They were Horace Walpole, the son of the prime minister Sir Robert Walpole; the precocious poet Richard West, who was closest to Gray; and Thomas Ashton. The style of life Gray developed at Eton, devoted to quiet study, the pleasures of the imagination, and a few understanding friends, was to persist for the rest of his years.

In 1734 he entered Peterhouse, Cambridge, where he began to write Latin verse of considerable merit. He left in 1738 without a degree and set out in 1739 with Horace Walpole on a grand tour of France, Switzerland, and Italy at Walpole's father's expense. At first all went well, but in 1741 they quarreled—possibly over Gray's preferences for museums and scenery to Walpole's interest in lighter social pursuits—and Gray returned to England. They were reconciled in 1745 on Walpole's initiative and remained somewhat cooler friends for the rest of their lives.

In 1742 Gray settled at Cambridge. That same year West died, an event that affected him profoundly. Gray had begun to write English poems, among which some of the best were "Ode on the Spring," "Sonnet on the Death of Mr. Richard West," "Hymn to Adversity," and "Ode on a Distant Prospect of Eton College." They revealed his maturity, ease and felicity of expression, wistful melancholy, and the ability to phrase truisms in striking, quotable lines, such as "where ignorance is bliss, 'Tis folly to be wise." The Eton ode was published in 1747 and again in 1748 along with "Ode on the Spring." They attracted no attention.

It was not until "An Elegy Written in a Country Church Yard," a poem long in the making, was published in 1751 that Gray was recognized. Its success was instantaneous and overwhelming. A dignified elegy in eloquent Classical diction celebrating the graves of humble and unknown villagers was, in itself, a novelty. Its theme that the lives of the rich and poor alike "lead but to the grave" was already familiar, but Gray's treatment—which had the effect of suggesting that it was not only the "rude forefathers of the village" he was mourning but the death of all men and of the poet himself—gave the poem its universal appeal.

Gray's newfound celebrity did not make the slightest difference in his habits. He remained at Peterhouse until 1756, when, outraged by a prank played on him by students, he moved to Pembroke College. He wrote two Pindaric odes, "The Progress of Poesy" and "The Bard," published in 1757 by Walpole's private Strawberry Hill Press. They were criticized, not without reason, for obscurity, and in disappointment, Gray virtually ceased to write. He was offered the laureateship in 1757 but declined it. He buried himself in his studies of Celtic and Scandinavian antiquities and became increasingly retiring and hypochondriacal. In his last years his peace was disrupted by his friendship with a young Swiss nobleman, Charles Victor de Bonstetten, for whom he conceived a romantic devotion, the most profound emotional experience of his life.

Gray died at 55 and was buried in the country churchyard at Stoke Poges, Buckinghamshire, celebrated in his "Elegy."

BUSON

(b. 1716, Kema, Settsu province, Japan—d. January 17, 1784, Kyoto)

B uson was a Japanese painter of distinction but is even more renowned as one of the great haiku poets.

Buson (also called Yosa Buson, original surname Taniguchi) came of a wealthy family but chose to leave it behind to pursue a career in the arts. He traveled extensively in northeastern Japan and studied haiku under several masters, among them Hayano Hajin, whom he eulogized in *Hokuju Rōsen wo itonamu* (1745; "Homage to Hokuju Rōsen"). In 1751 he settled in Kyoto as a professional painter, remaining there for most of his life. He did, however, spend three years (1754–57) in Yosa, Tango province, a region noted for its scenic beauty. There he worked intensively to improve his technique in both poetry and painting. During this period he changed his surname from Taniguchi to Yosa.

Buson's fame as a poet rose particularly after 1772. He urged a revival of the tradition of his great predecessor

Matsuo Bashō but never reached the level of humanistic understanding attained by Bashō. Buson's poetry, perhaps reflecting his interest in painting, is ornate and sensuous, rich in visual detail. "Use the colloquial language to transcend colloquialism," he urged, and he declared that in haiku "one must talk poetry." To Buson this required not only an accurate ear and an experienced eye but also intimacy with Chinese and Japanese classics. Buson's interest in Chinese poetry is especially evident in three long poems that are irregular in form. His experimental poems have been called "Chinese poems in Japanese," and two of them contain passages in Chinese.

HORACE WALPOLE, 4TH EARL OF ORFORD

(b. September 24, 1717, London—d. March 2, 1797)

Horace Walpole, 4th earl of Orford, was an English writer, connoisseur, and collector who was famous in his day for his medieval horror tale *The Castle of Otranto*, which initiated the vogue for Gothic romances. He is also remembered today as perhaps the most assiduous letter writer in the English language.

The youngest son of the prime minister Sir Robert Walpole, he was educated at Eton and at King's College, Cambridge. In 1739 he embarked with his Eton schoolmate, the poet Thomas Gray, on a grand tour of France and Italy, in the midst of which they quarrelled and separated. They were later reconciled, and Walpole remained throughout his life an enthusiastic admirer of Gray's poetry. On his return to England in 1741, Walpole entered Parliament, where his career was undistinguished, although he attended debates regularly until 1768. In 1791 he inherited the peerage from a nephew, a grandson of Robert Walpole. He remained unmarried, and on his death the earldom became extinct.

The most absorbing interests of his life were his friendships and a small villa that he acquired at Twickenham in 1747 and transformed into a pseudo-Gothic showplace known as Strawberry Hill. Over the years he added cloisters, turrets, and battlements, filled the interior with pictures and curios, and amassed a valuable library. The house was open to tourists and became widely known in Walpole's own lifetime. He established a private press on the grounds, where he printed his own works and those of his friends, notably Gray's *Odes* of 1757. Strawberry Hill was the stimulus for the Gothic revival in English domestic architecture.

Walpole's literary output was extremely varied. *The Castle of Otranto* (1765), which was first published anonymously, succeeded in restoring the element of romance to contemporary fiction. In it he furnished the machinery for a genre of fiction wherein the wildest fancies found refuge. He also wrote *The Mysterious Mother* (1768), a tragedy with the theme of incest; amateur historical speculations such as *Historic Doubts on the Life and Reign of King Richard the Third* (1768); and a contribution to art history, *Anecdotes of Painting in England*, 4 vol. (1762–71).

His most important works were intended for posthumous publication. His private correspondence of some 4,000 letters constitutes a survey of the history, manners, and taste of his age. Walpole revered the letters of Mme de Sévigné (1626–96) and, following her example, consciously cultivated letter writing as an art. His most substantial correspondence was with Horace Mann, a British diplomat whom Walpole met on his grand tour and with whom he maintained contact for 45 years, although the two never met again. Walpole's correspondence, edited by W.S. Lewis and others, was published in 48 volumes (1937–83).

Walpole also left *Memoirs* (first published 1822–59) of the reigns of George II and III, a record of political events of his time.

TOBIAS SMOLLETT

(baptized March 19, 1721, Cardross, Dumbartonshire, Scotland—
d. September 17, 1771, near Livorno, Tuscany [Italy])

Tobias George Smollett was a Scottish satirical novelist who is best known for his picaresque novels *The Adventures of Roderick Random* (1748) and *The Adventures of Peregrine Pickle* (1751) and his epistolary novel *The Expedition of Humphry Clinker* (1771).

Smollett came of a family of lawyers and soldiers, Whig in politics and Presbyterian in religion. In 1727 or 1728 he entered Dumbarton grammar school, proceeding from there to the University of Glasgow and apprenticeship to William Stirling and John Gordon, surgeons of that city. His first biographer states that he "attended the anatomical and medical lectures," and, if his first novel, *Roderick Random*, may be taken as evidence, he also studied Greek, mathematics, moral and natural philosophy, and logic. He left the university in 1739 without a degree and went to London, taking with him his play *The Regicide*. A year later he was commissioned surgeon's second mate in the Royal Navy and appointed to HMS *Chichester*, which reached Port Royal, Jamaica, on January 10, 1741. It is probable that Smollett saw action in the naval bombardment of

Cartagena (now in Colombia). The expedition was disastrous; he would later describe its horrors in *Roderick Random*. In Jamaica he met and was betrothed to—and perhaps there married—an heiress, Anne Lassells.

He returned to London alone to set up as a surgeon on Downing Street, Westminster, his wife joining him in 1747. He failed to secure a production of *The Regicide*, but in 1746, after the defeat of the Jacobite rebels at Culloden, he wrote his most famous poem, "The Tears of Scotland." He had by now moved to cheaper accommodations in Chapel Street, Mayfair, no doubt because, despite litigation, he had managed to recover only a fraction of his wife's considerable dowry, which was invested in land and slaves. It was in Chapel Street that he wrote *Advice* and *Reproof*, verse satires in the manner of the Roman poet Juvenal.

In 1748 Smollett published his novel *The Adventures of Roderick Random*, in part a graphic account of British naval life at the time, and also translated from the French the great picaresque romance *Gil Blas*, published by Alain-René Lesage in four volumes from 1715 to 1735. In 1750 Smollett obtained the degree of M.D. from Marischal College, Aberdeen. Later in the year he was in Paris, searching out material for *The Adventures of Peregrine Pickle*. This work contains a great comic figure in Hawser Trunnion, a retired naval officer who, though living on dry land, insists on behaving as though he were still on the quarterdeck of one of his majesty's ships at sea.

In 1752 he published "An Essay on the External Use of Water," an attack on the medicinal properties of the waters of a popular English health resort, Bath (he would resume the attack in his later novel *The Expedition of Humphry Clinker*). The essay made him many enemies and little money. His financial difficulties were intensified by his generosity in lending money to a hack writer called Peter Gordon, who employed legal stratagems to avoid repayment. Smollett came to blows with Gordon and his landlord and was sued by them for £1,000 and £500, respectively, on charges of trespass and assault. In the event, Smollett was required to pay only small damages. He was now living at Monmouth House, Chelsea, where he was host to such leading literary figures as the authors Samuel Johnson and Oliver Goldsmith, as well as to the actor David Garrick and John Hunter, a famous surgeon and anatomist. On Sundays, if one may take a passage in *Peregrine Pickle* as autobiographical, Smollett threw his house open to "unfortunate brothers of the quill," whom he regaled with "beer, pudding, and potatoes, port, punch, and Calvert's entire butt-beer." He himself seems to have been a man irascible, pugnacious, infinitely energetic, courageous, and generous.

The Adventures of Ferdinand, Count Fathom (now, with *The History and Adventures of an Atom*, the least regarded of his novels) appeared in 1753. It sold poorly, and Smollett was forced into borrowing from friends and into further hack writing. In June 1753 he visited Scotland for the first time in 15 years; his mother, it is said, recognized him only because of his "roguish smile." Back in London, Smollett set about a commitment to translate *Don Quixote* from the Spanish of Miguel de Cervantes, and this translation was published in 1755. Smollett was already suffering from tuberculosis.

Early in 1756 he became editor of *The Critical Review*, at the same time writing his *Complete History of England*, which was financially successful. This work relieved the financial pressure that he had felt all his adult life. A year later, his farce *The Reprisal: or, The Tars of Old England* was produced at Drury Lane and brought him a profit of almost £200. In 1758 he became what today might perhaps be called general editor of *Universal History*, a compilation of 58 volumes; Smollett himself wrote on France, Italy, and Germany. His friendship with the politician John Wilkes enabled him to secure the release of Francis Barber, Samuel Johnson's black servant, from the press-gang. But a libel on Admiral Sir Charles Knowles in *The Critical Review* led to Smollett's being sentenced to a fine of £100 and three months' imprisonment in the King's Bench Prison. He seems to have lived there in some comfort and drew on his experiences for his novel *The Adventures of Sir Launcelot Greaves* (1762), which was serialized in *The British Magazine*, of which Smollett became editor in 1760.

Two years later he became editor of *The Briton*, a weekly founded to support the prime minister John Stuart, 3rd earl of Bute. He was also writing an eight-volume work entitled *The Present State of All Nations*, and he had begun a translation, in 36 volumes, of the varied works of the French writer Voltaire. Smollett was now seriously ill; attempts to secure a post as physician to the army in Portugal and as British consul in Marseille or Madrid were fruitless. In 1763 the death of his only child, Elizabeth, who was 15 years old, overwhelmed him "with unutterable sorrow." He severed his connection with *The Critical Review* and, as he said, "every other literary system," retiring with his wife to France, where he settled at Nice.

In 1766 Smollett published *Travels Through France and Italy*. It is a satire on both tourists and those who profit from them, and its jaundiced version of traveling on the Continent led to Smollett's appearance as the splenetic Smelfungus in Laurence Sterne's novel *A Sentimental Journey* (1768). He returned to England in that year, visited Scotland, and at Christmas was again in England (at Bath), where he probably began what is his finest work, *The Expedition of Humphry Clinker,* an epistolary novel that recounts the adventures of a family traveling through Britain. In 1768, steadily weakening in health, he retired to Pisa, Italy. During the autumn of 1770 he seems to have written the bulk of *Humphry Clinker*, which was published on June 15, 1771.

Scholars may not consider Smollett the equal of the novelists Samuel Richardson and Henry Fielding, his older contemporaries, but he is unrivaled for the pace and vigour that sustain his comedy. He is especially brilliant in the rendering of comic characters in their externals, thus harking back to the manner of the Jacobean playwright Ben Jonson and looking forward to that of the Victorian novelist Charles Dickens. His panoramic picture of the life of his times is surpassed only by that given by Fielding, and his account of conditions in the Royal Navy is especially valuable.

WILLIAM COLLINS

(b. December 25, 1721, Chichester, Sussex, England—
d. June 12, 1759, Chichester)

The English poet William Collins wrote lyrical odes that adhered to the Neoclassical forms dominant during the time but that in theme and feeling looked forward to the Romantic movement. Though his literary career was brief and his output slender, he is considered one of the finest English lyric poets of the 18th century.

He was educated at Winchester College, where he formed one of the most stable and fruitful relationships of his unstable life: his friendship with the poet and critic Joseph Warton. When only 17, under the influence of the poet Alexander Pope's *Pastorals*, he composed his four *Persian Eclogues* (1742; 2nd ed., *Oriental Eclogues*, 1757), the only one of his works to be esteemed in his lifetime. In 1744 he published his verse *Epistle: Addrest to Sir Thomas Hanmer on his Edition of Shakespeare's Works*, containing his exquisite "Dirge from Cymbeline."

Collins graduated from Magdalen College, Oxford (1743), and went to London in 1744. An inheritance, supplemented by an allowance from his uncle, enabled him to live as a man-about-town. He made friends with Samuel Johnson, who expressed respect for his talents and, later, concern for his fate. By 1746 extravagance and dissipation had put Collins deeply in debt. He agreed to collaborate with Warton on a volume of odes. The two men's poems eventually appeared separately that December (the title page of Collins's *Odes* being dated 1747). Warton's collection was well received, but Collins's *Odes on Several Descriptive and Allegorical Subjects* was barely noticed. Though disappointed, Collins continued to perfect the style exemplified in his "Ode to Simplicity."

In 1749 Collins's uncle died, leaving him enough money to extricate himself from debt. In the next few months he wrote his "Ode on the Popular Superstitions of the Highlands of Scotland," which anticipates many of the attitudes and interests of the Romantic poets. Threatened after 1751 by mental illness and physical debility, which he tried to cure by travel, Collins was confined in a mental asylum in 1754. Released to the care of his sister, he survived wretchedly in Chichester for five more years, neglected and forgotten by his literary friends, who believed him dead. His work, however, became influential and admired after his death.

GORONWY OWEN

(b. January 1, 1723, Llanfair Mathafarn Eithaf, Anglesey, Wales —
d. July 1769, Brunswick, Virginia [U.S.])

Goronwy Owen (also called Goronwy Ddu o Fôn) was a clergyman and poet who revived the bardic tradition in 18th-century Welsh literature.

Owen was taught an appreciation of medieval Welsh poetry from his youth. He studied briefly to be a priest and then taught school for some years. While serving as master of the local school and curate of Uppington, Owen began to attract attention as a poet. Other poets gathered around him, and, influenced by Owen's vision (his letters are a foundation stone of Welsh literary criticism), they formed a neoclassical school of poetry whose influence lasted until the 20th century. In 1757 Owen obtained an appointment, through the efforts of friends, as headmaster of the grammar school attached to the College of William and Mary, in Williamsburg, Virginia. After losing this mastership (for excessive drinking and "riotous living"), he became a planter and the minister of St. Andrew's, Brunswick county, where he remained until he died.

Through his poetry, Owen breathed new life into two Welsh bardic meters: the *cywydd*, a short ode in rhyming couplets in which one rhyme is accented and the other unaccented, and the *awdl*, a long ode written in *cynghanedd* (a complex system of alliteration and internal rhyme) and in one or more of 24 strict bardic metres. He used these forms as vehicles for the expression of classic ideals rather than in praise of patrons. Owen's best-known poems were written before his departure for America; among them are "Cywydd y Farn Fawr" ("Cywydd of the Great Judgment"), "Cywydd y Gem neu'r Maen Gwerthfawr" ("Cywydd of the Gem or the Precious Stone"), and "Cywydd yn ateb Huw'r Bardd Coch o Fôn" ("Cywydd in Answer to Huw the Red Poet [Hugh Hughes]").

FRIEDRICH GOTTLIEB KLOPSTOCK

(b. July 2, 1724, Quedlinburg, Saxony [Germany]—
d. March 14, 1803, Hamburg)

The subjective vision of the German epic and lyric poet Friedrich Gottlieb Klopstock marked a break with the rationalism that had dominated German literature in the early 18th century.

Klopstock was educated at Schulpforta, a prestigious Protestant boarding school, where he read *Paradise Lost* by the great 17th-century English poet John Milton in a translation by the influential Swiss critic Johann Jakob Bodmer. That experience prompted Klopstock to begin planning a great religious epic poem. In 1749 the first three cantos of his *Der Messias* (*The Messiah*), written in unrhymed hexameters, appeared in the *Bremer Beiträge* and created a sensation.

To fulfill what he considered his poetic mission, Klopstock left his studies at the University of Leipzig and became a private tutor at Langensalza, Thuringia. There he fell in love with a cousin, the "Fanny" of his odes. Disappointed in romance, he went to Zürich (1750), staying for six months with Bodmer.

An invitation and an annuity from Frederick V of Denmark took him to Copenhagen, where he remained for 20 years. While there Klopstock composed historical plays dealing with the ancient Germanic hero Arminius. In 1754 he married Margarethe (Meta) Moller of Hamburg, who was the "Cidli" of his odes. Grief over her early death affected his creativity. A collection of his *Oden* ("Odes") was published in 1771. In 1770 he retired to Hamburg, where the last five cantos of *Der Messias* were produced with waning inspiration three years later. In 1791 he married Johanna Elisabeth von Winthem, his first wife's niece and a close friend for many years.

Although widely known as the author of *Der Messias* —the work was translated into 17 languages—Klopstock established his reputation chiefly as a lyric poet. The free verse forms he used in his hymnlike odes permitted a more natural and expressive use of language.

GIOVANNI GIACOMO CASANOVA

(b. April 2, 1725, Venice [Italy]   d. June 4, 1798, Dux, Bohemia [now Duchcov, Czech Republic])

Giovanni Giacomo Casanova was a sometime ecclesiastic, writer, soldier, and spy who is chiefly remembered as the prince of Italian adventurers and as the person whose name is today defined by Merriam-Webster's Collegiate Dictionary as "a man who is a promiscuous and unscrupulous lover." His autobiography, which perhaps exaggerates some of his escapades, is a splendid description of 18th-century society in the capitals of Europe.

The son of an actor, Casanova was expelled as a young man from the seminary of St. Cyprian for scandalous conduct and launched on a colourful career. After a time in the service of a Roman Catholic cardinal, he was a violinist in Venice, joined the Masonic Order (1750) in Lyon, then traveled to Paris, Dresden, Prague, and Vienna. Back in Venice in 1755, Casanova was denounced as a magician and sentenced to five years in the Piombi, prisons under the roof of the Doges' Palace. On October 31, 1756, he achieved a spectacular escape and made his way to Paris, where he introduced the lottery in 1757 and made a financial reputation and a name for himself among the aristocracy. Wherever he went, Casanova relied on personal charm to win influence and on gambling and intrigue to support himself.

Fleeing from his creditors in Paris in 1760, he assumed the name Jean-Jacques, Chevalier de Seingalt (which he retained for the rest of his life). He traveled to southern Germany, Switzerland (where he met Voltaire), Savoy, southern France, Florence (whence he was expelled), and Rome. He also spent some time in London. In Berlin (1764) Frederick II offered him a post. Casanova moved on to Riga, St. Petersburg, and Warsaw. A scandal followed by a duel forced him to flee, and he eventually sought refuge in Spain. Permitted to return to Venetian territory between 1774 and 1782, he acted as a spy for the Venetian inquisitors of state. He spent his final years (1785–98) in Bohemia as librarian for the Count von Waldstein in the château of Dux.

As versatile in his writing as he was in his career, Casanova wrote occasional verse, criticism, a translation of the *Iliad* (1775), and a satirical pamphlet on the Venetian patriciate, especially the powerful Grimani family. His most important work, however, is his vivid autobiography, first published after his death as *Mémoires de J. Casanova de Seingalt,* 12 vol. (1826–38). (A definitive edition, based on the original manuscripts, was published in 1960–62 with the title *Histoire de ma vie* [*History of My Life*].) This work provides an account of Casanova's dissolute life and established his reputation as an archetypal seducer of women.

MERCY OTIS WARREN

(b. September 14 [September 25, New Style], 1728, Barnstable,
Massachusetts [U.S.]—d. October 19, 1814, Plymouth,
Massachusetts, U.S.)

M ercy Otis Warren was an American poet, dramatist, and historian whose proximity to political leaders and critical national events gives particular value to her writing on the American Revolutionary period.

Mercy Otis was born to a prosperous Cape Cod family. One of her brothers was the political activist and firebrand James Otis, who was early involved in events leading to the American Revolution. She received no formal schooling but managed to absorb something of an education from her uncle, the Rev. Jonathan Russell, who tutored her brothers and allowed her to study by their side in all subjects except Latin and Greek. In 1754 she married James Warren, a merchant and farmer who went on to serve in the Massachusetts state legislature (1766–78). Together they had five children. Because of her husband's political associations, Warren was personally acquainted with most of the leaders of the Revolution and was continually at or near the centre of events for more than two decades, from the Stamp Act crisis of 1765 to the establishment of the federal republic in 1789.

After her brother James was brutally beaten by colonial revenue officers in 1769, Warren was increasingly drawn to political activism and hosted protest meetings at her home that resulted in the organization of the Committees of Correspondence. Combining her unique vantage point and fervent beliefs with a talent for writing, she then became both a poet and a historian of the Revolutionary era, beginning with a trio of scathingly polemical plays in verse that were published serially in a Boston newspaper. *The Adulateur* (1772) foretold the War of Revolution through the actions of Rapatio, a haughty, imperious official obviously modeled on Massachusetts's royal governor, Thomas Hutchinson. *The Defeat*, also featuring Rapatio, followed a year later, and in 1775 Warren published *The Group*, a satire conjecturing what would happen if the British king abrogated the Massachusetts charter of rights. The anonymously published prose dramas *The Blockheads* (1776) and *The Motley Assembly* (1779), no less acerbic, are also attributed to her.

As the young United States, and Massachusetts in particular, began to move in a Federalist direction following the war, Warren remained steadfastly Republican. In 1788 she published *Observations on the New Constitution*, detailing her opposition to the document on account of its emphasis on a strong central government. Warren maintained social and political correspondences with her friends John and Abigail Adams. She wrote the latter about her belief that the relegation of women to minor concerns reflected not their inferior intellect but the inferior opportunities offered them to develop their capacities. In 1790 she published *Poems, Dramatic and Miscellaneous*, a collection of her works that contained two new plays, *The Sack of Rome* and *The Ladies of Castille*. In 1805 Warren completed a three-volume history titled *A History of the Rise, Progress, and Termination of the American Revolution*. The work deliberately avoided dull accounts of "military havoc" in favour of knowledgeable comments on the important personages of the day, which remain especially useful. Its marginalizing and sharply critical treatment of John Adams, whose term as the president of the United States ended in 1801, led to a heated correspondence and a breach in Warren's friendship with the Adamses that lasted until 1812.

Mercy Otis Warren, 19th century. Kean Collection/Archive Photos/ Getty Images

GOTTHOLD EPHRAIM LESSING

(b. January 22, 1729, Kamenz, Upper Lusatia, Saxony [Germany]—
d. February 15, 1781, Braunschweig, Brunswick [Germany])

The German dramatist, critic, and writer on philosophy and aesthetics Gotthold Ephraim Lessing helped free German drama from the influence of classical and French models and wrote plays of lasting importance. His critical essays greatly stimulated German arts and letters, and they combated conservative dogmatism and cant while affirming religious and intellectual tolerance and the unbiased search for truth.

Education and First Dramatic Works

Lessing's father, a highly respected theologian, found it difficult to support his large family even though he occupied the position of *pastor primarius* (chief pastor). At the age of 12, Lessing, even then an avid reader, entered the famous *Fürstenschule* ("elector's school") of St. Afra, in Meissen. A gifted and eager student, Lessing acquired a good knowledge of Greek, Hebrew, and Latin, while his admiration for the plays of the ancient Latin dramatists Plautus and Terence fired him with the ambition to write comedies himself.

In the autumn of 1746 Lessing entered the University of Leipzig as a student of theology. His real interests, however, were in literature, philosophy, and art. Lessing became fascinated by the theatre in Leipzig, which had recently been revitalized by the work of a talented and energetic actress, Caroline Neuber. Neuber took an interest in the young poet and in 1748 successfully produced his comedy *Der junge Gelehrte* ("The Young Scholar"). The play is a satire on an arrogant, superficial, vain, and easily offended scholar, a figure through which Lessing mocked his own bookishness. The other comedies belonging to this Leipzig period of 1747–49 (*Damon, Die alte Jungfer* ["The Old Maid"], *Der Misogyn* ["The Misogynist"], *Die Juden* ["The Jews"], *Der Freigeist* ["The Free Thinker"]) are witty commentaries on human weaknesses—bigotry, prejudice, nagging, fortune hunting, matchmaking, intrigue, hypocrisy, corruption, and frivolity.

Early in 1748 Lessing's parents, who disapproved of his association with the theatre in Leipzig, summoned him home. But he managed to win their consent to begin studying medicine and was soon allowed to return to Leipzig. He quickly found himself in difficulties because he had generously stood surety for some members of the Neuber theatrical company—although he was himself heavily in debt. When the company folded, he fled from Leipzig in order to avoid being arrested for debt. He eventually reached Berlin in 1748, where he hoped to find work as a journalist through a cousin who was by this time an established editor. In the next four years he undertook a variety of jobs, mainly translating French and English historical and philosophical works into German. But he also began to make a name for himself through his brilliant and witty criticism for a newspaper at which he was book review editor.

Rising Reputation as Dramatist and Critic

From 1751 to 1752 Lessing was in Wittenberg, where he took his degree in medicine. He then returned to Berlin, where he started a short-lived periodical, *Theatralische Bibliothek* ("Theatrical Library"). The most significant event during this time was the publication in 1753–55 of a six-volume edition of his works. Apart from some witty epigrams, the edition contained the most important of his Leipzig comedies. It also contained *Miss Sara Sampson*, which is the first major *bürgerliches Trauerspiel*, or domestic tragedy, in German literature. Middle-class writers had long wanted to do away with the traditional class distinctions in literature, whereby heroic and tragic themes were played out by aristocratic figures, while middle-class characters appeared only in comedy. Lessing was, in fact, not the first German writer to challenge this tradition, but it is fair to say that his play marks the decisive break with the classical French drama that still dominated the German stage.

Miss Sara Sampson was inspired by the English dramatist George Lillo's *London Merchant* (1731) and by the novels of Samuel Richardson—with their praise of middle-class feminine virtue—and, to a lesser degree, by the sentimental *comédie larmoyante* ("tearful comedy"), originated in France by the early 18th-century dramatist Pierre-Claude de La Chausée. It is the first German play in which *bürgerlich* (middle-class) characters bear the full burden of a tragic fate, and it had its successful premiere at Frankfurt an der Oder in 1755. The plot centres on an innocent, sensitive heroine of a bourgeois family; she becomes the victim of Lady Marwood, her vampirelike rival in love, who disregards all restraints and inhibitions, and of Mellefont, a weak man who vacillates between the two women but finally atones for his guilt by his death.

Characteristic of Lessing's writings at this period is his *Rettungen* ("Vindications"), which is outstanding for its incisive style and clarity of argument. In its four essays he aimed to defend independent thinkers such as the Reformation-period writers Johannes Cochlaeus and Gerolamo Cardano, who, he felt, had been unjustly slandered and persecuted. In 1754 he directed a scintillating and biting polemic against the carelessly corrupt translations of the ancient Roman poet Horace by the scholar S.G. Lange, whose literary reputation was demolished by Lessing's attack. From this point on, Lessing was justly feared as a literary adversary who used his command of style as a finely honed weapon. The philosopher Moses Mendelssohn and the writer and publisher C.F. Nicolai stand out among Lessing's Berlin friends. With these men Lessing conducted a truly epoch-making correspondence (*Briefwechsel über das Trauerspiel*, 1756–57; "Correspondence About Tragedy") on the aesthetic of tragic drama.

Between November 1755 and April 1758 Lessing lived again at Leipzig, but in May he moved back to Berlin. There he contributed regularly to Nicolai's weekly, *Briefe, die neueste Literatur betreffend* ("Letters Concerning the Latest Literature"), writing a number of essays on contemporary literature. The central point of these was a vigorous attack on the influential theatre critic J.C. Gottsched for his advocacy of a theatre modeled on French drama, especially that of the 17th-century tragedian Pierre Corneille. Lessing maintained that the courtly, mannered drama of France was alien to the German mentality. Instead, he demanded a truly national drama, belonging to the people, based on faithfulness to nature and reality. He urged German playwrights to take the greatest of all English dramatists, William Shakespeare, as their model. In the 17th *Literaturbrief* he published a stirring scene from his own fragmentary Faust drama. In this scene, Lessing sketches out a "Faust without evil" whose relentless spirit of inquiry is justified before God, notwithstanding his pact with the devil. He thus paved the way for his young contemporary Johann Wolfgang von Goethe and the great dramatic version of the Faust story that he worked on during much of his adult life.

In 1760 Lessing went to Breslau as secretary to General Tauentzien, the military governor of Silesia. Lessing's studies in philosophy and aesthetics there brought forth two important literary works. One is the great treatise *Laokoon: oder über die Grenzen der Malerei und Poesie* (1766; "Laocoon; or, On the Limits of Painting and Poetry"). Here he took issue with the contemporary art historian Johann Winckelmann, specifically over his interpretation of the "Laocoon," a famous sculpture of Hellenistic times (C. 1st century BCE), which shows the priest Laocoon and his sons as they are about to be killed by the serpents that hold them entwined. In the *Laokoon* Lessing attempted to fundamentally define the separate functions of painting and of poetry. He pointed out that whereas painting is bound to observe spatial proximity—and must, therefore, select and render the most expressive moment in a chain of events—poetry has the task of depicting an event organically and in its temporal sequence. The essence of poetry thus lies not in description but in the representation of the transitory.

The second great Breslau work is *Minna von Barnhelm* (1767), which marks the birth of classical German comedy. The central characters are a Prussian officer, Major Tellheim, and a young gentlewoman from Thuringia, Minna. The upright officer's conscientiousness and rigid interpretation of the code of honour has endangered his relationship with Minna. Charming and spirited, Minna takes matters into her own hands and, prompted by her heart's perceptions, resolutely overcomes the obstacles that war and occupation have placed in the way of their union. Thus, in thinking and acting like true representatives of the Enlightenment, the two eventually behave like ordinary people and so bear witness to Lessing's concept of humanity.

On returning to Berlin in 1765 Lessing applied for the post of director of the royal library. Since he had quarreled with Voltaire, who lived as a favourite at Frederick the Great's court, the king (who in any case thought little of German authors) rejected his application. Lessing then accepted the offer of some Hamburg merchants to act as adviser and critic in their privately funded venture of a national theatre, which failed within a year. His reviews of more than 50 performances were published in the form of 104 brief essays on basic principles of the drama in 1767–69. Here Lessing argued against tragedy modeled on that of Corneille and Voltaire, although he praised the realism of the contemporary French writer Denis Diderot's descriptions of middle-class life.

Final Years

Being extremely poor, in 1770 Lessing had no choice but to accept the badly paid post of librarian at Wolfenbüttel, which he had earlier visited in 1766. His years there were unhappy and tempestuous but rich in achievement. His tragedy *Emilia Galotti* was performed in 1772. Written in intense and incisive prose, this brilliantly constructed play deals with a conflict of conscience at the court of an Italian prince. Lessing became involved in perhaps the most bitter controversy of his career when he also published extracts containing extremely radical ideas from the papers of the recently deceased biblical critic and scholar H.S. Reimarus under the title *Fragmente eines Ungenannten* (1774–77; "Fragments of an Unknown"). Lessing went into battle against the orthodox clergy, involving himself in violent controversies with their leader, the chief pastor of Hamburg, J.M. Goeze. Against this rigid dogmatist, Lessing launched some of his most cutting polemics, notably "Anti-Goeze" (1778), in which he expounded his belief that the search for truth is more valuable than the certainty gained by clinging to doctrinaire orthodoxy.

This controversy culminated in *Nathan der Weise* (1779), Lessing's "dramatic poem" in iambic pentameter. This is a didactic play of a theological and philosophical nature, combining ethical profundity with many comic touches, and is a work of high poetic quality and dramatic tension. *Nathan der Weise* symbolizes the equality of Islam, Christianity, and Judaism in regard to their ethical basis, for the play celebrates humanity's true religion—love, acting without prejudice and devoted to the service of humankind.

Lessing's last work, *Die Erziehung des Menschengeschlechts* (1780; *The Education of the Human Race*), is a treatise that expresses his belief in the perfectibility of the human race. In the history of the world's religions, Lessing saw a developing moral awareness that would, he believed, eventually attain the peak of universal brotherhood and moral freedom that would transcend all dogmas and doctrines.

Thus the last decade of his life spent at Wolfenbüttel produced a rich harvest of philosophical and literary works. But his life there was otherwise full of tribulations. His health had begun to give way, and it was a lonely existence, with only a few trips to break the monotony. In October 1776 he had finally been able to marry Eva König, the widow of a Hamburg merchant and a friend of long standing. In December 1777 she gave birth to their only child, a son, but he died soon after; she herself died the following month. Lessing's last years were lonely and poor.

CHARLOTTE LENNOX

(b. 1729/30, probably Gibraltar—
d. January 4, 1804, London, England)

Charlotte Lennox was an English novelist whose work, especially *The Female Quixote*, was much admired by leading literary figures of her time, including Samuel Johnson and the novelists Henry Fielding and Samuel Richardson.

Born Charlotte Ramsay, Lennox was the daughter of a British army officer who was said to have been lieutenant governor of the colony of New York. (This claim has been dismissed, however, in light of evidence that she went to live in or near Albany, New York, in 1739, when her father was posted there as captain of a company of foot soldiers.) In 1743, after her father's death, she returned to England, apparently to live with relatives. She attempted to earn a living as an actress but was not successful and is said to have turned to literary work. Her *Poems on Several Occasions* was published in 1747, and that same year she married Alexander Lennox. She made the first comparative study of William Shakespeare's source material, published in 1753–54, a project in which she may have been assisted by Johnson. The book takes Shakespeare to task for his plot adaptations and his lack of morality.

Lennox's first novel was *The Life of Harriot Stuart* (1751). *The Female Quixote* (1752) and *Henrietta* (1758) followed. She attempted to write for the stage as well but met with only slight success. Despite the friendship of Johnson and Richardson and the approbation of Fielding, Lennox made little from the sale of her books. She died in poverty.

OLIVER GOLDSMITH

(b. November 10, 1730, Kilkenny West, County Westmeath, Ireland—d. April 4, 1774, London, England)

The Anglo-Irish essayist, poet, novelist, and dramatist Oliver Goldsmith was made famous by such works as the series of essays *The Citizen of the World; or, Letters from a Chinese Philosopher* (1762), the poem *The Deserted Village* (1770), the novel *The Vicar of Wakefield* (1766), and the play *She Stoops to Conquer* (1773).

Goldsmith was the son of an Anglo-Irish clergyman, the Rev. Charles Goldsmith, curate in charge of Kilkenny West, County Westmeath. At about the time of his birth, the family moved into a substantial house at nearby Lissoy, where Oliver spent his childhood. Much has been recorded concerning his youth, his unhappy years as an undergraduate at Trinity College, Dublin, where he received the B.A. degree in February 1749, and his many misadventures before he left Ireland in the autumn of 1752 to study in the medical school at Edinburgh. His father was now dead, but several of his relations had undertaken to support him in his pursuit of a medical degree. Later on, in London, he came to be known as Dr. Goldsmith—Doctor being the courtesy title for one who held the Bachelor of Medicine—but he took no degree while at Edinburgh nor, so far as anyone knows, during the two-year period when, despite his meagre funds, which were eventually exhausted, he somehow managed to make his way through Europe. The first period of his life ended with his arrival in London, penniless, early in 1756.

Goldsmith's rise from total obscurity was a matter of only a few years. He worked as an apothecary's assistant, school usher, physician, and as a hack writer—reviewing, translating, and compiling. Much of his work was for Ralph Griffiths's *Monthly Review*. It remains amazing that this young Irish vagabond was able within a few years to climb from obscurity to mix with aristocrats and the intellectual elite of London. Such a rise was possible because Goldsmith had one quality, soon noticed by booksellers and the public, that his fellow literary hacks did not possess—the gift of a graceful, lively, and readable style. His rise began with the *Enquiry into the Present State of Polite Learning in Europe* (1759), a minor work. Soon he emerged as an essayist, in *The Bee* and other periodicals, and above all in his *Chinese Letters*. These essays were first published in the journal *The Public Ledger* and were collected as *The Citizen of the World* in 1762. The same year brought his *Life of Richard Nash, of Bath, Esq.* Already Goldsmith was acquiring those distinguished and often helpful friends whom he alternately annoyed and amused, shocked and charmed—the critic Samuel Johnson, the painter Sir Joshua Reynolds, the actor David Garrick, the statesman and political thinker Edmund Burke, and Johnson's eventual biographer, James Boswell. The obscure drudge of 1759 became in 1764 one of the nine founder-members of the famous Club, a select body, including Reynolds, Johnson, and Burke, which met weekly for supper and talk. Goldsmith could now afford to live more comfortably, but his extravagance continually ran him into debt, and he was forced to undertake more hack work. He thus produced histories of England and of ancient Rome and Greece, biographies, verse anthologies, translations, and works of popular science. These were mainly compilations of works by other authors, which Goldsmith then distilled and enlivened by his own gift for fine writing. Some of these makeshift compilations went on being reprinted well into the 19th century, however.

By 1762 Goldsmith had established himself as an essayist with his *Citizen of the World*, in which he used the device of satirizing Western society through the eyes of a visitor to London. By 1764 he had won a reputation as a poet with *The Traveller,* the first work to which he put his name. It embodied both his memories of tramping through Europe and his political ideas. In 1770 he confirmed that reputation with the more famous *Deserted Village*, which contains charming vignettes of rural life while denouncing the evictions of the country poor at the hands of wealthy landowners. In 1766 Goldsmith revealed himself as a novelist with *The Vicar of Wakefield* (written in 1762), a portrait of village life whose idealization of the countryside, sentimental moralizing, and melodramatic incidents are underlain by a sharp but good-natured irony. In 1768 Goldsmith turned to the theatre with *The Good Natur'd Man*, which was followed in 1773 by the much more effective *She Stoops to Conquer*, which was immediately successful. This play has outlived almost all other English-language comedies from the early 18th to the late 19th century by virtue of its broadly farcical horseplay and vivid, humorous characterizations.

During his last decade Goldsmith's conversational encounters with Johnson and others, his lack of sound judgment, and his wit were preserved in Boswell's *Life of Samuel Johnson*. Goldsmith eventually became deeply embroiled in mounting debts despite his considerable earnings as an author, though, and after a short illness in the spring of 1774 he died. It was Johnson who best summed up Goldsmith's reputation among his contemporaries: "No man," he declared, "was more foolish when he had not a pen in his hand, or more wise when he had." In his novel and plays Goldsmith helped to humanize his era's literary imagination without growing sickly or mawkish. Goldsmith saw people, human situations, and indeed the human predicament from the comic point of view. He was a realist, something of a satirist, but in his final judgments he was unfailingly charitable.

LUCY TERRY

(b. 1730, West Africa—d. 1821, Vermont, U.S.)

Lucy Terry was a poet, storyteller, and activist of colonial and postcolonial America who is among the earliest figures in African American literature.

Terry was taken from Africa to Rhode Island by slave traders at a very young age. She was baptized a Christian at age five, with the approval of her owner, Ebenezer Wells of Deerfield, Massachusetts; she became a full church member in 1744. Terry remained a slave in the Wells household until 1756, when she married Abijah Prince, a free black man. (Her marriage gave her the name Lucy Prince; she was also called Bijah's [Abijah's] Luce, or Luce [Lucy] Abijah.) It is not certain if Prince purchased her freedom or if she was manumitted by Wells. In 1764 the Princes settled in Guilford, Vermont, where all six of their children were born.

Terry was considered a born storyteller and poet. Her only surviving work, the poem "Bars Fight" (1746), is the earliest existing poem by an African American. It was transmitted orally for more than 100 years, first appearing in print in 1855. Consisting of 28 lines in irregular iambic tetrameter, the poem commemorates white settlers who were killed in an encounter with Indians in 1746.

Later in life, Terry also proved to be a persuasive orator. Although she and her husband had hired Isaac Ticknor, a future governor of Vermont, to handle their case, Terry herself successfully argued before the U.S. Supreme Court their case against false land claims made by Colonel Eli Bronson. Less successful was her three-hour address to the board of trustees of Williams College in Massachusetts, in an attempt to gain admittance for one of her sons.

WILLIAM COWPER

(b. November 26, 1731, Great Berkhamstead, Hertfordshire, England—d. April 25, 1800, East Dereham, Norfolk)

William Cowper (pronounced "Cooper") was one of the most widely read English poets of his day. His most characteristic work, such as *The Task* or the melodious short lyric "The Poplar Trees," brought a new directness to 18th-century nature poetry.

Cowper wrote of the joys and sorrows of everyday life and was content to describe the minutiae of the countryside. In his sympathy with rural life, his concern for the poor and downtrodden, and his comparative simplicity of language, he may be seen as one in revolt against much 18th-century verse and as a forerunner of the poets Robert Burns, William Wordsworth, and Samuel Taylor Coleridge. While he is often gently humorous in his verse, the sense of desolation that was never far below the surface of his mind is revealed in many of his poems, notably "The Castaway."

After the death of his mother when he was six, Cowper, the son of an Anglican clergyman, was sent to a local boarding school. He then moved to Westminster School, in London, and in 1750 began to study law. He was called to the bar in 1754 and took chambers in London's Middle Temple in 1757. During his student days he fell in love with his cousin, Theodora Cowper, and for a while the two were engaged. But Cowper was beginning to show signs of the mental instability that plagued him throughout his

William Cowper. © Photos.com/Thinkstock

life. His father had died in 1756, leaving little wealth, and Cowper's family used its influence to obtain two administrative posts for him in the House of Lords, which entailed a formal examination. This prospect so disturbed him that he attempted suicide and was confined for 18 months in an asylum, troubled by religious doubts and fears and persistently dreaming of his predestined damnation.

Religion, however, also provided the comfort of Cowper's convalescence, which he spent at Huntingdon, lodging with the Reverend Morley Unwin, his wife Mary, and their small family. Pious Calvinists, the Unwins supported the evangelical revival, then a powerful force in English society. In 1767 Morley Unwin was killed in a riding accident, and his family, with Cowper, took up residence at Olney, in Buckinghamshire. The curate there, John Newton, a leader of the revival, encouraged Cowper in a life of practical evangelism; however, the poet proved too frail, and his doubt and melancholy returned. Cowper collaborated with Newton on a book of religious verse, eventually published as *Olney Hymns* (1779).

In 1773 thoughts of marriage with Mary Unwin were ended by Cowper's relapse into near madness. When he recovered the following year, his religious fervour was gone. Newton departed for London in 1780, and Cowper again turned to writing poetry; Mrs. Unwin suggested the theme for "The Progress of Error," six moral satires. Other works, such as "Conversation" and "Retirement," reflected his comparative cheerfulness at this time.

Cowper was friendly with Lady Austen, a widow living nearby, who told him a story that he made into a ballad, "The Journey of John Gilpin," which was sung all over London after it was printed in 1783. She also playfully suggested that he write about a sofa—an idea that grew into *The Task*. This long discursive poem, written "to recommend rural ease and leisure," was an immediate success on its publication in 1785. Cowper then moved to Weston, a neighbouring village, and began translating Homer. His health suffered under the strain, however, and there were occasional periods of mental illness. His health continued to deteriorate, and in 1795 he moved with Mary Unwin to live near a cousin in Norfolk, finally settling at East Dereham. Unwin, a permanent invalid since 1792, died in December 1796, and Cowper sank into despair from which he never emerged.

Robert Southey, who was Britain's poet laureate at the time, edited his writings in 15 volumes between 1835 and 1837. Cowper is also considered one of the best letter writers in English, and some of his hymns, such as "God Moves in a Mysterious Way" and "Oh! For a Closer Walk with God," have become part of the folk heritage of Protestant England.

SOPHIE VON LA ROCHE

(b. December 6, 1731, Kaufbeuern, Bavaria [Germany]—
d. February 18, 1807, Offenbach, Hesse)

Sophie von La Roche was a German writer whose first and most important work, *Geschichte des Fräuleins von Sternheim* (1771; *History of Lady Sophia Sternheim*), was the first German novel written by a woman. It is considered to be among the best works from the period in which English novels, particularly those of Samuel Richardson, had great influence on many German writers.

Born Sophie Gutermann, she was engaged to her close friend and cousin, the well-known writer Christoph Martin Wieland, but the betrothal was dissolved, and in 1754 she married G.M. Franck von La Roche. (Years later, she would become the grandmother of Bettina von Arnim and Clemens Brentano, both writers who would be central to the German Romantic movement.) From 1771 she maintained a literary salon in Ehrenbreitstein to which the young Johann Wolfgang von Goethe belonged; Goethe would become one of the greatest of German literary figures.

In 1771 Wieland also edited and published her first novel. Both its insistent didacticism and its partially epistolary form follow English models, but it also is related to the new phase of fiction introduced by Jean-Jacques Rousseau's novel *La Nouvelle Héloïse*; in La Roche's novel, passion begins to take a place beside rational morality and virtue. Fräulein von Sternheim's melancholy moods and the "confessional" aspect lent to the novel by its letter form won it fame. This, like all La Roche's works, is imbued with the rational spirit of the Enlightenment and shows her interest in economic and social problems, including women's education.

CHRISTOPH MARTIN WIELAND

(b. September 5, 1733, Oberholzheim, near Biberach [Germany] — d. January 20, 1813, Weimar, Saxe-Weimar)

Christoph Martin Wieland was a transitional figure in German literature, a poet and man of letters of the German Rococo period whose work spans the major trends of his age, from rationalism and the Enlightenment to classicism and pre-Romanticism.

Wieland was the son of a Pietist parson, and his early writings from the 1750s were sanctimonious and strongly devotional. During the 1760s, however, he discovered another, more sensual aspect of his nature and moved toward a more worldly, rationalistic philosophy. Although some of Wieland's work of this period includes erotic poetry, he began to find the balance between sensuality and rationalism that marked his mature writing. His *Geschichte des Agathon*, 2 vol. (1766–67; *History of Agathon*), which describes the process, is considered the first *Bildungsroman*, or novel of psychological development.

Between 1762 and 1766 Wieland published the first German translations of 22 of William Shakespeare's plays, which were to be influential models for *Sturm und Drang* ("Storm and Stress") dramatists. Wieland was professor of philosophy at Erfurt (1769–72) and was then appointed tutor to the Weimar princes. He was not a successful teacher but spent the rest of his life in or near the court circle as an admired man of letters. In 1773 he established *Der teutsche Merkur* ("The German Mercury"), which was a leading literary periodical for 37 years. Late in life, he considered himself a classicist and devoted most of his time to translating Greek and Roman authors. His allegorical verse epic *Oberon* (1780) foreshadows many aspects of Romanticism.

UEDA AKINARI

(b. July 25, 1734, Osaka, Japan—d. August 8, 1809, Kyoto)

Ueda Akinari (pseudonym of Ueda Senjiro) was a preeminent writer and poet of late 18th-century Japan, best known for his tales of the supernatural.

Ueda was adopted into the family of an oil and paper merchant and brought up with great kindness. A childhood attack of smallpox left him with some paralysis in his hands, and it may have caused his blindness late in life. Ueda became interested in classical Japanese and Chinese literature around the age of 25. He had started to write *ukiyo-zōshi*, "tales of the floating world," the popular fiction of the day, when in 1771 the business he had managed since his stepfather's death (1761) burned down. He took that as his opportunity to devote his full time to writing. In 1776, after eight years of work, he produced *Ugetsu monogatari* (*Tales of Moonlight and Rain*). These ghost tales showed a concern for literary style not present in most popular fiction of the time, in which the text was usually simply an accompaniment for the illustrations that formed the main part of the books.

A student of history and language, Ueda called for a revival of classical literature and language reform. His late years were spent in poverty-stricken wandering. His *Harusame monogatari* (1808; *Tales of the Spring Rain*) is another fine story collection. *Ugetsu monogatari* was the basis for the film *Ugetsu* (1953), directed by Mizoguchi Kenji.

MICHEL-GUILLAUME-SAINT-JEAN DE CRÈVECOEUR

(b. January 31, 1735, Caen, France—d. November 12, 1813, Sarcelles)

Michel-Guillaume-Saint-Jean de Crèvecoeur—also known as Hector Saint John de Crèvecoeur or J. Hector St. John—was a French American author whose work provided a broad picture of life in the New World.

After study in Jesuit schools and four years as an officer and mapmaker in Canada, Crèvecoeur chose in 1759 to remain in the New World. He wandered the Ohio and Great Lakes region, took out citizenship papers in New York in 1765, became a farmer in Orange county, and in 1769 married Mehitable Tippet, with whom he had three children.

When the American Revolution broke out, Crèvecoeur found himself in an untenable position: his wife was from a loyalist family and he had friends and neighbours among the opposite faction. Persecuted by both sides, he left rebel country only to languish for months in a British army prison in New York City before sailing for Europe in 1780, accompanied by one son. In London, using his American name, J. Hector St. John, he arranged for the publication in 1782 of 12 essays called *Letters from an American Farmer*.

Within two years this book —charmingly written, optimistic, and timely—saw eight editions in five countries and made its author famous, gaining him such influential patrons as the naturalist the comte de Buffon and Benjamin

Michel-Guillaume-Saint-Jean de Crèvecoeur. Library of Congress, Washington, D.C. (neg. no. LC-USZ62-53348)

Franklin, who in the early 1780s was acting as a diplomat in France; it also earned Crèvecoeur a membership in France's Academy of Sciences and an appointment as French consul to three of the new states in America. Before assuming his consular duties in 1784, Crèvecoeur translated and added to the original 12 essays, in *Lettres d'un cultivateur Américain*, 2 vol. (Paris, 1784).

In America again, Crèvecoeur found his home burned, his wife dead, and his daughter and second son with strangers in Boston. Reunited with his children, he set about organizing a packet service between the United States and France, continued an interest in botany, and published articles on agriculture and medicine. A two-year furlough in Europe resulted in a larger, second edition of the French *Lettres*, 3 vol. (1790). Recalled from his consulship in 1790, Crèvecoeur wrote one other book on America, *Voyage dans la haute Pennsylvanie et dans l'État de New York*, 3 vol. (1801; *Travels in Upper Pennsylvania and New York*, 1961). He lived quietly in France and Germany until his death.

Because of his letters, Crèvecoeur was not only for a while the most widely read commentator on America but also a great favourite with such Romantic-era English writers as Charles Lamb and Thomas Campbell and with the French revolutionist Jacques-Pierre Brissot. His reputation was further increased in the 1920s when a bundle of his unpublished English essays was discovered in an attic in France. These were brought out as *Sketches of Eighteenth Century America, or More Letters from an American Farmer* (1925). Crèvecoeur's books outline the steps through which new immigrants passed, analyze the religious problems of the New World, describe the life of the whalers of Nantucket, reveal much about the Indians and the horrors of the Revolution, and present the colonial farmer—his psychology and his daily existence—more completely than any contemporaneous writings were able to do. The passage containing his "melting pot" theory and answering the question "What is an American?" is widely quoted, and historians of the frontier depend heavily on his documented account of the stages by which the log cabin became the opulent farmhouse.

JAMES MACPHERSON

(b. October 27, 1736, Ruthven, Inverness, Scotland—
d. February 17, 1796, Belville, Inverness)

The Ossianic controversy initiated by the Scottish poet James Macpherson, which revolved around the authenticity of poems he "discovered" and claimed to be of the 3rd century, has obscured his genuine contributions to Gaelic studies.

Macpherson's first book of poems, *The Highlander* (1758), was undistinguished. After collecting Gaelic manuscripts and having orally transmitted Gaelic poems transcribed with the encouragement of the poet John Home and the financial support of the rhetorician Hugh Blair, he published *Fragments of Ancient Poetry...Translated from the Gallic or Erse Language* (1760), *Fingal* (1762), and *Temora* (1763), stating that much of their content was based on a 3rd-century Gaelic poet, Ossian. This would have been a revolutionary discovery, because no Gaelic manuscripts date back beyond the 10th century, but it soon came to be questioned.

The authenticity of Ossian was supported by Blair, looked on with skepticism by the Scottish philosopher David Hume, admired with doubt by the English poet Thomas Gray, and denied by the critic and lexicographer Samuel Johnson. None of the critics knew Gaelic.

Macpherson often injected a good deal of Romantic mood into the originals, sometimes closely followed them, and other times did not. His language was strongly influenced by the Authorized Version of the Bible. The originals were published only after Macpherson's death.

THOMAS PAINE

(b. January 29, 1737, Thetford, Norfolk, England—
d. June 8, 1809, New York, New York, U.S.)

Thomas Paine was an English American writer and political pamphleteer whose *Common Sense* and "Crisis" papers were important influences on the American Revolution. Other works that contributed to his reputation as one of the greatest political propagandists in history were *Rights of Man*, a defense of the French Revolution and of republican principles; and *The Age of Reason*, an exposition of the place of religion in society.

Life in England and America

Paine was born of a Quaker father and an Anglican mother. His formal education was meagre, just enough to enable him to master reading, writing, and arithmetic. At 13 he began work with his father as a corset maker and then tried various other occupations unsuccessfully. Paine's life in England was marked by repeated failures. He had two brief marriages. He was unsuccessful or unhappy in every job he tried. He was dismissed as an excise officer after he published a strong argument in 1772 for a raise in pay as the only way to end corruption in the service. Just when his situation appeared hopeless, he met Benjamin Franklin in London, who advised him to seek his fortune in America and gave him letters of introduction.

Paine arrived in Philadelphia on November 30, 1774, where he edited a magazine and published numerous articles and some poetry, anonymously or under pseudonyms. His arrival in America came at a time when the conflict between the colonists and England was reaching its height. After blood was spilled at the Battle of Lexington and Concord in April 1775, Paine argued that the cause of America should not be just a revolt against taxation but a demand for independence. He put this idea into *Common Sense*, which came off the press on January 10, 1776. The 50-page pamphlet sold more than 500,000 copies within a few months. More than any other single publication, *Common Sense* paved the way for the Declaration of Independence, adopted on July 4, 1776.

During the American Revolution, Paine served as a volunteer aide-de-camp. His great contribution to the patriot cause was the 16 "Crisis" papers issued between 1776 and 1783, each one signed *Common Sense*. "The American Crisis. Number I," published on December 19, 1776, when George Washington's army was on the verge of disintegration, opened with the flaming words: "These are the times that try men's souls." Washington ordered the pamphlet read to all the troops at Valley Forge.

In 1777 Congress appointed Paine secretary to the Committee for Foreign Affairs. He held the post until early in 1779, when he became involved in a controversy that resulted in his being forced to resign his post, and in November 1779 he was appointed clerk of the General Assembly of Pennsylvania. Paine raised money and acquired supplies for American troops struggling during the Revolution during this time, and he also appealed

Thomas Paine, detail of a portrait by John Wesley Jarvis; in the Thomas Paine Memorial House, New Rochelle, N.Y. Courtesy of the Thomas Paine National Historical Association

to the separate states to cooperate for the well-being of the entire nation (e.g., "Public Good" [1780]).

When the American Revolution ended in 1783, Paine found himself poverty-stricken. His patriotic writings had sold by the hundreds of thousands, but he had refused to accept any profits in order that cheap editions might be widely circulated. In a petition to Congress endorsed by Washington, he pleaded for financial assistance. It was buried by Paine's opponents, but Pennsylvania gave him a relatively small amount of money, and New York presented him with a farm in New Rochelle, where Paine devoted his time to scientific inventions.

In Europe: Rights of Man

In April 1787 Paine left for Europe to promote his plan to build a single-arch bridge near Philadelphia, but in England he was soon diverted. In December 1789 he published anonymously a warning against the attempt of Prime Minister William Pitt to involve England in a war with France over the Dutch Republic. But it was the French Revolution that wholly filled Paine's thoughts. He was enraged by the English statesman Edmund Burke's attack on the uprising of the French people in his *Reflections on the Revolution in France*, and, though Paine admired Burke's stand in favour of the American Revolution, he rushed into print with his celebrated answer, *Rights of Man* (March 13, 1791). The book immediately created an international sensation. When Burke replied, Paine came back with *Rights of Man, Part II*, published on February 17, 1792.

What began as a defense of the French Revolution evolved into an analysis of the basic reasons for discontent in European society and a remedy for the evils of arbitrary government, poverty, illiteracy, unemployment, and war. To the ruling class Paine's proposals spelled "bloody revolution," and the government ordered the book banned and the publisher jailed. Paine himself was indicted for treason, and an order went out for his arrest. But he was en route to France, having been elected to a seat in the National Convention, before the order for his arrest could be delivered. Paine was tried in absentia, found guilty of seditious libel, and declared an outlaw, and *Rights of Man* was ordered permanently suppressed.

In France Paine hailed the abolition of the monarchy but deplored the terror against the royalists and fought unsuccessfully to save the life of King Louis XVI, favouring banishment rather than execution. He was to pay for his efforts to save the king's life when the radicals under Maximilien de Robespierre, one of the leaders of the French Revolution during its Reign of Terror, took power. Paine was imprisoned from December 28, 1793, to November 4, 1794, when, with the fall of Robespierre, he was released and, though seriously ill, readmitted to the National Convention.

The first part of Paine's *Age of Reason* was published (1794) while Paine was in prison, and it was followed by *Part II* after his release (1796). Although Paine made it clear that he believed in a Supreme Being and opposed only organized religion, the work won him a reputation as an atheist among the orthodox. Paine remained in France until September 1, 1802, when he sailed for the United States, where he found that his services to the country had been all but forgotten. Despite his poverty and his physical condition, worsened by occasional drunkenness, Paine continued his attacks on privilege and religious superstitions until his death in 1809.

EDWARD GIBBON

(b. May 8 [April 27, old style], 1737, Putney, Surrey, England —
d. January 16, 1794, London)

The English historian and scholar Edward Gibbon is best known as the author of *The History of the Decline and Fall of the Roman Empire* (1776–88), a continuous narrative from the 2nd century CE to the fall of Constantinople (now Istanbul) in 1453.

Early Life and Adulthood

Gibbon's grandfather, Edward, had made a considerable fortune and his father, also Edward, was able to live an easy-going life in society and Parliament. He married Judith, a daughter of James Porten, whose family had originated in Germany. Edward, too, had independent means throughout his life. He was the eldest and the only survivor of seven children, the rest dying in infancy.

Gibbon's own childhood was a series of illnesses and more than once he nearly died. Neglected by his mother, he owed his life to her sister, Catherine Porten, whom he also called "the mother of his mind," and after his mother's death in 1747 he was almost entirely in his aunt's care. He early became an omnivorous reader and could indulge his tastes the more fully since his schooling was most irregular. In 1749 he was admitted to Westminster School. He was taken in 1750 to Bath and Winchester in search of health and after an unsuccessful attempt to return to Westminster was placed for the next two years with tutors from whom he learned little. His father took him on visits to country houses where he had the run of libraries filled with old folios. He noted his

12th year as one of great intellectual development and says in his *Memoirs* that he had early discovered his "proper food," history. Apart from his aunt's initial guidance, Gibbon followed his intellectual bent in solitary independence. This characteristic remained with him throughout his life.

In his *Memoirs* Gibbon remarked that with the onset of puberty his health suddenly improved and remained excellent throughout his life. Never a strong or active man, he was of diminutive stature and very slightly built and he became corpulent in later years. The improvement in his health apparently accounts for his father's sudden decision to enter him at Magdalen College, Oxford, on April 3, 1752, about three weeks before his 15th birthday. He was now privileged and independent. Any expectations of study at Oxford were soon disappointed. The authorities failed to look after him intellectually or spiritually or even to note his absences from the college. Left to himself, Gibbon turned to theology and read himself into the Roman Catholic faith. It was a purely intellectual conversion. Yet he acted on it and was received into the Roman Catholic Church by a priest in London on June 8, 1753.

His father, outraged because under the existing laws his son had disqualified himself for all public service and office, acted swiftly, and Edward was dispatched to Lausanne and lodged with a Calvinist minister, the Rev. Daniel Pavillard. Though the change was complete, and Gibbon was under strict surveillance, in great discomfort, and with the scantiest allowance, he later spoke of this period with gratitude. He mastered the bulk of classical Latin literature and studied mathematics and logic. He also became perfectly conversant with the language and literature of France, which exercised a permanent influence on him. These studies made him not only a man of considerable learning but a stylist for life. He began his first work, written in French, *Essai sur l'étude de la littérature* (1761; *An Essay on the Study of*

Literature). Meanwhile, the main purpose of his exile had not been neglected. Not without weighty thought, Gibbon at last rejected his new faith and was publicly readmitted to the Protestant communion at Christmas 1754.

In the latter part of his exile Gibbon entered more freely into Lausanne society. He attended Voltaire's parties. He formed an enduring friendship with a young Swiss, Georges Deyverdun, and also fell in love with and rashly committed himself to Suzanne Curchod, a pastor's daughter of great charm and intelligence. In 1758 his father called Gibbon home shortly before his 21st birthday and provided him with a regular income. On the other hand, he found that his father and his stepmother were implacably opposed to his engagement, and he was compelled to break it off. He never again thought seriously of marriage. After an estrangement he and Curchod became lifelong friends. She was well known as the wife of Jacques Necker, the French finance minister under King Louis XVI. During the next five years Gibbon read widely and considered many possible subjects for a historical composition. From 1760 until the end of 1762, his studies were seriously interrupted by his service on home defense duties with the Hampshire militia. With the rank of captain he did his duty conscientiously and later claimed that his experience of men and camps had been useful to him as a historian.

Gibbon left England on January 25, 1763, and spent some time in Paris, making the acquaintance of Denis Diderot and Jean Le Rond d'Alembert, among other French thinkers and men of letters of the time who have come to be known as the *philosophes*. During the autumn and winter spent in study and gaiety at Lausanne, he gained a valuable friend in John Baker Holroyd (later Lord Sheffield), who was to become his literary executor. In 1764 Gibbon went to Rome, where he made an exhaustive study of the antiquities and, on October 15, 1764, while musing amid the ruins of the Capitol, was inspired to write of the decline and fall of the city. Some time was yet to pass before he decided on the history of the empire.

At home, the next five years were the least satisfactory in Gibbon's life. He was dependent on his father and although nearly 30 had achieved little in life. Although bent on writing a history, he had not settled on a definite subject. Impressed by the supremacy of French culture in Europe, he began in that language a history of the liberty of the Swiss, but was dissuaded from continuing it. He and Deyverdun published two volumes of *Mémoires littéraires de la Grande Bretagne* (1768–69). In 1770 he sought to attract some attention by publishing *Critical Observations on the Sixth Book of the Aeneid*.

His father died in 1770. Two years later Gibbon was established in London and concentrated on his Roman history. At the same time he entered fully into social life. He joined the fashionable clubs and was also becoming known among men of letters. In 1775 he was elected to the Club, the brilliant circle that the painter Sir Joshua Reynolds had formed around the writer and lexicographer Samuel Johnson. Although Johnson's biographer, James Boswell, openly detested Gibbon, and it may be inferred that Johnson disliked him, Gibbon took an active part in the Club and developed close friendships with Reynolds and the actor David Garrick. In the previous year he had entered Parliament and was an assiduous, though silent, supporter of the prime minister, Lord North.

Publication of The Decline and Fall

The first quarto volume of *The Decline and Fall of the Roman Empire*, published on February 17, 1776, immediately scored a success that was resounding, if somewhat scandalous because of the last two chapters in which he dealt with great irony with the rise of Christianity. Both in his lifetime and after, he was attacked by those who feared that his skepticism would shake the existing establishment. But Gibbon himself was not militantly opposed to organized religion, because in his England and Switzerland he saw no danger in the ecclesiastical systems. His concern was past history. While he treated the supernatural with irony, his main purpose was to establish the principle that religions must be treated as phenomena of human experience.

Gibbon went on to prepare the next volumes. Meanwhile, he was assailed by many pamphleteers and subjected to much ridicule. His ugliness and elaborate clothes made him an easy target. For the most part he ignored his critics. Only to those who had accused him of falsifying his evidence did he make a devastating reply in *A Vindication of Some Passages in the Fifteenth and Sixteenth Chapters of the Decline and Fall of the Roman Empire* (1779).

In the same year he obtained a position as a commissioner of trade and plantations. Shortly after that, in 1779, he composed a masterly paper in reply to continental criticism of the British government's policy in America. In 1781 he published the second and third volumes of his history, bringing the narrative down to the end of the empire in the West. Gibbon paused at this point to consider continuing his history. In 1782, however, Lord North's government fell, and soon Gibbon's commission was abolished. This was a serious loss of income. To economize he left England and joined Deyverdun in a house at Lausanne. There he quietly completed his history in three more volumes, writing the last lines of it on June 27, 1787. He soon returned to England with the manuscript, and these volumes were published on his 51st birthday, May 8, 1788. The completion of this great work was acclaimed on all sides.

The Decline and Fall is thus comprised of two divisions, equal in bulk but inevitably different in treatment. The first half covers a period of about 300 years to the end of the empire in the West, about 480 CE. In the second half nearly 1,000 years are compressed. Yet the work is a coherent whole by virtue of its conception of the Roman Empire as a single entity throughout its long and diversified course. Gibbon imposed a further unity on his narrative by viewing it as an undeviating decline from those ideals of political and, even more, intellectual freedom that he had found in classical literature. The material decay that had inspired him in Rome was the effect and symbol of moral decadence. However well this attitude suited the history of the West, its continuance constitutes the most serious defect of the second half of Gibbon's history. He asserted, for example, that the long story of empire in the East is one of continuous decay, yet for 1,000 years Constantinople stood as a bulwark of eastern Europe. The fact is that Gibbon was not only out of sympathy with Byzantine civilization; he was less at home with Greek sources than with Latin and had no access to vast stores of material in other languages that subsequent scholars have assembled. Nevertheless, this second half contains much of Gibbon's best work.

The vindication of intellectual freedom is a large part of Gibbon's purpose as a historian. When toward the end of his work he remarks, "I have described the triumph of barbarism and religion," he reveals epigrammatically his view of the causes of the decay of the Greco-Roman world. But there is the further question of whether the changes brought about are to be regarded as ones of progress or retrogression. Writing as a mid-18th-century "philosopher," Gibbon saw the process as retrogression, and his judgment remains of perpetual interest.

Returning to Lausanne, Gibbon turned mainly to writing his memoirs. His happiness was broken first by Deyverdun's death in 1789, quickly followed by the outbreak of the French Revolution and the subsequent apprehension of an invasion of Switzerland. He had now become very fat and his health was declining. In 1793 he suddenly returned to England on hearing of Lady Sheffield's death. The journey aggravated his ailments, and he died in London. His remains were placed in Lord Sheffield's family vault in Fletching Church, Sussex.

HESTER LYNCH PIOZZI

(b. January 27, 1740, Bodvel, Carnarvonshire, Wales —
d. May 2, 1821, Clifton, Bristol, England)

Hester Lynch Piozzi was an English writer who is best known today for her friendship with critic and lexicographer Samuel Johnson.

In 1763 Hester Lynch Salusbury married a wealthy brewer named Henry Thrale. In January 1765 Johnson was brought to dinner, and the next year, following a severe illness, he spent most of the summer in the country with the Thrales. Gradually, he became part of the family circle, living about half the time in their homes. A succession of distinguished visitors came there to see Johnson and socialize with the Thrales.

In 1781 Thrale died, and his wife was left a wealthy widow. To everyone's dismay, she fell in love with her daughter's music master, Gabriel Piozzi, an Italian singer and composer, married him in 1784, and set off for Italy on a honeymoon. Johnson openly disapproved. The resulting estrangement saddened his last months of life.

Johnson died in 1784. When that news reached her, she hastily compiled and sent back to England copy for *Anecdotes of the Late Samuel Johnson, LL.D., During the Last*

Twenty Years of His Life, published in 1786, which thrust her into open rivalry with James Boswell, whose biography of Johnson, known to be underway at the time, would eventually appear in 1791. The breach was further widened when, after her return to England in 1787, she brought out a two-volume edition of *Letters to and from the Late Samuel Johnson, LL.D.* (1788). Although less accurate in some details than Boswell's, her accounts show other aspects of Johnson's character, especially the more human and affectionate side of his nature.

When many old friends remained aloof, Piozzi drew around her a new artistic circle, including the actress Sarah Siddons. Her pen remained active, and thousands of her letters have survived.

MARQUIS DE SADE

(b. June 2, 1740, Paris, France—
d. December 2, 1814, Charenton, near Paris)

The Marquis de Sade—the byname of Donatien-Alphonse-François, Comte de Sade—was a French nobleman whose sexual preferences and erotic writings gave rise to the term *sadism*, defined today in Merriam-Webster's Collegiate Dictionary variously as "a sexual perversion in which gratification is obtained by the infliction of physical or mental pain on others" and as "delight in cruelty." His best-known work is the novel *Justine* (1791).

Heritage and Youth

Related to the royal house of Condé, the de Sade family numbered among its ancestors Laure de Noves, whom the

14th-century Italian poet Petrarch immortalized in verse. When the marquis was born at the Condé mansion, his father was away from home on a diplomatic mission. De Sade's mother, Marie Elénore Maillé de Carman, was a lady-in-waiting to the princesse de Condé.

After early schooling with his uncle, Abbé de Sade of Ebreuil, the marquis continued his studies at the Lycée Louis-le-Grand in Paris. His aristocratic background entitled him to various ranks in the king's regiments, and in 1754 he began a military career, which he abandoned in 1763 at the end of the Seven Years' War. In that year he married the daughter of a high-ranking bourgeois family *de robe* ("of the magistracy"), the Montreuils. By her he had two sons, Louis-Marie and Donatien-Claude-Armand, and one daughter, Madeleine-Laure.

In the very first months of his marriage he began an affair with an actress, La Beauvoisin. He invited prostitutes to his house at Arcueil and subjected them to various sexual abuses. For this he was imprisoned, on orders of the king, in the fortress of Vincennes. Freed several weeks later, he resumed his life of debauchery and went deeply into debt. In 1768 the first public scandal erupted: the Rose Keller affair. Keller was a young prostitute he had met on Easter Sunday in Paris. He took her to Arcueil, where he locked her up and abused her sexually. She escaped and related the unnatural acts and brutality to persons in the neighbourhood and showed them her wounds. De Sade was sentenced to the fortress of Pierre-Encise, near Lyon, for his offenses.

After his release he retired to his château of La Coste. In June 1772 he went to Marseille to get some much-needed money, but, while there, he again committed various sexual outrages that resulted in de Sade and his servant Latour's fleeing to the estates of the king of Sardinia, who had them arrested. The Parlement at Aix sentenced them to death

The Marquis de Sade in prison. The Bridgeman Art Library/Getty Images

by default and, on September 12, 1772, executed them in effigy. After escaping from the fortress of Miolans, de Sade took refuge in his château at La Coste, rejoining his wife. She became his accomplice and shared his pleasures, until the parents of the neighbourhood boys and girls he had abducted complained to the crown prosecutor. De Sade fled to Italy accompanied by his sister-in-law, the canoness de Launay, who had become his mistress. He returned to La Coste on November 4, 1776. One incident followed another in an atmosphere of continual scandal, and, on his return to Paris, the marquis was arrested and sent to the dungeon of Vincennes on February 13, 1777.

Writings

De Sade overcame his boredom and anger in prison by writing sexually graphic novels and plays. In July 1782 he finished his *Dialogue entre un prêtre et un moribond* (*Dialogue Between a Priest and a Dying Man*), in which he declared himself an atheist. On February 27, 1784, he was transferred to the Bastille in Paris. On a roll of paper some 12 metres (39 feet) long, he wrote *Les 120 Journées de Sodome* (*One Hundred and Twenty Days of Sodom*), in which he graphically describes numerous varieties of sexual perversion. In 1787 he wrote his most famous work, *Les Infortunes de la vertu* (an early version of *Justine*), and in 1788 the novellas, tales, and short stories later published in the volume entitled *Les Crimes de l'amour* (*Crimes of Passion*).

A few days before the French Revolutionaries stormed the Bastille on July 14, 1789, de Sade had shouted through a window, "They are massacring the prisoners; you must come and free them." He was transferred to the insane asylum at Charenton, where he remained until April 2, 1790.

On his release, de Sade offered several plays to the Comédie-Française as well as to other theatres. Though five of them were accepted, not all of them were performed. Separated from his wife, he lived now with a young actress, the widow Quesnet, and wrote his novels *Justine, ou les malheurs de la vertu* (*Justine; or, The Misfortunes of Virtue*) and *Juliette.* In 1792 he became secretary of the Revolutionary Section of Les Piques in Paris, was one of the delegates appointed to visit hospitals in Paris, and wrote several patriotic addresses. During the Reign of Terror he saved the life of his father-in-law, Montreuil, and that of the latter's wife, even though they had been responsible for his various imprisonments. He gave speeches on behalf of the Revolution but was nevertheless accused of *modérantisme* ("moderatism"). He escaped the guillotine by chance the day before the revolutionary leader Robespierre was overthrown. At the time he was living with the widow Quesnet in conditions of abject poverty.

On March 6, 1801, he was arrested at his publisher's, where copies of *Justine* and *Juliette* were found with notes in his hand and several handwritten manuscripts. Again he was sent to Charenton, where he caused new scandals. His repeated protests had no effect on Napoleon, who saw to it personally that de Sade was deprived of all freedom of movement. Nevertheless, de Sade succeeded in having his plays put on at Charenton, with the inmates themselves as the actors. He began work on an ambitious 10-volume novel, at least two volumes of which were written. After his death his elder son burned these writings, together with other manuscripts.

His remains were scattered. In his will, drawn up in 1806, he asked that "the traces of my grave disappear from the face of the earth, as I flatter myself that my memory will be effaced from the mind of men." Although banned in France until the 1960s, his works were still widely read there and elsewhere. While some consider de Sade an incarnation of absolute evil whose life and works advocate the unleashing of instincts even to the point of crime, his writings belong to the history of ideas and may be considered as much a part of Enlightenment literary culture as those of such immediate contemporaries as Thomas Paine or James Boswell. None created works of enduring literary value comparable to the giants of the era, such as Molière or Alexander Pope, but all three provide vivid perspectives on what was possible during the 18th century.

JAMES BOSWELL

(b. October 29, 1740, Edinburgh, Scotland—
d. May 19, 1795, London, England)

James Boswell was a friend and biographer of Samuel Johnson (*Life of Johnson*, 2 vol., 1791). The 20th-century publication of his journals proved him to be also one of the world's greatest diarists and provided an intimate, intensely detailed portrait of an enlightened yet tormented man, a participant in the intellectual debates of his time who was often driven by sensual appetites and religious fears and who may be seen as representative of his era.

Edinburgh and London

Boswell's father, Alexander Boswell, advocate and laird of Auchinleck in Ayrshire from 1749, received the judicial title of Lord Auchinleck in 1754. The Boswells were an old and well-connected family, and James was subjected to the strong pressure of an ambitious family.

Boswell hated the select day school to which he was sent at age 5, and from 8 to 13 he was taught at home by tutors. From 1753 to 1758 he went through the arts course at the University of Edinburgh. Returning to the university in 1758 to study law, he became enthralled by the theatre and fell in love with an actress. Lord Auchinleck thought it prudent to send him to the University of Glasgow, where he attended the lectures of the philosopher and political economist Adam Smith. In the spring of 1760 he ran away to London. He was, he soon found, passionately fond of metropolitan culture, gregarious, high-spirited, sensual, and attractive to women, and London offered the pleasures that seemed to fulfill him. At this time he contracted gonorrhea, an affliction that he was to endure many times in the course of his life. His escape to London, however, was rewarded with a two-year period, from 1760 to 1762, during which he studied law at home under strict supervision.

When Boswell came of age, he was eager to enter the military. Lord Auchinleck agreed that if he passed his trials in civil law, he would receive a supplementary annuity and be allowed to go to London to seek a commission through influence. Boswell passed the examination in July 1762.

Anticipating great happiness, Boswell began, in the autumn, the journal that was to be the central expression of his genius. His great zest for life was not fully savoured until life was all written down, and he had a rare faculty for imaginative verbal reconstruction. His journal is much more dramatic than most because he wrote up each event as though he were still living through it, as if he had no knowledge of anything that had happened later.

Boswell's second London visit lasted from November 1762 to August 1763. It was during that visit, on May 16, 1763, in the back parlour of the actor and bookseller Thomas Davies, that he secured an unexpected introduction to Samuel Johnson, whose works he admired and whom he had long been trying to meet. Johnson was rough with him, but Boswell kept his temper, went to call a week later, and found himself liked—a great friendship was initiated. Johnson was 53 years old when they met, Boswell 22. There was condescension on both sides on account of differences in rank and intelligence. Having become genuinely convinced that the scheme to join the guards was not practicable, Boswell capitulated to his father and consented to become a lawyer. It was agreed that he should spend a winter studying civil law at Utrecht and should then make a modest foreign tour.

Continental Tour

In Holland Boswell befriended and unsuccessfully courted the novelist Isabella van Tuyll van Serooskerken (later called Isabelle de Charrière). He had been deeply affected by Johnson's piety and on Christmas Day, in the ambassador's chapel at The Hague, received communion for the first time in the Church of England. His pious program proved stimulating for a time but palled when it had lost its novelty. He received word that his little boy had died. In the depression that ensued he had recurring nightmares of being hanged. He was discouraged to find that the pursuit of sensual pleasures brought him more happiness than hard work and piety did, and he soon abandoned the way of life inspired by Johnson.

From Utrecht, Boswell traveled to Berlin, and, passing through Switzerland (December 1764), he secured interviews with both Voltaire, who had by that time achieved wide fame and was known as the "Innkeeper of Europe," and Jean-Jacques Rousseau, whose writings were yet to see their fullest influence, which was achieved during the French Revolution and the Romantic movement. Boswell stayed nine months in Italy, devoting himself systematically to sightseeing.

The most original act of his life followed when he made a six weeks' tour of the island of Corsica (autumn 1765) to interview the heroic Corsican chieftain Pasquale de Paoli, then engaged in establishing his country's independence of Genoa. Paoli succumbed to his charm and became his lifelong friend. On his return to the mainland, Boswell sent off paragraphs to the newspapers, mingling facts with fantastic political speculation.

Scottish Lawyer and Laird

Back in Scotland, Boswell was admitted to the Faculty of Advocates on July 26, 1766, and, as such, became a member of the bar in Scotland. For 17 years he practiced law at Edinburgh with complete regularity and a fair degree of assiduity. His cherished trips to London were by no means annual and until 1784 were always made during the vacations. He was an able courtroom lawyer, especially in criminal cases.

In February 1768 Boswell published *An Account of Corsica, The Journal of a Tour to That Island; and Memoirs of Pascal Paoli* and stepped into fame. France had unmasked its intention of annexing the island, and people were greedy for information about Corsica and Paoli. Motives of propaganda caused him to present himself in the book as completely naive and to cut the tour to a mere frame for the memoirs of Paoli.

Between 1766 and 1769 Boswell amused himself with various well-hedged schemes of marriage, maintaining meantime a liaison with a young Mrs. Dodds. Their daughter, Sally, like Charles, seems to have died in infancy. Boswell ended by marrying (November 1769) his first cousin, Margaret Montgomerie.

During the first few years of his marriage, Boswell was on the whole happy, hard-working, faithful to his wife, and confident of getting a seat in Parliament, a good post in the government, or at the very least a Scots judgeship. Paoli visited him in Scotland in 1771; in 1773 Boswell was elected to the Club, the brilliant circle that the painter Sir Joshua Reynolds had formed around Johnson; and later in the year Johnson made with him the famous tour of the Hebrides. Boswell ultimately had five healthy and promising children. But by 1776 he began to feel strong intimations of failure. A headlong entry into Ayrshire politics had ranged him in opposition to Henry Dundas, who was then emerging as a political despot in the management of the Scottish elections. Boswell's practice was not becoming more notable. He began to drink heavily to replenish his spirits, not, as formerly, to give them vent. He returned to the use of prostitutes when separated from his wife by distance, by her pregnancy, or by her frequent complaints. As early as 1778 it was obvious that she was critically ill with tuberculosis.

Between 1777 and 1783 Boswell published in *The London Magazine* a series of 70 essays entitled *The Hypochondriack*. At the end of 1783, in the hope of attracting the attention of the new government of prime minister William Pitt, he published a pamphlet attacking the East India Bill that had been introduced by Charles James Fox, Pitt's great rival. Pitt sent a note of thanks but made no move to employ him. Boswell succeeded to Auchinleck in 1782 and managed his estate with attention and some shrewdness. But he thought he could be happy only in London and encouraged himself in the groundless notion that he could be more successful at the English than at the Scottish bar.

Life of Johnson *and London*

Johnson died on December 13, 1784. Boswell decided to take his time in writing the *Life* but to publish his journal of the Hebridean tour as a first installment. In the spring of 1785 he went to London to prepare the work for the press. *The Journal of a Tour to the Hebrides, with Samuel Johnson, LL.D.* (1785) tops all the others published later. It comes from the soundest and happiest period of Boswell's life, the narrative of the tour is interesting in itself, and it provides us with 101 consecutive days with Johnson. The book was a best-seller, but it provoked the scornful charge of personal fatuity that has dogged Boswell's name ever since. Boswell analyzed and recorded his own vanity and weakness with the objectivity of a historian, and in his Johnsonian scenes he ruthlessly subordinated his own personality, reporting the blows that Johnson occasionally gave him without constantly reassuring the reader that he understood the implications of what he had written.

In 1786 Boswell was called to the English bar from the Inner Temple and moved his family to London. Thereafter he had almost no legal practice. His principal business was the writing of the *Life of Johnson*, which he worked at irregularly but with anxious attention.

Though he had limited income, Boswell gave his children expensive educations. He visited Edinburgh only once after his emigration and then almost surreptitiously. His wife pined for Auchinleck and insisted on being taken there when her health grew desperate. Boswell felt that he had to be in London in order to finish the *Life* and to be at the call of the earl of Lonsdale, who had given him unexpected encouragement and caused him to be elected recorder of Carlisle. When his wife died (June 4, 1789), he was not at her side; and when he tried to detach himself from Lonsdale, he was treated with brutality.

The Life of Samuel Johnson, LL.D. was published in two volumes on May 16, 1791. Contemporary criticism set the pattern of acclaim for the work and derision for its author. Boswell took intense pleasure in his literary fame but felt himself to be a failure. His later years were prevailingly unhappy. People were afraid to talk freely in his presence, fearing that their talk would be reported, and his habit of getting drunk and noisy at other people's tables (he was never a solitary drinker) made him a difficult guest in any case. His five children, however, loved him deeply, and he never lost the solicitous affection of a few friends, including the great Shakespeare editor Edmund Malone, who had encouraged him in his writing of the *Life of Johnson*. Boswell saw the second edition of the *Life* through the press (July 1793) and was at work on the third when he died in 1795.

BASÍLIO DA GAMA

(b. 1740, São José do Rio das Mortes, Brazil—
d. July 31, 1795, Lisbon, Portugal)

The neoclassical poet José Basílio da Gama wrote the Brazilian epic poem *O Uraguai* (1769), an account of the Portuguese-Spanish expedition against the Jesuit-controlled reservation Indians of the Uruguay River basin.

Gama completed his novitiate with the Jesuits in 1759. In that same year the order was expelled from Brazil and all other Portuguese possessions, and he eventually left Brazil for Rome. On his return to Brazil in 1767 he was sent by the Inquisition to Lisbon where, as a Jesuit, he faced deportation to Angola. He won his pardon from the chief minister of the realm, the marquês de Pombal, by composing a poem for Pombal's daughter's wedding; he subsequently became Pombal's protégé. The original version of *O Uraguai* was openly pro-Jesuit; the anti-Jesuit theme of the published version—in which the Indian princess Lindóia commits suicide in order to avoid marriage to the illegitimate son of a Jesuit—was no doubt Gama's supreme gesture to establish himself in the good graces of his new patrons.

In spite of its questionable historicity, the poem became the most important Brazilian work of the colonial period. Gama shows himself to be a sensitive and original poet in breaking away from the strict epic model established by Luis de Camões, Portugal's great 16th-century poet, and creating a Brazilian epic in blank verse. He substitutes descriptions of indigenous animism and fetishism for the standard Classical mythology of the epic genre and elaborates vivid and moving scenes of Indian life and the Brazilian natural environment. His poem opened the way for the romantic nationalism that was to flower in 19th-century Brazilian literature.

JOHANNES EWALD

(b. November 18, 1743, Copenhagen, Denmark—
d. March 17, 1781, Copenhagen)

Johannes Ewald was one of Denmark's greatest lyric poets and was the first to use themes from early Scandinavian myths and sagas.

On the death of his father, a poorhouse chaplain, Ewald was sent to school at Slesvig (Schleswig), where his reading of *Tom Jones* and *Robinson Crusoe* (by the 18th-century English novelists Henry Fielding and Daniel Defoe, respectively) aroused his spirit of adventure. In 1758 he went to Copenhagen to study theology, fell in love, and, in search of quickly gained glory, ran away to fight in the Seven Years' War. He returned to find that his beloved

Arendse, whom he immortalized as his muse, had married another. He passed his final examination when he was 19 and was then already becoming known as a writer of prose and occasional poetry. When finishing *Adam og Eva* (1769; "Adam and Eve"), a dramatic poem in the style of French tragedy, he met the German epic poet Friedrich Klopstock, and at about the same time he read William Shakespeare's plays and James Macpherson's controversial Ossian poems. Their influence resulted in the historical drama *Rolf Krage* (1770), taken from an old Danish legend that was recorded by the medieval historian Saxo Grammaticus.

Ewald's life began to show signs of serious disorder, especially an addiction to alcohol. In the spring of 1773 his mother and a Pietistic pastor secured his removal from Copenhagen to the relative isolation of Rungsted. There he produced his first mature works: *Rungsteds lyksaligheder* (1775; "The Joys of Rungsted"), a lyric poem in the elevated new style of the ode; *Balders død* (1775; *The Death of Balder*), a lyric drama on a subject from Saxo and Old Norse mythology; and the first chapters of his memoirs, *Levnet og meninger* (written *c.* 1774–78: "Life and Opinions"), explaining his enthusiasm for the adventurous and fantastic. In 1775 he was transferred to a still more solitary place near Elsinore, where he went through a religious crisis—a struggle between self-denial and his own proud independence. In 1777 he was allowed to return to Copenhagen. His poetic genius was recognized, and his life became calmer despite increasingly severe illness. On his deathbed he wrote the heroic Pietist hymn "Udrust dig, helt fra Golgotha" ("Gird Thyself, Hero of Golgotha").

Ewald renewed Danish poetry in all of its genres. Of his dramatic works, only *Fiskerne* (1779; "The Fishermen"), an operetta, is still performed. His greatest work in prose is his posthumously published memoirs, in which lyrically pathetic chapters about his lost Arendse intermingle with humorous passages. He is known best as a lyric poet, especially for his great personal odes and for songs such as "Kong Kristian stod ved højen mast" (translated by the American poet Henry Wadsworth Longfellow as "King Christian Stood by the Lofty Mast"), which is used as a national anthem, and "Lille Gunver" ("Little Gunver"), the first Danish romance. Both these songs form part of *Fiskerne*.

Ewald's work was radical for its time in its aesthetic transformation of loss into imaginatively achieved insight and meaning. Thus, though its form is rooted in the classical tradition, his poetry heralded the works of Adam Oehlenschläger and the Romantic movement, and it anticipated the Romantics in its use of themes drawn from Old Norse literature. It was Ewald's genius that he transformed his sense of an unreadable reality into an autonomous poetic world. While his heroic efforts to imbue his real-life experience with heightened sensibility and poetic imagery may have been tempered by an occasional retreat to Christianity and patriotism, his achievement resonated in diverse 20th-century writers such as Isak Dinesen, the playwright Kaj Munk, and lyrical poets as dissimilar as Jens August Schade and Per Lange.

OLAUDAH EQUIANO

(b. c. 1745, Essaka [in present-day Nigeria]? —
d. March 31, 1797, London, England)

Olaudah Equiano was a self-proclaimed West African sold into slavery and later freed. His autobiography, *The Interesting Narrative of the Life of Olaudah Equiano; or,*

Gustavus Vassa, the African, Written by Himself (1789), with its strong abolitionist stance and detailed description of life in Nigeria, was so popular that in his lifetime it ran through nine English editions and one U.S. printing and was translated into Dutch, German, and Russian. At the turn of the 21st century, newly discovered documents suggesting that Equiano may have been born in North America raised questions, still unresolved, about whether his accounts of Africa and the Middle Passage are based on memory, reading, or a combination of the two.

According to his own account, Equiano was kidnapped at age 11 and taken to the West Indies. From there he went to Virginia, where he was purchased by a sea captain, Michael Henry Pascal, with whom he traveled widely. He received some education before he bought his own freedom in 1766. After he settled in England, he became an active abolitionist, agitating and lecturing against the cruelty of British slave owners in Jamaica. He briefly was commissary to Sierra Leone for the Committee for the Relief of the Black Poor; his concerns for the settlers—some 500 to 600 freed slaves—and for their ill treatment before their journey ultimately led to his replacement.

Publication of his autobiography was aided by British abolitionists, including Hannah More, Josiah Wedgwood, and John Wesley, who were collecting evidence on the sufferings of slaves. In that book and in his later *Miscellaneous Verses...* (1789), he idealizes Africa and shows great pride in the African way of life, while attacking those Africans who trafficked in slavery (a perspective further shown by his setting forth not only the injustices and humiliations endured by slaves but also his own experience of kindness, that of his master and a community of English women). As a whole, Equiano's work shows both broad human compassion and realism.

Equiano is often regarded as the originator of the slave narrative because of his firsthand literary testimony against the slave trade. Despite the controversy regarding his birth, *The Interesting Narrative* remains an essential work both for its picture of 18th-century Africa as a model of social harmony defiled by Western greed and for its eloquent argument against the barbarous slave trade. A critical edition of *The Interesting Narrative*, edited by Werner Sollors—which includes an extensive introduction, selected variants of the several editions, contextual documents, and early and modern criticism—was published in 2001.

HANNAH MORE

(b. February 2, 1745, Stapleton, Gloucestershire, England—
d. September 7, 1833, Bristol, Gloucestershire)

The English religious writer Hannah More is best known as a writer of popular tracts and as an educator of the poor.

As a young woman with literary aspirations, More made the first of her visits to London in 1773–74. She was welcomed into a circle of female wits (often referred to condescendingly as Bluestockings) and was befriended by the painter Sir Joshua Reynolds, the critic Samuel Johnson, and the statesman and political thinker Edmund Burke and, particularly, by the actor David Garrick, who produced her plays *The Inflexible Captive* (1775) and *Percy* (1777). After Garrick's death in 1779 she forsook writing for the stage, and her strong piety and Christian attitudes, already intense, became more marked.

Through her friendship with the abolitionist philanthropist William Wilberforce, she was drawn to the Evangelicals. From her cottage in Somerset, she began to admonish society in a series of treatises beginning with *Thoughts on the Importance of the Manners of the Great to General Society* (1788). In the climate of alarm over the French Revolution, her fresh and forceful defense of traditional values met with strong approval.

Her *Village Politics* (1792; under the pseudonym of Will Chip), written to counteract Thomas Paine's *Rights of Man*, was so successful that it led to the production of a series of "Cheap Repository Tracts." Produced at the rate of three a month for three years with the help of her sisters and friends, the tracts sold for a penny each, two million being circulated in a single year. They advised the poor to cultivate the virtues of sobriety and industry and to trust in God and in the kindness of the gentry.

As was the case for most of her educated contemporaries, More believed that society was static and that civilization depended upon a large body of the poor, for whom the best education was one that reconciled them to their fate. Hence she established clubs for women and schools for children, in which the latter were taught the Bible, catechism, and skills thought to befit their station. She persevered in her efforts in spite of much opposition and abuse from country neighbours, who thought that even the most limited education of the poor would destroy their interest in farming, and from the clergy, who accused her of Methodism.

Her final popular success as a writer was her didactic novel *Coelebs in Search of a Wife* (1808). The feminist movement in the second half of the 20th century revived interest in her *Strictures on the Modern System of Female Education*, 2 vol. (1799).

VITTORIO, COUNT ALFIERI

(b. January 16, 1749, Asti, Piedmont [Italy] —
d. October 8, 1803, Florence)

The predominant theme of the Italian poet Vittorio, Count Alfieri, was the overthrow of tyranny. In his tragedies, he hoped to provide Italy with dramas comparable to those of other European nations. Through his lyrics and dramas he helped to revive the national spirit of Italy and so earned the title of precursor of the Risorgimento.

Educated at the Military Academy of Turin, Alfieri became an ensign. A distaste for military life led him to obtain leave to travel through most of Europe. In England he found the political liberty that became his ideal, and in France the literature that influenced him most profoundly. He studied the major 18th-century writers and thinkers Voltaire and Jean-Jacques Rousseau and, above all, the political philosopher Montesquieu.

Alfieri settled in Turin in 1772 and resigned his commission the following year. To divert himself, he wrote *Cleopatra*, a tragedy performed with great success in 1775. Thereupon Alfieri decided to devote himself to literature. He began a methodical study of the classics and of the Italian poets, and since he expressed himself mainly in French, the language of the ruling classes in Turin, he went to Tuscany to familiarize himself with pure Italian.

By 1782 he had written 14 tragedies as well as many poems (including four odes in the series *L'America libera*, on American independence, to which a fifth ode was added in 1783) and a political treatise on tyranny, in prose,

Della tirannide (1777). He also hailed the fall of the Bastille with an ode, "Parigi sbastigliata" (1789). Ten of the tragedies were printed at Siena in 1783.

Meanwhile, in Florence in 1777, Alfieri had met the Countess of Albany, wife of the Stuart pretender to the English throne, Charles Edward. He remained deeply attached to her for the rest of his life.

Alfieri's genius was essentially dramatic. His rough, forthright, and concise style was chosen deliberately, so that he could persuade the oppressed and the resigned to accept his political ideas and inspire them to heroic deeds. Nearly always, Alfieri's tragedies present the struggle between a champion of liberty and a tyrant.

Of the 19 tragedies that he approved for publication in the Paris edition of 1787–89, the best are *Filippo*, in which Philip II of Spain is presented as the tyrant; *Antigone*, *Oreste*, and, above all, *Mirra* and *Saul*. *Saul*, his masterpiece, is often considered the most powerful drama in the Italian theatre.

Alfieri's autobiography, published posthumously as *Vita di Vittorio Alfieri scritta da esso* (1804; *The Life of Vittorio Alfieri Written by Himself*), is his chief work in prose. He also wrote sonnets, comedies, satires, and epigrams.

ROBERT FERGUSSON

(b. September 5, 1750, Edinburgh, Scotland—
d. October 16, 1774, Edinburgh)

The Scottish poet Robert Fergusson was one of the leading figures of the 18th-century revival of Scots vernacular writing and the chief forerunner of Robert Burns.

Fergusson was educated at the University of St. Andrews and became a copying clerk in a lawyer's office in Edinburgh. In 1771 he began to contribute poems to the *Weekly Magazine*. Although he was noted for the vivacity of temperament reflected in his verse, from 1773 his good spirits were encroached upon by fits of depression and religious guilt, and after suffering a severe head injury in a fall he became insane. He died in the Edinburgh asylum at the age of 24.

Fergusson's poems were popular from their first appearance, and a collected volume came out in 1773. He wrote in both Scots and English, but the English verse has been deemed of little lasting value. His Scots poems —racy, realistic, wittily descriptive and humorous—had a stimulating effect on Burns, whose "Holy Fair" and "The Cotter's Saturday Night" stem from Fergusson's "Leith Races" and "The Farmer's Ingle." But vigorous poems such as "The Daft Days," "Address to the Tron Kirk Bell," and the famous "Auld Reekie" prove how well Fergusson can stand as a poet in his own right.

RICHARD BRINSLEY SHERIDAN

(baptized November 4, 1751, Dublin, Ireland—
d. July 7, 1816, London, England)

Richard Brinsley Sheridan was an Irish-born playwright, impresario, orator, and Whig politician. His plays, notably *The School for Scandal* (1777), form a link in the history of the dramatic genre known as the comedy of manners between the end of the 17th century and the end of the 19th century, when Oscar Wilde wrote some of the genre's greatest examples.

Formative Years

Sheridan was the third son of Thomas and Frances Sheridan. His grandfather Thomas Sheridan had been a companion and confidant of Jonathan Swift; his father was the author of a pronouncing dictionary and the advocate of a scheme of public education that gave a prominent place to elocution; and his mother gained some fame as a playwright.

The family moved to London, and Sheridan never returned to Ireland. He was educated (1762–68) at Harrow, and in 1770 he moved with his family to Bath. There Sheridan fell in love with Elizabeth Ann Linley (1754–92), whose fine soprano voice delighted audiences at the concerts and festivals conducted by her father, Thomas. In order to avoid the unpleasant attentions of a Welsh squire, Thomas Mathews of Llandaff, she decided to take refuge in a French nunnery. Sheridan accompanied her to Lille in March 1772 but returned to fight two duels that same year with Mathews. Meanwhile, Elizabeth had returned home with her father, and Sheridan was ordered by his father to Waltham Abbey, Essex, to pursue his studies. He was entered at the Middle Temple in April 1773 but after a week broke with his father, gave up a legal career, and married Elizabeth at Marylebone Church, London.

Theatrical Career

After his marriage Sheridan turned to the theatre for a livelihood. His comedy *The Rivals* opened at Covent Garden Theatre, London, in January 1775. It ran an hour longer than was usual, and, because of the offensive nature and poor acting of the character of Sir Lucius O'Trigger, it was hardly a success. Drastically revised and with a new actor as Sir Lucius, its second performance 11 days later won immediate applause. The play is characteristic of Sheridan's work in its genial mockery of the affectation displayed by some of the characters. It also gave rise to the English word *malapropism*, derived from the name of the character Mrs. Malaprop and her propensity for extravagant verbal fumbling.

Some of the play's success was due to the acting of Lawrence Clinch as Sir Lucius. Sheridan showed his gratitude by writing the amusing little farce *St. Patrick's Day; or, The Scheming Lieutenant* for the benefit performance given for Clinch in May 1775. Another example of his ability to weave an interesting plot from well-worn materials is seen in *The Duenna,* produced the following November. The characters are generally undeveloped, but the intrigue of the plot and charming lyrics and the music by his father-in-law, Thomas Linley, and his son gave this ballad opera great popularity. Its 75 performances exceeded the 62, a record for that time, credited to John Gay's *The Beggar's Opera* (1728).

Thus, in less than a year Sheridan had brought himself to the forefront of contemporary dramatists. David Garrick, looking for someone to succeed him as manager and proprietor of Drury Lane Theatre, saw in Sheridan a young man with energy, shrewdness, and a real sense of theatre. A successful physician, James Ford, agreed with Garrick's estimate and increased his investment in the playhouse. In 1776, Sheridan and Linley became partners with Ford in a half-share of Drury Lane Theatre. Two years later they bought the other half from Willoughby Lacy, Garrick's partner.

In fact, Sheridan's interest in his theatre soon began to seem rather fitful. Nevertheless, he was responsible for the renewed appreciation of Restoration-era comedy that followed the revival of the plays of William Congreve at Drury Lane. In February 1777 he brought out his version of Sir John Vanbrugh's *The Relapse* (1696) as *A Trip to Scarborough*, again showing his talent for revision. He gave the rambling plot a neater shape and removed much indelicacy from the dialogue, but the result was disappointing, probably because of the loss of much of the earlier play's gusto.

What Sheridan learned from the Restoration dramatists can be seen in *The School for Scandal*, produced at Drury Lane in May 1777. That play earned him the title of "the modern Congreve." Although resembling Congreve in that its satirical wit is so brilliant and so general that it does not always distinguish one character from another, *The School for Scandal* does contain two subtle portraits in Joseph Surface and Lady Teazle. There were several Restoration models (e.g., Mrs. Pinchwife in William Wycherley's *The Country-Wife* and Miss Hoyden in Vanbrugh's *The Relapse*) for the portrayal of a country girl amazed and delighted by the sexual freedom of high society. Sheridan softened his Lady Teazle, however, and the part combined innocence and sophistication. The other parts were written with equal care to suit the members of the company, and the whole work was a triumph of intelligence and imaginative calculation. With its spirited ridicule of affectation and pretentiousness, it is often considered the greatest comedy of manners in English.

Sheridan's flair for stage effect, exquisitely demonstrated in scenes in *The School for Scandal*, was again demonstrated in his delightful satire on stage conventions, *The Critic*, which since its first performance in October 1779 has been thought much funnier than its model, *The Rehearsal* (1671), by George Villiers, the 2nd duke of Buckingham. Sheridan himself considered the first act to be his finest piece of writing.

Political Career

Sheridan continued to adapt plays and to improvise spectacular shows at Drury Lane, but as a succession of acting managers took over the burden of direction his time was increasingly given to politics. His only full-length later play was the artistically worthless but popular patriotic melodrama *Pizarro* (1799), based on a German play on the conquest of Peru. Sheridan had become member of Parliament for Stafford in September 1780 and was undersecretary for foreign affairs (1782) and secretary to the treasury (1783). Later he was treasurer of the navy (1806–07) and a privy councillor. The rest of his 32 years in Parliament were spent as a member of the minority Whig party in opposition to the governing Tories.

Sheridan's critical acumen and command over language had full scope in his oratory and were seen at their best in his speeches as manager of the unsuccessful impeachment of Warren Hastings, governor general of India. Sheridan was recognized as one of the most persuasive orators of his time but never achieved greater political influence in Parliament because he was thought to be an unreliable intriguer. Some support for this view is to be found in his behaviour during the regency crisis (1788–89) following the temporary insanity of George III, when Sheridan acted as adviser to the unpopular, self-indulgent prince of Wales (later George IV). He encouraged the prince to think that there would be a great majority for his being regent with all the royal powers simply because he was heir apparent. In the country at large this was seen as a move by the Whig statesman Charles James Fox and his friends to take over the government and drive out the prime minister, William Pitt. Sheridan was also distrusted because of his part in the Whigs' internecine squabbles

(1791–93) with Edmund Burke over the latter's implacable hostility to the French Revolution. He was one of the few members courageous enough openly to defend those who suffered for their support of the French Revolution. He also came out on the side of the Tory administration when he condemned mutineers who had rebelled against living conditions in the British Navy (1797).

In November 1806, Sheridan succeeded Fox as member for Westminster—although not, as he had hoped, as leader of the Whigs—but he lost the seat in May 1807. The prince of Wales then returned him as member for the "pocket borough" (an election district that is controlled by, or "in the pocket" of, one person or family) of Ilchester, but his dependence on the prince's favour rankled with Sheridan, for they differed in their attitude on Catholic emancipation. Sheridan, who was determined to support emancipation, stood for election as member from Stafford again in 1812, but he could not pay those who had previously supported him as much as they expected and, as a result, was defeated.

Last Years

Sheridan's financial difficulties were largely brought about by his own extravagance and procrastination, as well as by the destruction of Drury Lane Theatre by fire in February 1809. With the loss of his parliamentary seat and his income from the theatre, he became a prey to his many creditors. His last years were beset by these and other worries—his circulatory complaints and the cancer that afflicted his second wife, Esther Jane Ogle. She was the daughter of the dean of Winchester and was married to Sheridan in April 1795, three years after Elizabeth's death. Pestered by bailiffs to the end, Sheridan died in 1816.

PHILIP FRENEAU

(b. January 2, 1752, New York, New York [U.S.] — d. December 18, 1832, Monmouth County, New Jersey, U.S.)

The American poet, essayist, and editor Philip Morin Freneau is known as the "poet of the American Revolution."

After graduating from Princeton University in 1771, Freneau taught school and studied for the ministry until the outbreak of the American Revolution, when he began to write vitriolic satire against the British and Tories. Not until his return from two years in the Caribbean islands, where he produced two of his most ambitious poems, "The Beauties of Santa Cruz" and "The House of Night," did he become an active participant in the war, joining the New Jersey militia in 1778 and sailing through the British blockade as a privateer to the West Indies. Captured and imprisoned by the British in 1780, Freneau wrote in verse bitterly, on his release, *The British Prison-Ship* (1781).

During the next several years he contributed to the *Freeman's Journal* in Philadelphia. Freneau became a sea captain until 1790, when he again entered partisan journalism, ultimately as editor from 1791 to 1793 of the strongly Republican *National Gazette* in Philadelphia. Freneau alternated quiet periods at sea with periods of active newspaper work, until he retired early in the 19th century to his farm in Monmouth county.

Well schooled in the classics and in the Neoclassical English poetry of the period, Freneau strove for a fresh idiom that would be unmistakably American, but, except in a few poems, he failed to achieve it.

Fanny Burney

(b. June 13, 1752, King's Lynn, Norfolk, England—
d. January 6, 1840, London)

Fanny Burney was an English novelist and letter writer, the daughter of the musician Charles Burney.

Born Frances Burney, she educated herself by omnivorous reading at home. Her literary apprenticeship was much influenced by her father's friend Samuel Crisp, a disappointed author living in retirement. It was to "Daddy" Crisp that she addressed her first journal letters, lively accounts of the musical evenings at the Burneys' London house where the elite among European performers entertained informally for gatherings that might include the actor David Garrick, the critic Samuel Johnson, the statesman and political thinker Edmund Burke, and the playwright Richard Brinsley Sheridan. Considered the least promising of the clever Burney children, she moved unnoticed in the circles of the great, confiding her observations to Crisp.

Her practice of observing and recording society led eventually to her novel *Evelina, or The History of a Young Lady's Entrance into the World*. *Evelina* revealed its author to be a keen social commentator with an attentive ear for dialect and the differentiation of London speech. It concerns the development of a young girl, unsure of herself in society and subject to errors of manners and judgment. The plot terminates with Evelina's marriage after the mistakes stemming from her untutored girlhood have been surmounted. A novel treating contemporary manners in an elegant and decorous way and depending for the development of its plot upon the erring and uncertain conduct of the heroine was an innovation that pointed the way for the novels of Jane Austen. Published anonymously in 1778, *Evelina* took London by storm. No one guessed it was by shy Fanny Burney, then 26.

When the secret was out, Burney's debut into literary society was launched by the fashionable hostess Hester Thrale. Once the young woman overcame her shyness she could match wits with Johnson himself, who was very kind to her between 1779 and 1783 when they both made long visits to Thrale and her husband, Henry. Burney's journals from this period have been prized for their vignettes of contemporary scenes and celebrities and for Burney's own secretly expressed delight in being famous.

Her next novel, *Cecilia, or Memoirs of an Heiress*, 5 vol. (1782), incorporated morally didactic themes along with the social satire of Burney's first novel into a more complex plot. Though lacking the freshness and spontaneity of *Evelina*, this novel was equally well received, but Burney's success was shadowed by the death of Henry Thrale in 1781, of Crisp in 1783, and of Johnson in 1784. These years also brought a disappointment in love, when the ambiguous attentions of a young clergyman came to nothing.

In 1785 Burney was presented to Queen Charlotte and King George III and in 1786 she accepted a position at the royal court, where she remained for five unhappy years. Eventually her health suffered, and she was allowed to resign in 1791. Her journals of the period loyally repress court gossip of the years of the king's madness (1788–89) but contain interesting accounts of public events such as the trial (1788–95) of Warren Hastings, a governor-general of India.

In 1793, when she was 41, Burney married Alexandre d'Arblay, a former adjutant general to Lafayette, then a penniless French émigré living in England. They had one son. In 1796 she wrote *Camilla; or, A Picture of Youth*, and on

Fanny Burney. Rischgitz/Hulton Archive/Getty Images

its proceeds the d'Arblays built a house in Surrey, where they moved in 1797. While on a visit to France with her husband and son in 1802, the trio was forced by the renewal of the Napoleonic Wars to stay for 10 years. After Napoleon's final defeat at the Battle of Waterloo (1815) the d'Arblays returned and settled at Bath, where d'Arblay died in 1818. Mme d'Arblay then retired to London, where she devoted her attention to her son's career and to the publication of her father's *Memoirs* (1832). An edition of her journals and letters in eight volumes was published 1972–80.

THOMAS CHATTERTON

(b. November 20, 1752, Bristol, Gloucestershire, England—
d. August 24, 1770, London)

Thomas Chatterton was the chief poet of the 18th-century "Gothic" literary revival, England's youngest writer of mature verse, and a precursor of the Romantic Movement.

At first considered slow in learning, Chatterton had a tearful childhood, choosing the solitude of an attic and making no progress with his alphabet. One day, seeing his mother tear up as wastepaper one of his father's old French musical folios, the boy was entranced by its illuminated capital letters, and his intellect began to be engaged. He learned to read far in advance of his age but only from old materials taken by his father from a chest in the Church of St. Mary Redcliffe. At age seven Chatterton entered Colston's Hospital, but his learning was acquired independently.

Chatterton's first known poem, written when he was 10, was a scholarly piece, *On the Last Epiphany*, written in the style of the great 17th-century poet John Milton. About a year later an old parchment he had inscribed with a pastoral eclogue, *Elinoure and Juga,* supposedly of the 15th century, deceived its readers, and thereafter what had begun merely as a childish deception became a poetic activity quite separate from Chatterton's acknowledged writings. These poems were supposedly written by a 15th-century monk of Bristol, Thomas Rowley, a fictitious character created by Chatterton. The name was taken from a civilian's monument brass at St. John's Church in Bristol. The poems had many shortcomings both as medieval writings and as poetry. Yet Chatterton threw all his powers into the poems, supposedly written by Rowley, in such a manner as to mark him a poet of genius and an early Romantic pioneer, both in metrics and in feeling.

In 1767 Chatterton was apprenticed to John Lambert, a Bristol attorney, but spent most of his time on his own writing, which for a while he turned to slight profit in *Felix Farley's Bristol Journal* and *Town and Country Magazine.* The life was irksome to him, however, and pressures began to build up, compounded of a fight for a free press, contempt for Bristol and his dowdy family, a philandering attitude to local girls, and the "death" of Rowley.

Chatterton sent James Dodsley, the publisher, letters offering some of Rowley's manuscripts, but Dodsley ignored him. The writer and connoisseur Horace Walpole received similar offers and at first was enchanted with the "old" poems; but, when advised by friends that the manuscripts were modern, he treated Chatterton with chilly contempt, advising him in a letter to stick to his calling. Chatterton rewarded him with bitter but noble lines. By a mock suicide threat ("The Last Will and Testament of me, Thomas Chatterton of Bristol"), he forced Lambert to release him from his contract and set out for London to storm the city with satires and pamphlets. A lively burletta (comic opera), *The Revenge*, brought some money, but the death of a prospective patron quenched Chatterton's hopes. At this time he wrote the most pathetic of his Rowley poems, *An Excelente Balade of Charitie*. Though literally starving, Chatterton refused the food of friends and, on the night of August 24, 1770, took arsenic in his Holborn garret and died.

The aftermath was fame. The just tributes of many poets came after controversy between the "Rowleians" and those who rightly saw Chatterton as the sole author. Chatterton drew the attention—and sympathy—of the major figures of English Romanticism: Samuel Taylor Coleridge wrote a poem to him; William Wordsworth saw him as "the marvelous boy"; Percy Bysshe Shelley gave him a stanza in *Adonais*; and John Keats dedicated *Endymion: A Poetic Romance* to him and was heavily influenced by him. Lord Byron and Sir Walter Scott added their praise. In France the Romantics hailed his example, and Alfred de Vigny's historically inaccurate play *Chatterton* was the model for an opera by Ruggero Leoncavallo.

PHILLIS WHEATLEY

(b. *c.* 1753, present-day Senegal?, West Africa—
d. December 5, 1784, Boston, Massachusetts, U.S.)

Phillis Wheatley was the first black female poet of note in the United States.

The young girl who was to become Phillis Wheatley was kidnapped and taken to Boston on a slave ship in 1761 and purchased by a tailor, John Wheatley, as a personal servant for his wife, Susanna. Phillis was treated kindly in the Wheatley household, almost as a third child.

The Wheatleys soon recognized her talents and gave her privileges unusual for a slave, allowing her to learn to read and write. In less than two years, under the tutelage of Susanna and her daughter, Phillis had mastered English; she went on to learn Greek and Latin and caused a stir among Boston scholars by translating a tale from Ovid. Beginning in her early teens she wrote exceptionally mature, if conventional, verse that was stylistically influenced by Neoclassical poets such as Alexander Pope and was largely concerned with morality, piety, and freedom.

Wheatley's first poem to appear in print was *On Messrs. Hussey and Coffin* (1767), but she did not become widely known until the publication of *An Elegiac Poem, on the Death of the Celebrated Divine...George Whitefield* (1770), a tribute to Whitefield, a popular preacher with whom she may have been personally acquainted. The piece is typical of Wheatley's poetic ouevre both in its formal reliance on couplets and in its genre; more than one-third of her extant works are elegies to prominent figures or friends. A number of her other poems celebrate

Phillis Wheatley, engraving attributed to Scipio Moorhead, from the frontispiece of her 1773 book. Library of Congress Prints and Photographs Division

the nascent United States of America, whose struggle for independence was sometimes employed as a metaphor for spiritual or, more subtly, racial freedom. Though Wheatley generally avoided the topic of slavery in her poetry, her best-known work, *On Being Brought from Africa to America* (written 1768), contains a mild rebuke toward some white readers: "Remember, Christians, Negroes, black as Cain / May be refined, and join th' angelic train." Other notable poems include "To the University of Cambridge in New England" (written 1767), "To the King's Most Excellent Majesty" (written 1768), and "On the Death of Rev. Dr. Sewall" (written 1769).

Phillis was escorted by the Wheatleys' son to London in May 1773. Her first book, *Poems on Various Subjects, Religious and Moral*, where many of her poems first saw print, was published there the same year. Wheatley's personal qualities, even more than her literary talent, contributed to her great social success in London. She returned to Boston in September because of the illness of her mistress. At the desire of friends she had made in England, she was soon freed. Both Mr. and Mrs. Wheatley died shortly thereafter. In 1778 she married John Peters, a free black man who eventually abandoned her. Though she continued writing, fewer than five new poems were published after her marriage. At the end of her life Wheatley was working as a servant, and she died in poverty.

Two books issued posthumously were *Memoir and Poems of Phillis Wheatley* (1834)—in which Margaretta Matilda Odell, a descendant of Susanna Wheatley, provides a short biography of Phillis as a preface to a collection of her poems—and *Letters of Phillis Wheatley, the Negro Slave-Poet of Boston* (1864). Wheatley's work was frequently cited by abolitionists to combat the charge of innate intellectual inferiority among blacks and to promote educational opportunities for African Americans.

GEORGE CRABBE

(b. December 24, 1754, Aldeburgh, Suffolk, England—d. February 3, 1832, Trowbridge, Wiltshire)

George Crabbe was an English writer of poems and verse tales memorable for their realistic details of everyday life.

Crabbe grew up in the then-impoverished seacoast village of Aldeburgh, where his father was collector of salt duties, and he was apprenticed to a surgeon at 14. Hating his surroundings and unsuccessful occupation, he abandoned both in 1780 and went to London. In 1781 he wrote a desperate letter of appeal to the statesman and political thinker Edmund Burke, who read Crabbe's writings and persuaded James Dodsley to publish one of his didactic, descriptive poems, *The Library* (1781). Burke also used his influence to have Crabbe accepted for ordination, and in 1782 he became chaplain to the duke of Rutland at Belvoir Castle.

In 1783 Crabbe demonstrated his full powers as a poet with *The Village*. Written in part as a protest against Oliver Goldsmith's *The Deserted Village* (1770), which Crabbe thought too sentimental and idyllic, the poem was his attempt to portray realistically the misery and degradation of rural poverty. Crabbe made good use in *The Village* of his detailed observation of life in the bleak countryside from which he himself came. *The Village* was popular but was followed by an unworthy successor, *The Newspaper* (1785), and after that Crabbe published nothing for the next 22 years. Apparently happily married (1783) and the father of a family, he no longer felt impelled to write poetry.

In 1807, however, spurred by the increasing expenses associated with his sons' education, Crabbe began to publish again. He reprinted his poems, together with a new work, "The Parish Register," in which he made use of the register of births, deaths, and marriages to create a compassionate depiction of the life of a rural community. Other verse tales followed, including *The Borough* (1810), *Tales in Verse* (1812), and *Tales of the Hall* (1819).

Crabbe is often called the last of the Augustan poets because he followed John Dryden, Alexander Pope, and Samuel Johnson in using the heroic couplet, which he came to handle with great skill. Like the Romantics, who esteemed his work, he was a rebel against the realms of genteel fancy that poets of his day were forced to inhabit, and he pleaded for the poet's right to describe the commonplace realities and miseries of human life.

JULIAN URSYN NIEMCEWICZ

(b. February 6, 1757 or 1758, Skoki, Poland—
d. May 21, 1841, Paris, France)

Julian Ursyn Niemcewicz was a Polish playwright, poet, novelist, and translator whose writings, inspired by patriotism and concern for social and governmental reform, reflect the turbulent political events of his day. He was the first Polish writer to know English literature thoroughly, and he translated works of such authors as John Dryden, John Milton, Alexander Pope, and Samuel Johnson during a period of imprisonment in 1794–96. Further, he introduced the historical novel to

Poland with his three-volume *Jan z Tęczyna* (1825; "Jan of Tęczyn"), which was influenced by the Scottish novelist Sir Walter Scott.

Educated in the Warsaw cadet corps between 1770 and 1777, Niemcewicz spent most of the period 1783–88 in western Europe and in 1788 was elected deputy to the Sejm (parliament) of Poland. In 1790 he wrote *Powrót posła* ("The Deputy's Return"), a political comedy very popular in its day. After participating in the unsuccessful insurrection against Russia of 1794, when he served as an aide-de-camp to Tadeusz Kościuszko, he was captured at Maciejowice and imprisoned in St. Petersburg for two years. Upon his release, he traveled to England and then with Kościuszko to the United States, where he met George Washington, Thomas Jefferson, and other American political leaders. He married in the United States and remained there until 1807, when he returned to Poland. His recollections of that period—*Podróże po Ameryce 1797–1807*—were translated into English as *Under Their Vine and Fig Tree: Travels Through America in 1797–1799, 1805, with Some Further Account of Life in New Jersey* (1965).

While Niemcewicz strove to add a moderate voice to the social and political unrest in Poland between 1807 and 1831, he devoted himself primarily to literary work, publishing *Śpiewy historyczne* (1816; "Historical Songs"), a series of simple song poems that became very popular, and the novel *Lebje i Sióra* (1821; *Levi and Sarah*). In 1831 he journeyed to England to attempt to persuade the western European powers to intervene on behalf of the Polish insurrection against the Russians. He failed to do so, however, and spent the last years of his life in Paris, campaigning for Polish freedom. His memoirs appeared in 1848.

ROYALL TYLER

(b. July 18, 1757, Boston—d. August 26, 1826,
Brattleboro, Vermont, U.S.)

The American lawyer, teacher, and dramatist Royall Tyler was the author of the first American comedy, *The Contrast* (1787).

After graduating from Harvard University, Tyler —who was born William Clark Tyler—served in the U.S. Army and later became a lawyer. A meeting with Thomas Wignell, the star comedian of the American Company, in New York City, led him to write *The Contrast*, which premiered in 1787 at the John Street Theatre. A light comedy echoing the English playwrights Oliver Goldsmith and Richard Sheridan (especially *The School for Scandal*), *The Contrast* contains a Yankee character, the predecessor of many such in years to follow, that brought something native to the stage. His other plays, some no longer extant, did not equal *The Contrast*.

GÂLIB DEDE

(b. 1757, Constantinople—d. January 5, 1799, Constantinople)

The Turkish poet Gâlib Dede—also called Şeyh Gâlib, both names pseudonyms of Mehmed Es' Ad—was one of the last great classical poets of Ottoman literature.

Gâlib Dede was born into a family that was well-connected with the Ottoman government and with the Mawlawīyah, or Mevlevîs, an important order of Muslim dervishes. Continuing in the family tradition by becoming an official in the Divan-ı Hümayun, the Ottoman imperial council, he thus established a career for himself in the Ottoman bureaucracy. Later, after giving up this government position, he became the sheikh (superior) of the Galata monastery, in Constantinople, the renowned centre of the Mawlawī yah order. Remaining in this position for the rest of his life, he continued to write poetry. His work was much appreciated by the reigning Ottoman sultan, Selim III (himself a poet, musician, and Mawlawī dervish), and by other members of the court, who showed him great favour and respect.

Gâlib Dede is primarily known for his masterpiece, *Hüsn ü Aşk* ("Beauty and Love"). This allegorical romance describes the courtship of a youth (Hüsn, or "Beauty") and a girl (Aşk, or "Love"). After many tribulations, the couple are finally brought together, allegorizing the fundamental unity of love and beauty. In addition to this famous work, Gâlib Dede is known for his *Divan* (collection of poems). These poems illustrate his preoccupation with mystical religious themes and are characterized by highly symbolic language and complex conceits and wordplay.

ROBERT BURNS

(b. January 25, 1759, Alloway, Ayrshire, Scotland—
d. July 21, 1796, Dumfries, Dumfriesshire)

Robert Burns, who wrote lyrics and songs in the Scottish dialect of English, is considered the national poet of Scotland. He was also famous for his amours and for his rebellion against orthodox religion and morality.

Life

Burns's father had come to Ayrshire from Kincardineshire in an endeavour to improve his fortunes, but, though he worked immensely hard first on the farm of Mount Oliphant, which he leased in 1766, and then on that of Lochlea, which he took in 1777, ill luck dogged him, and he died in 1784, worn out and bankrupt. It was watching his father being thus beaten down that helped to make Robert both a rebel against the social order of his day and a bitter satirist of all forms of religious and political thought that condoned or perpetuated inhumanity. He received some formal schooling from a teacher as well as sporadically from other sources. He acquired a superficial reading knowledge of French and a bare smattering of Latin, and he read most of the important 18th-century English writers as well as William Shakespeare, John Milton, and John Dryden. His knowledge of Scottish literature was confined in his childhood to orally transmitted folk songs and folk tales together with a modernization of the late 15th-century poem "Wallace." His religion throughout his adult life seems to have been a humanitarian deism.

Proud, restless, and full of a nameless ambition, the young Burns did his share of hard work on the farm. His father's death made him tenant of the farm of Mossgiel to which the family moved and freed him to seek male and female companionship where he would. He took sides against the dominant extreme Calvinist wing of the church in Ayrshire and championed a local gentleman, Gavin Hamilton, who had got into trouble with the Kirk Session for sabbath breaking. He had an affair with a servant girl at the farm, Elizabeth Paton, who in 1785 bore

Robert Burns. Hulton Archive/Getty Images

his first child out of wedlock, and on the child's birth he welcomed it with a lively poem.

Burns developed rapidly throughout 1784 and 1785 as an "occasional" poet who more and more turned to verse to express his emotions of love, friendship, or amusement or his ironical contemplation of the social scene. But these were not spontaneous effusions by an almost-illiterate peasant. Burns was a conscious craftsman; his entries in the commonplace book that he had begun in 1783 reveal that from the beginning he was interested in the technical problems of versification.

Though he wrote poetry for his own amusement and that of his friends, Burns remained restless and dissatisfied. He won the reputation of being a dangerous rebel against orthodox religion, and, when in 1786 he fell in love with Jean Armour, her father refused to allow her to marry Burns even though a child was on the way and under Scots law mutual consent followed by consummation constituted a legal marriage. Jean was persuaded by her father to go back on her promise; Robert, hurt and enraged, took up with another girl, Mary Campbell, who died soon after; on September 3 Jean bore him twins out of wedlock. Meanwhile, the farm was not prospering, and Burns, harassed by insoluble problems, thought of emigrating. But he first wanted to show his country what he could do. In the midst of his troubles he went ahead with his plans for publishing a volume of his poems at the nearby town of Kilmarnock. It was entitled *Poems, Chiefly in the Scottish Dialect* and appeared on July 31, 1786. Its success was immediate and overwhelming. Simple country folk and sophisticated Edinburgh critics alike hailed it, and the upshot was that Burns set out for Edinburgh on November 27, 1786, to be lionized, patronized, and showered with well-meant but dangerous advice.

The Kilmarnock volume was a remarkable mixture. It included a handful of first-rate Scots poems: "The Twa

Dogs," "Scotch Drink," "The Holy Fair," "An Address to
the Deil," "The Death and Dying Words of Poor Maillie,"
"To a Mouse," "To a Louse," and some others, including
a number of verse letters addressed to various friends.
There were also a few Scots poems in which he was unable
to sustain his inspiration or that are spoiled by a confused
purpose. In addition, there were six gloomy and histrionic
poems in English, four songs, of which only one, "It Was
Upon a Lammas Night," showed promise of his future
greatness as a song writer, and what to contemporary
reviewers seemed the stars of the volume, "The Cotter's
Saturday Night" and "To a Mountain Daisy."

Burns selected his Kilmarnock poems with care: he
was anxious to impress a genteel Edinburgh audience.
In his preface he played up to contemporary sentimental views about the natural man and the noble peasant,
exaggerated his lack of education, pretended to a lack of
natural resources and in general acted a part. The trouble
was that he was only half acting. He was uncertain enough
about the genteel tradition to accept much of it at its face
value, and though, to his ultimate glory, he kept returning
to what his own instincts told him was the true path for
him to follow, far too many of his poems are marred by a
naive and sentimental moralizing.

Edinburgh unsettled Burns, and, after a number of
amorous adventures there and several trips to other parts
of Scotland, he settled in the summer of 1788 at a farm in
Ellisland, Dumfriesshire. At Edinburgh, too, he arranged
for a new and enlarged edition (1787) of his *Poems*, but little
of significance was added to the Kilmarnock selection. He
found farming at Ellisland difficult, though he was helped
by Jean Armour, with whom he had been reconciled and
whom he finally married in 1788.

In Edinburgh Burns had met James Johnson, a keen
collector of Scottish songs who was bringing out a series of

volumes of songs with the music and who enlisted Burns's help in finding, editing, improving, and rewriting items. Burns was enthusiastic and soon became virtual editor of Johnson's *The Scots Musical Museum*. Later, he became involved with a similar project for George Thomson, but Thomson was a more consciously genteel person than Johnson, and Burns had to fight with him to prevent him from "refining" words and music and so ruining their character. Johnson's *The Scots Musical Museum* (1787–1803) and the first five volumes of Thomson's *A Select Collection of Original Scotish Airs for the Voice* (1793–1818) contain the bulk of Burns's songs. Burns spent the latter part of his life in assiduously collecting and writing songs to provide words for traditional Scottish airs. He regarded his work as service to Scotland and quixotically refused payment. The only poem he wrote after his Edinburgh visit that showed a hitherto unsuspected side of his poetic genius was *Tam o'Shanter* (1791), a spirited, narrative poem in brilliantly handled eight-syllable couplets based on a folk legend.

Meanwhile, Burns corresponded with and visited on terms of equality a great variety of literary and other people who were considerably "above" him socially. He was an admirable letter writer and a brilliant talker, and he could hold his own in any company. At the same time, he was still a struggling tenant farmer, and the attempt to keep himself going in two different social and intellectual capacities was wearing him down. After trying for a long time, he finally obtained a post in the excise service in 1789 and moved to Dumfries in 1791, where he lived until his death. His life at Dumfries was active. He wrote numerous "occasional" poems and did an immense amount of work for the two song collections in addition to carrying out his duties for the excise service. The outbreak of the French Revolution excited him, and some indiscreet outbursts nearly lost him his job, but his reputation as a good worker and a politic but humiliating recantation saved him.

Legacy

Burns was a man of great intellectual energy and force of character who, in a class-ridden society, never found an environment in which he could fully exercise his personality. The fact is that Scottish culture in his day could provide no intellectual background that might replace the Calvinism that Burns rejected. That Burns produced so much fine poetry shows the strength of his unique genius, and that he has become the Scottish national poet is a tribute to his hold on the popular imagination.

Burns perhaps exhibited his greatest poetic powers in his satires. There is also a remarkable craftsmanship in his verse letters. But it is by his songs that Burns is best known, and it is his songs that have carried his reputation round the world. Burns is without doubt one of the greatest songwriters Great Britain has ever produced.

Burns wrote all his songs to known tunes, sometimes writing several sets of words to the same air in an endeavour to find the most apt poem for a given melody. Many songs which, it is clear from a variety of evidence, must have been substantially written by Burns he never claimed as his. He never claimed "Auld Lang Syne," for example, which he described simply as an old fragment he had discovered, but the song we have is almost certainly his, though the chorus and probably the first stanza are old. (Burns wrote it for a simple and moving old air that is *not* the tune to which it is now sung, as Thomson set it to another tune.) The full extent of Burns's work on Scottish song will probably never be known.

It is positively miraculous that Burns was able to enter into the spirit of older folk song and re-create, out of an old chorus, such songs as "I'm O'er Young to Marry Yet," "Green Grow the Rashes, O," and a host of others. It is this uncanny ability to speak with the great anonymous voice of the Scottish people that explains the special feeling that Burns arouses, feelings that manifest themselves in the "Burns cult."

MARY WOLLSTONECRAFT

(b. April 27, 1759, London, England—d. September 10, 1797, London)

The English writer Mary Wollstonecraft was a passionate advocate of educational and social equality for women.

The daughter of a farmer, Wollstonecraft taught school and worked as a governess, experiences that inspired her views in *Thoughts on the Education of Daughters* (1787). In 1788 she began working as a translator for the London publisher James Johnson, who published several of her works, including the novel *Mary: A Fiction* (1788). Her mature work on woman's place in society is *A Vindication of the Rights of Woman* (1792), which calls for women and men to be educated equally.

In 1792 Wollstonecraft left England to observe the French Revolution in Paris, where she lived with an American, Captain Gilbert Imlay. In the spring of 1794 she gave birth to a daughter, Fanny. The following year, distraught over the breakdown of her relationship with Imlay, she attempted suicide.

Wollstonecraft returned to London to work again for Johnson and joined the influential radical group that gathered at his home and that included the writers William Godwin, Thomas Paine, and Thomas Holcroft, the artist William Blake, and, after 1793, the poet William Wordsworth. In 1796 she began a liaison with Godwin,

Mary Wollstonecraft, oil painting on canvas by John Opie, C. *1797; in the National Portrait Gallery, London.* DEA Picture Library/De Agostini/ Getty Images

and on March 29, 1797, Mary being pregnant, they were married. The marriage was happy but brief; Mary Wollstonecraft Godwin died 11 days after the birth of her second daughter, Mary.

A Vindication of the Rights of Woman is one of the trailblazing works of feminism. Published in 1792, Wollstonecraft's work argued that the educational system of her time deliberately trained women to be frivolous and incapable. She posited that an educational system that allowed girls the same advantages as boys would result in women who would be not only exceptional wives and mothers but also capable workers in many professions. Other early feminists had made similar pleas for improved education for women, but Wollstonecraft's work was unique in suggesting that the betterment of women's status be effected through such political change as the radical reform of national educational systems. Such change, she concluded, would benefit all society.

The publication of *Vindication* caused considerable controversy but failed to bring about any immediate reforms. From the 1840s, however, members of the incipient American and European women's movements resurrected some of the book's principles. It was a particular influence on American women's rights pioneers such as Elizabeth Cady Stanton and Margaret Fuller.

The life of Mary Wollstonecraft has been the subject of several biographies, beginning with her husband's *Memoirs of the Author of A Vindication of the Rights of Woman* (1798, reissued 2001, in an edition edited by Pamela Clemit and Gina Luria Walker). Those written in the 19th century tended to emphasize the scandalous aspects of her life and not her work. With the renewed interest in women's rights in the later 20th century, she again became the subject of several books. *The Collected Letters of Mary Wollstonecraft*, assembled by Janet Todd, was published in 2003.

WILLIAM BECKFORD

(b. September 29, 1760, London, England—
d. May 2, 1844, Bath, Somerset)

The English writer William Beckford is best known as the author of the Gothic novel *Vathek* (1786). He also is renowned for having built Fonthill Abbey, the most sensational building of the English Gothic revival.

Beckford was the only legitimate son of William Beckford the Elder, twice lord mayor of London, and was the heir to a vast fortune accumulated by three generations of his Beckford ancestors, who were sugar planters in Jamaica. His mother was descended from Mary Stuart. He was a precocious child, and his natural talents were given every encouragement. At five he received piano lessons from the nine-year-old Wolfgang Amadeus Mozart. He also received training in architecture and drawing from prominent teachers. He inherited his fortune in 1770, upon the death of his father.

In 1778, after a period of travel and study in Europe, Beckford returned to England, where he later met the 11-year-old son and heir of Viscount Courtenay, a boy for whom Beckford felt strong romantic (but probably not sexual) attraction. Following a lavish three-day Christmas party held in the boy's honour at Fonthill, Beckford conceived the story of Vathek, a monarch as impious as he is voluptuous, who builds a tower so high that from it he can survey all the kingdoms of the world. Vathek challenges the founder of Islam, Muhammad, in the seventh heaven and so brings about his own damnation and his banishment to the subterranean kingdom ruled by Eblis, prince of darkness.

Completed in outline in three days and two nights, the tale was written in French during the first four months of 1782, in all the gaiety of a London society greeting the inheritor of a fortune. A protégé of Lord Chancellor Edward Thurlow, with a seat in the House of Commons, and married to the beautiful Lady Margaret Gordon, Beckford was expecting to be elevated to the peerage in December 1784. In the autumn of that year, scandal broke when he was charged with sexual misconduct with young Courtenay. Reports of the scandal were quickly spread, and, though Beckford's guilt was never proved, in mid-1785 he—with his wife and baby daughter—was forced into exile. In May 1786, in Switzerland, his wife died after giving birth to a second daughter. About that time, Beckford also learned that *Vathek*, which he had given to the Reverend Samuel Henley for translation, would be published anonymously, with a preface in which Henley claimed that it had been taken directly from the Arabic. Beckford remained abroad for many years.

From 1796, after his return to England, he devoted his energies to his Gothic "abbey" at Fonthill. His architect was James Wyatt, but Beckford himself supervised the planning and building of what became the most extraordinary house in England. He lived there as a recluse, collecting curios, costly furnishings, and works of art and reading the library of the historian Edward Gibbon, which he had purchased in its entirety. In 1807 the house's great central tower collapsed and was rebuilt. Beckford's extravagances forced him to sell his estate in 1822. The tower later collapsed again, destroying part of the building.

Beckford's literary reputation rests solely on *Vathek*. Though all agree that it is uneven and stylistically uncertain, the strength of its final image has sustained Beckford's reputation for more than two centuries. A classic among Gothic novels, the book is a masterpiece of fantastic invention and bizarre detail. Among Beckford's other published works are accounts of his travels, two parodies of Gothic and sentimental novels, and a journal, *Life at Fonthill, 1807–22*.

André de Chénier

(b. October 30, 1762, Istanbul—d. July 25, 1794, Paris, France)

André-Marie de Chénier was a poet and political journalist, generally considered the greatest French poet of the 18th century. His work was scarcely published until 25 years after his death. When the first collected edition of Chénier's poetry appeared in 1819, it had an immediate success and was acclaimed not only by the poets of the Romantic movement but also by the anti-Romantic liberal press. Not only was Chénier's influence felt on poetic trends throughout the 19th century but the legend of his political struggle and heroic death also made him a European symbol of the poet-hero.

His mother was Greek, and he always had a deep affection for Classical literature, in particular for elegiac poetry. He was educated in the progressive Collège de Navarre and, after an unsuccessful attempt at a military career in 1782–83, devoted himself for five years to study. In 1787 he reluctantly accepted a post in the French embassy in London. He was obsessed at that time by epic themes, notably a project for a poem on the New World, but he was psychologically inhibited from completing these works. His years in London were unhappy: he suffered from frustrated ambition and from self-doubt.

The upheavals of the French Revolution in 1789 offered an opportunity to escape from this frustration. He returned to Paris that year and began to take an active part in political journalism, attacking the extremes both of monarchist reaction and of Revolutionary terror. Chénier was not a political innocent and realized the dangers of his position. At times he exposed himself unnecessarily, from the sense of moral integrity that is a fundamental theme of his work and perhaps also from an obscure hunger for self-destruction. In March 1794 he was arrested, imprisoned at Saint-Lazare, and, four months later, guillotined, a few days before the fall of the Revolutionary leader Maximilien Robespierre, an event that would have saved him.

Chénier's achievement was to have demonstrated how the qualities of the Greek lyrics could revitalize French poetry. In his works of the Revolutionary period, including poems that he smuggled out of prison in a laundry basket, he makes a passionate defense of ideals of liberty and justice: the *Iambes*, the last of which dates from very shortly before his execution, are a moving testimonial to the human spirit in the face of persecution.

JEAN PAUL

(b. March 21, 1763, Wunsiedel, Principality of Bayreuth [Germany]—d. November 14, 1825, Bayreuth, Bavaria)

Jean Paul (the pseudonym of Johann Paul Friedrich Richter) was a German novelist and humorist whose works were immensely popular in the first 20 years of the 19th century. His pen name reflected his admiration for the French writer Jean-Jacques Rousseau. Jean Paul's writing bridged the shift in literature from the formal ideals of

Weimar Classicism to the intuitive transcendentalism of early Romanticism.

Jean Paul, the son of a poor teacher and pastor, studied theology at Leipzig but soon gave up his studies for freelance writing. He published two collections of satiric essays in the style of the Anglo-Irish writer Jonathan Swift, *Grönländische Prozesse* (1783; *The Greenland Lawsuits*) and *Auswahl aus des Teufels Papieren* (1789; "Selection from the Devil's Papers"), but these were unsuccessful, and he was forced to support himself as a private tutor (1787–90) and schoolmaster (1790–94). About 1790 a personal crisis prompted him to forsake bitter satire for sentimental humour in his writings, and the English novelist Laurence Sterne replaced Swift as his model. His reputation began with the sentimental novel *Die unsichtbare Loge,* 2 parts (1793; *The Invisible Lodge*), and was established by *Hesperus* (1795). He became a celebrity and was lionized by the critic Johann Herder and by a patron, Frau von Kalb, who brought him to Weimar. In 1801 he married Karoline Mayer and in 1804 settled in Bayreuth, his home for the rest of his life.

The second period in Jean Paul's work is marked by his attempts to reconcile the comic satirist and the sentimental enthusiast in himself. The novels of this period include *Blumen-, Frucht-, und Dornenstücke*, 3 vol. (1796; *Flower, Fruit and Thorn Pieces*), commonly known as *Siebenkäs*, for its hero; *Leben des Quintus Fixlein* (1796; "Life of Quintus Fixlein"); *Titan*, 4 vol. (1800–03), which he considered his classical masterpiece; and the unfinished *Flegeljahre*, 4 vol. (1804–05; "Adolescence," Eng. trans. *Walt and Vult*).

The novels of his third period mirror his disillusionment with both Classicism and Romanticism. But his idyllic novels, always marked by humour, treat his predicament in a comic style. The forced figurative style of his earliest books had become second nature by this time;

he thought, talked, and wrote wittily. *Dr. Katzenbergers Badereise*, 2 vol. (1809; "Dr. Katzenberger's Journey to the Spa"), and *Des Feldpredigers Schmelzle Reise nach Flätz* (1809; *Army Chaplain Schmelzle's Journey to Flätz*) were the last of his extremely popular novels. In 1808 he received a pension from Prince Karl Theodore von Dalberg, later paid by the Bavarian government, which guaranteed him financial security. He continued to write novels and treatises on education and aesthetics.

Jean Paul's novels are peculiar combinations of sentiment, irony, and humour expressed in a highly subjective and involuted prose style that is marked by rapid transitions of mood. His books are formless, lacking in action, and studded with whimsical digressions, but to some extent they are redeemed by the author's profuse imagination and equal capacity for realistic detail and dreamlike fantasy. One favourite theme is the tragicomic clash between the soul's infinite aspirations and the trivial restrictions of everyday life. Jean Paul greatly influenced his contemporaries by his simple piety, humanity and warmth, his religious attitude toward nature, and his beguiling mixture of sentimentality, fantasy, and humour. After the mid-19th century the unevenness and undisciplined form of his novels began to detract rather than add to his reputation, but the deep humanity of his finest works has preserved them from oblivion.

ANN RADCLIFFE

(b. July 9, 1764, London, England—d. February 7, 1823, London)

Ann Radcliffe (née Ward) remains the most representative of English Gothic novelists. She stands apart

Ann Radcliffe. DEA Picture Library/De Agostini/Getty Images

in her ability to infuse scenes of terror and suspense with an aura of romantic sensibility.

Her father was in trade, and the family lived in well-to-do gentility. In 1787, at the age of 23, she married William Radcliffe, a journalist who encouraged her literary pursuits. Radcliffe led a retired life and never visited the countries where the fearful happenings in her novels took place. Her only journey abroad, to Holland and Germany, was made in 1794 after most of her books were written. The journey was described in her *A Journey Made in the Summer of 1794* (1795).

Her first novels, *The Castles of Athlin and Dunbayne* (1789) and *A Sicilian Romance* (1790) were published anonymously. She achieved fame with her third novel, *The Romance of the Forest* (1791), a tale of 17th-century France. Her next work, *The Mysteries of Udolpho* (1794), by which she became the most popular novelist in England, tells how the orphaned Emily St. Aubert is subjected to cruelties by guardians, threatened with the loss of her fortune, and imprisoned in castles but is finally freed and united with her lover. Strange and fearful events take place in the haunted atmosphere of the solitary castle of Udolpho, set high in the dark and majestic Apennines.

With *The Italian* (1797), Radcliffe realized her full stature as a writer. It shows not only improved dialogue and plot construction, but its villain, Schedoni, a monk of massive physique and sinister disposition, is treated with a psychological insight unusual in her work. She made considerable sums of money from *The Mysteries of Udolpho* and *The Italian*, selling the copyright of the former for £500 and that of the latter for £800. Radcliffe published no more fiction in her lifetime; it seems likely that she ceased to write novels as soon as it was no longer financially necessary to do so. She was notoriously shy about being addressed in person as an author.

In the last 20 years of her life Radcliffe wrote mostly poetry. Her poems (1816) and her posthumous novel *Gaston de Blondeville* (1826), which includes a good deal of verse, were comparatively unsuccessful.

There is little physical horror in Radcliffe's "tales of terror," and elements that seem to be supernatural are usually found to have some rather disappointing natural explanation. Her characterization is usually weak, her historical insight is almost nonexistent, and her stories abound in anachronisms and impossibilities. But Radcliffe's admirers cared as little for "realism" or accuracy as she did. They reveled in her romanticized views of nature, her intimations of evil, and her prolonged scenes of suspense.

The Scottish novelist Sir Walter Scott called her "the first poetess of romantic fiction," and her many admirers included the poets Lord Byron, Samuel Taylor Coleridge, and Christina Rossetti. Writing in the tradition of the novel of sensibility, she boldly focused the themes of nascent Romanticism in her stories and paved the way for the greater talents of Scott and the Romantic poets.

WILLIAM HILL BROWN

(b. November 1765, Boston—d. September 2, 1793, Murfreesboro, North Carolina, U.S.)

William Hill Brown was a novelist and dramatist whose anonymously published *The Power of Sympathy, or the Triumph of Nature Founded in Truth* (1789) is considered the first American novel. An epistolary novel about tragic, incestuous love, it followed the sentimental style developed by the English novelist

Samuel Richardson; its popularity began a flood of sentimental novels.

The son of the Boston clockmaker who made the timepiece in Old South Church, Boston, Brown wrote the romantic tale "Harriot, or the Domestic Reconciliation" (1789), which was published in the first issue of *Massachusetts Magazine,* and the play *West Point Preserved* (1797), a tragedy about the death of a Revolutionary spy. He also wrote a series of verse fables, a comedy in West Indies style (*Penelope*), essays, and a short second novel about incest and seduction, *Ira and Isabella* (published posthumously, 1807). Brown went south to study law and died shortly thereafter.

MARIA EDGEWORTH

(b. January 1, 1767, Blackbourton, Oxfordshire, England—d. May 22, 1849, Edgeworthstown, Ireland)

The Anglo-Irish writer Maria Edgeworth is best known for her children's stories and for her novels of Irish life.

She lived in England until 1782, when the family went to Edgeworthstown, County Longford, in midwestern Ireland, where Maria, then 15 and the eldest daughter, assisted her father in managing his estate. In this way she acquired the knowledge of rural economy and of the Irish peasantry that was to be the backbone of her novels. Domestic life at Edgeworthstown was busy and happy. Encouraged by her father, Maria began her writing in the common sitting room, where the 21 other children in the family provided material and audience for her stories.

She published them in 1796 as *The Parent's Assistant*. Even the intrusive moralizing, attributed to her father's editing, does not wholly suppress their vitality, and the children who appear in them, especially the impetuous Rosamond, are the first real children in English literature since Shakespeare.

Her first novel, *Castle Rackrent* (1800), written without her father's interference, reveals her gift for social observation, character sketch, and authentic dialogue and is free from lengthy lecturing. It established the genre of the "regional novel," and its influence was enormous; Sir Walter Scott acknowledged his debt to Edgeworth in writing *Waverley*. Her next work, *Belinda* (1801), a society novel unfortunately marred by her father's insistence on a happy ending, was particularly admired by Jane Austen.

Edgeworth never married. She had a wide acquaintance in literary and scientific circles. Between 1809 and 1812 she published her *Tales of Fashionable Life* in six volumes. They include one of her best novels, *The Absentee*, which focused attention on a great contemporary abuse in Irish society: absentee English landowning.

Before her father's death in 1817 she published three more novels, two of them, *Patronage* (1814) and *Ormond* (1817), of considerable power. After 1817 she wrote less. She completed her father's *Memoirs* (1820) and devoted herself to the estate. She enjoyed a European reputation and exchanged cordial visits with Scott. Her last years were saddened by the Irish famine of 1846, during which she worked for the relief of stricken peasants.

The feminist movement of the 1960s led to the reprinting of her *Moral Tales for Young People*, 5 vol. (1801) and *Letters for Literary Ladies* (1795) in the 1970s. Her novels continued to be regularly reprinted afterward.

GLOSSARY

abrogate To abolish by authoritative action; annul.

adjutant general Chief administrative officer of an army who is responsible especially for the administration and preservation of personnel records.

alexandrine Verse form that is the most popular measure in French poetry.

amanuenses Those employed to write from dictation or to copy a manuscript.

antiquary One who collects or studies antiquities.

aphorism An expression of some generally accepted truth expressed in a memorable, short statement.

ascetic One who applies strict self-discipline and self-denial as a means of self-improvement, especially as an act of religious devotion.

assiduous Marked by careful unremitting attention or persistent application.

avaunt Away; hence.

awdl In Welsh verse, a long ode written in *cynghanedd* (a complex system of alliteration and internal rhyme) and in one or more of the 24 strict bardic metres, though only 4 bardic metres are commonly used. The *awdl* was, by the 15th century, the vehicle for many outstanding Welsh poems.

baptize To dip in water or sprinkle water on as a part of the ceremony of gaining admission into the Christian church.

benefice Ecclesiastical office to which the revenue from an endowment is attached.

Bluestockings Group of women who in mid-18th-century England held "conversations" to which they invited men of letters and members of the aristocracy with literary interests. The word came to be applied derisively to women who affected literary or learned interests.

bombast Pretentious inflated speech or writing.

bourgeois Belonging to or typical of the middle class.

bursar Officer (as of a monastery or college) in charge of funds.

canon law The usually codified law governing a church.

canto One of the major divisions of a long poem.

catechism A manual of religious instruction, often written in question-and-answer form.

Cavalier Adherent of Charles I of England.

codicil Legal instrument made to modify an earlier will.

colloquial Conversational.

comedy of manners Comedy that satirically portrays the manners and fashions of a particular class or set.

commedia dell'arte A form of Italian popular theatre with an emphasis on ensemble acting that flourished throughout Europe in the 16th–18th centuries.

cuckold Man whose wife is unfaithful.

curate Clergyman in charge of a parish.

deil Scottish for devil.

dervish Member of a Muslim religious group noted for its customs (as bodily movements leading to a trance).

didactic Designed or intended primarily to teach rather than to entertain.

disputatious Provoking debate; controversial.

Dissenting Of or relating to the English Nonconformists.

dissimulation Concealment or hiding of one's true feelings.

dissolute Marked by a self-indulgent lack of restraint.

diurnal Active during the day, as opposed to during the night (nocturnal).

divine right of kings Doctrine in defense of monarchical absolutism, which asserted that kings derived their authority from God and could not therefore be held accountable for their actions by any earthly authority such as a parliament.

Duke of Monmouth Claimant to the English throne who led an unsuccessful rebellion against King James II in 1685.

eclogue Short pastoral poem, usually in dialogue, on the subject of rural life and the society of shepherds, depicting rural life as free from the complexity and corruption of more civilized life.

edema An abnormal collection of watery fluid in a bodily tissue or cavity.

effigy An image or representation of a person, especially depicted as a crude figure representing a hated person.

elegy Song or poem expressing sorrow or lamentation especially for one who is dead.

Epicurean A follower of Epicurus, who identified the supreme good with the absence of bodily and mental pain and advocated the limitation of all desire, the practice of virtue, withdrawal from public life, and the cultivation of friendship.

epigram A concise poem on a single theme with a turn of thought at the end.

epistle A formal or elegant letter.

epitome Ideal example.

exchequer A treasury of a state or nation.

excoriate To denounce severely or berate.

exegesis The critical analysis of a text, especially a religious text.

extant Still in existence; not destroyed or lost.

fabulist A creator or writer of fables especially that carry a moral lesson.

facile Shallow; simplistic.

fatuous Silly.

Glorious Revolution In English history, the Revolution of 1688–89 is known as the Glorious Revolution and the Bloodless Revolution because the monarch, James II, was toppled from his throne without a war.

gout A disease marked by a painful inflammation and swelling of the joints and by the deposit of salts of uric acid in and around the joints.

historiographer One who writes about history; historian.

idyll A simple descriptive work in poetry or prose that deals with rustic life or pastoral scenes or suggests a mood of peace and contentment.

impecunious Habitually having very little or no money.

impresario One who who puts on or sponsors an entertainment.

internecine Of, relating to, or involving conflict within a group.

jōruri Chanted dramatic narrative used in *bunraku* (Japanese traditional puppet theatre).

Kabuki Traditional Japanese popular drama performed with highly stylized singing and dancing.

laird Chiefly Scottish word for a landed proprietor.

legal fiction Rule assuming as true something that is clearly false.

libertine One who who is unrestrained by convention or morality.

libretto Text of a work (as an opera) for the musical theatre.

licentious Unrestrained by law or general morality.

lord chancellor British officer of state who presides over the House of Lords in both its legislative and judicial capacities, serves as the head of the British judiciary, and is usually a leading member of the cabinet.

magistracy The state of being a magistrate, that is, an official entrusted with administration of the laws.

malapropism The usually unintentionally humorous misuse or distortion of a word or phrase, especially the use of a word sounding somewhat like the one intended but ludicrously wrong in the context.

manumit To release from slavery.

mezzotint A method of engraving a metal plate by pricking its surface with innumerable small holes that hold ink and, when printed, produce large areas of tone.

Neoplatonism Platonism modified in later antiquity to accord with Aristotelian, post-Aristotelian, and Eastern conceptions that conceives of the world as an emanation from an ultimate indivisible being with whom the soul is capable of being reunited in trance or ecstasy.

Nonconformist One who does not conform to an established church, especially one who does not conform to the Church of England.

notary Public officer who attests or certifies writings (as a deed) to make them authentic and takes affidavits, depositions, and protests of negotiable paper.

novitiate The period or state of being a novice.

oeuvre French for a writer's or artist's body of work.

Ossianic Of, relating to, or resembling the legendary Irish bard Ossian, the poems ascribed to him, or the rhythmic prose style used by James Macpherson in the poems he claimed to have translated from Ossian.

panegyric A eulogistic oration or writing; formal praise.

parish A section of a church district in the care of a priest or minister.

parson Clergyman, especially a Protestant pastor.

pastoral A poem or play dealing with shepherds or rural life in an often artificial manner and typically drawing a contrast between the innocence and serenity of a simple rural life and the corruption of city or courtly life.

pathos An artistic representation that gives rise to feelings of pity or spurs compassion.

pecuniary Consisting of or measured in money.

pedantry The presentation or application of knowledge in a narrow, stodgy, and often ostentatious manner.

peerage The rank of any of the five degrees of nobility in Great Britain.

perfidy The quality or state of being faithless or disloyal.

picaresque Describes a story that involves a rogue or adventurer surviving mainly by his or her wits in a treacherous society.

Pietist A 17th-century religious movement originating in Germany in reaction to formalism and intellectualism, and stressing Bible study and personal religious experience.

pillory To expose to public contempt, ridicule, or scorn.

Pindaric Written in the manner or style characteristic of Pindar, the greatest lyric poet of ancient Greece.

plenipotentiary One invested with the authority to transact business on behalf of another.

polemic An aggressive attack on the opinions or principles of another.

posthumous Following or occurring after one's death.

precentor A leader of the singing of a choir or congregation.

prelate A high-ranking member of the clergy.

proscription An imposed restraint, restriction, or prohibition.

prosody The study of poetic metre and versification.

quixotic Foolishly impractical, especially in the pursuit of ideals; derived from the name of the hero of Cervantes's novel *Don Quixote*.

Rabelaisian Characteristic of French writer and priest François Rabelais or his works, which—his profession as a priest notwithstanding—are marked by bawdy humour and extravagance of caricature.

rector A member of the clergy (as of the Protestant Episcopal Church) in charge of a parish.

Risorgimento The 19th-century movement for Italian political unity.

sacrament Religious action or symbol in which spiritual power is believed to be transmitted through material elements or the performance of ritual.

sacrosanct Considered sacred.

splenetic Marked by bad temper, malevolence, or spite.

squib A short, humorous piece of writing that may be used as filler in a longer work.

stratagem. A cunning plan or scheme.

sycophant A person looking for recognition by flattering the influential and powerful.

tallow A fatty substance used in making of soap and candles.

Tory Member or supporter of a major British political group of the 18th and early 19th centuries, favouring at first the Stuarts and later royal authority and the established church, and seeking to preserve the traditional political structure and defeat parliamentary reform; conservative.

vellum The skin of a lamb, calf, or kid (baby goat) treated for use as a writing surface.

vicar A minister in charge of a church who serves under

the authority of another minister.

vicarage The house of a vicar.

vicereine The wife of a viceroy (or a woman who is a viceroy).

viceroy One who rules a country or province as the empowered representative of a monarch.

victual To supply with food.

viscount A nobleman below earl and above baron in rank.

ward Person (as a child) under the protection of a court or guardian.

Whig Member or supporter of a major British political group of the late 17th through early 19th centuries seeking to limit royal authority and increase parliamentary power.

Zen Japanese sect of Mahayana Buddhism that aims at enlightenment by direct intuition through meditation.

BIBLIOGRAPHY

G reat Britain and France were the most important centres of European literature during the
Enlightenment era. A useful analysis of the literature
of 18th-century England and its broader context can be
found in John Brewer, *The Pleasures of the Imagination:
English Culture in the Eighteenth Century* (1997). The essays
collected in Robert Darnton, *The Great Cat Massacre: And
Other Episodes in French Cultural History* (1984, reissued
2001), do much the same for the literature and culture
of 18th-century France. Michael McKeon, *The Origins of
the English Novel* (1987, reissued 2002); and John Richetti
(ed.), *The Cambridge Companion to the Eighteenth-Century
Novel* (1996), provide complicated but valuable insights
into the most important literary genre that developed in
England during the 18th century. Although this book does
not take the Enlightenment per se as its subject, many of
the writers described here contributed to or bear some
mark of that movement—and, for the British writers, this
is true of the Scottish Enlightenment in particular. Two
valuable studies of the Scottish Enlightenment are James
Buchan, *Crowded with Genius: The Scottish Enlightenment*
(also published as *Capital of the Mind: How Edinburgh
Changed the World*, 2003); and Arthur Herman, *How the
Scots Invented the Modern World* (2001; also published as
*The Scottish Enlightenment: The Scots' Invention of the Modern
World*, 2002).

Noteworthy biographical studies of some of the
major French authors covered in this volume include
Virginia Scott, *Molière: A Theatrical Life* (2000); Ronald

W. Tobin, *Jean Racine Revisited* (1999); and Ian Davidson, *Voltaire: A Life* (2010). Samuel Johnson has been the subject of numerous biographies, some of the most recent of which are Peter Martin, *Samuel Johnson* (2008); Jeffrey Meyers, *Samuel Johnson: The Struggle* (2008); and David Nokes, *Samuel Johnson: A Life* (2009). Studies of the earliest British novelists include Paula R. Backscheider, *Daniel Defoe* (1989); Martin C. Battestin and Ruthe R. Battestin, *Henry Fielding: A Life* (1989); Donald Thomas, *Henry Fielding* (1991); Arthur H. Cash, *Laurence Sterne. The Early & Middle Years* (1975, reissued 1992), and *Laurence Sterne: The Later Years* (1986, reissued 1992); and Ian Campbell Ross, *Laurence Sterne: A Life* (2001). An often overlooked novelist is described in Claire Harman, *Fanny Burney: A Biography* (2000).

Two books on the first black poet of note in the United States are Henry Louis Gates, Jr., *The Trials of Phillis Wheatley: America's First Black Poet and Her Encounters with the Founding Fathers* (2003); and Vincent Carretta, *Phillis Wheatley: Biography of a Genius in Bondage* (2011). Other writers important to American literature and culture of the 18th century are discussed in Edmund S. Morgan, *Benjamin Franklin* (2002); Craig Nelson, *Thomas Paine: Enlightenment, Revolution, and the Birth of Modern Nations* (2006); and Nancy Rubin Stuart, *The Muse of the Revolution: The Secret Pen of Mercy Otis Warren and the Founding of a Nation* (2008).

The number of books on the other writers covered in this volume can seem overwhelming. Among the most useful are Lyndall Gordon, *Vindication: A Life of Mary Wollstonecraft* (also published as *Mary Wollstonecraft: A New Genius*, 2005); David Nokes, *Jonathan Swift: A Hypocrite Reversed* (1985); Victoria Glendinning, *Jonathan Swift* (1998); Octavio Paz, *Sor Juana; or, The Traps of Faith* (1988; originally published in Spanish, 1983); Robert Crawford, *The Bard: Robert Burns, A Biography* (2009); Maynard Mack,

Alexander Pope: A Life (1985); Pat Rogers, *The Alexander Pope Encyclopedia* (2004); Paul Hammond, *John Dryden: A Literary Life* (1991); Patricia B. Craddock, *Edward Gibbon, Luminous Historian, 1772–1794* (1989); Maurice Lever, *Sade: A Biography* (1993; originally published in French, 1991); Peter Martin, *A Life of James Boswell* (2000); Derek Hughes and Janet Todd (eds.), *The Cambridge Companion to Aphra Behn* (2004); Fintan O'Toole, *A Traitor's Kiss: The Life of Richard Brinsley Sheridan* (1997); and Nick Groom (ed.), *Thomas Chatterton and Romantic Culture* (1999).

INDEX

A

Addison, Joseph, 110, 113–119,
    120, 121, 122–123, 133, 137, 140,
    170, 194, 201
Age of Reason, The, 248, 252
Alcoforado, Mariana, 37, 63–64
Alfieri, Vittorio, Count, 278–279
Anne, Queen, 93, 96, 112, 119,
    122, 139, 140
Arbuthnot, John, 95–96, 130,
    140, 143

B

Bashō, 71–74, 211
Beckford, William, 309–311
Beggar's Opera, The, 129, 131,
    132, 282
Behn, Aphra, 64–66, 84
Boileau, Nicolas, 9, 23, 36, 52–54,
    57, 137
Boswell, James, 163, 198, 235,
    236, 256, 260, 265–271
Brooke, Henry, 167–168
Brown, William Hill, 317–318
Burney, Fanny, 287–290
Burns, Robert, 132, 238, 279,
    299–306
Buson, 210–211
Butler, Samuel, 2–4, 6

C

Candide, 163
*Les Caractères de Théophraste traduits
    du grec avec Les Caractères ou les
    moeurs de ce siècle*, 75, 76
Casanova, Giovanni Giacomo,
    163, 221–222
Catherine II, 163
Charles I, 5, 13, 47
Charles II, 3, 4, 13, 14, 15, 17, 38,
    40, 41, 43–44, 47, 50, 64, 66,
    67, 70, 76, 77
Châtelet, Mme du, 159–160, 161
Chatterton, Thomas, 290–292
Chénier, André de, 311–312
Chesterfield, Philip Dormer
    Stanhope, 4th earl of, 153–154
Chikamatsu Monzaemon, 85–88
Cibber, Colley, 111–113
Clarissa, 147, 150–151, 152
Cleveland, John, 5–6
Collins, William, 201, 217–218
Congreve, William, 43, 67,
    106–111, 115, 140, 158,
    282–283
Cowper, William, 238–241
Crabbe, George, 295–296
Crèvecoeur, Michel-Guillaume-
    Saint-Jean de, 244–247
Cromwell, Oliver, 5, 15, 40, 47
Cruz, Sor Juana Inés de la, 78–84

D

Defoe, Daniel, 88–95, 272
*Dictionary of the English Language,
    A*, 196–197
Dryden, John, 4, 5, 6, 38–46, 53,
    70–71, 77, 107, 114, 136, 201,
    296, 300

E

École des femmes, L', 27, 30, 31
Edgeworth, Maria, 318–319
Equiano, Olaudah, 274–276
Evelyn, John, 13–15, 51
Ewald, Johannes, 272–274

F

Fables, 18–22, 23
Fergusson, Robert, 279–280
Fielding, Henry, 146, 151,
    180–188, 202, 216, 233, 272
Fielding, Sarah, 151, 183, 202–203
Franklin, Benjamin, 169–177,
    245–246, 248–249
Frederick II (the Great), 160,
    161–162, 163, 222, 230–231
French Revolution, 135, 165, 179,
    251, 252, 259, 263, 264, 267,
    277, 285, 304, 306, 312
Freneau, Philip, 286
Fronde, the, 6, 8, 10

G

Gâlib Dede, 298–299
Gama, Basílio da, 271–272
Garrick, David, 149, 192, 194, 196,
    199, 235, 256, 276, 282, 287
Gay, John, 96, 110, 129–131, 132,
    140, 146, 154, 282

George I, 94, 119
George II, 213
George III, 198, 213, 284, 288
Gibbon, Edward, 163, 199,
    253–259, 310
Goldoni, Carlo, 178–179
Goldsmith, Oliver, 198, 215,
    233–236, 298
Gray, Thomas, 201, 208–210,
    211, 247
Gresset, Jean-Baptiste-Louis,
    189–190
Grimmelshausen, Hans Jacob
    Christoph von, 25–26
Guilleragues, Gabriel-Joseph
    de Lavergne, viscount of,
    36–37
Gulliver's Travels, 97, 102–105, 129

H

*History of the Decline and Fall of
    the Roman Empire, The*, 253,
    256–258
Holberg, Ludvig, 125–129
Homer, 24, 110, 138, 139–140,
    142, 241
Hudibras, 2, 3–4, 6

I

Ihara Saikaku, 68–70

J

James II, 14, 45, 51, 68, 90, 183
Jean Paul, 312–314
Johnson, Samuel, 46, 53, 113,
    149, 154, 165, 166, 190–202,
    215, 218, 233, 235, 236, 247,
    256, 259–260, 265, 266–267,

269–270, 276, 287, 288, 296
Joseph Andrews, 180, 182–183,
185, 186

K

Kantemir, Antiokh
Dmitriyevich, 188–189
Klopstock, Friedrich Gottlieb,
220–221, 273

L

La Bruyère, Jean de, 13, 75–76
La Fontaine, Jean de, 18–24, 132
La Roche, Sophie von, 241–242
La Rochefoucauld, François VI,
duke de, 6–13, 23, 36
Lennox, Charlotte, 196, 232–233
Lessing, Gotthold Ephraim,
226–232
Lettres portugaises, 36, 37, 63–64
Louis XIII, 8
Louis XIV, 1, 6, 23, 29, 36, 57, 59,
91, 155
Louis XV, 161, 162
Louis XVI, 177, 252, 255

M

Macpherson, James, 247–248, 273
Maintenon, Françoise d'Aubigné,
marquise de, 1, 59
Marivaux, Pierre, 133–135
Marvell, Andrew, 15–17
Maximes, 9, 10–12, 13
Mazarin, Cardinal, 6–8, 55
Metaphysical poets, 5, 15
Milton, John, 15, 17, 118, 139, 201,
220, 291, 296, 300
Misanthrope, Le, 27, 30, 33

Molière, 1, 2, 23, 26–35, 36, 41, 56, 70,
71, 84, 109, 113, 127, 133, 178, 265
Moll Flanders, 88, 95
Montagu, Lady Mary Wortley,
145–147, 183
More, Hannah, 276–277

N

Nedim, Ahmed, 124–125
Niemcewicz, Julian Ursyn, 296–297

O

Otway, Thomas, 84–85
Owen, Goronwy, 218–219

P

Paine, Thomas, 248–252, 265,
277, 306
Pamela, 147, 148, 149–150, 151, 152,
179, 182
Pepys, Samuel, 14, 46–52
Peter the Great, 159, 188
Piozzi, Hester Lynch (Hester
Thrale), 199, 259–260, 288
Pompadour, Mme de, 134, 161
Poor Richard's almanac, 171, 173
Pope, Alexander, 53, 68, 96, 110,
113, 119, 130, 131, 135–144,
146, 154, 158, 166, 167, 191,
201, 217, 265, 293, 296

R

Racine, Jean, 23, 32, 54–62, 84, 157
Radcliffe, Ann, 314–317
Ramsay, Allan, 131–133
Richardson, Samuel, 134,
147–152, 179, 180, 182, 196,

202, 216, 228, 233, 241, 317–318

Richelieu, Cardinal de, 8, 30

Rights of Man, 248, 251–252, 277

Robinson Crusoe, 88, 94

Rochester, John Wilmot, 2nd earl of, 76–77

Rousseau, Jean-Jacques, 135, 162, 242, 267, 278, 312

S

Sade, Marquis de, 260–265

Savage, Richard, 165–166, 193

Scarron, Paul, 1–2, 3

Shadwell, Thomas, 44–45, 70–71

Shakespeare, William, 43, 45, 70, 71, 112, 113, 142, 158, 193, 199–200, 217, 233, 243, 273, 300

Sheridan, Richard Brinsley, 199, 280–285, 287, 298

Silva, Antônio José da, 168–169

Simplicissimus, 25, 26

Smollett, Tobias, 213–217

Spectator, The, 93, 113, 117–118, 120, 122–123, 133, 137, 170, 194

Steele, Sir Richard, 110, 113, 114, 115, 117–118, 120–124, 137, 140, 170

Sterne, Laurence, 203–208

Swift, Jonathan, 77, 96, 97–106, 110, 117, 130, 140, 142, 146, 158, 167, 192, 281, 313

T

Tartuffe, 27, 31, 33, 34

Tatler, The, 93, 113, 117, 120, 122–123

Terry, Lucy, 237–238

Thomson, James, 166–167

Tom Jones, 151, 180, 181, 183, 185, 186

Tristram Shandy, 203, 205–207

Tyler, Royall, 298

U

Ueda Akinari, 243–244

V

Vindication of the Rights of Woman, A, 306, 308

Voltaire, 27, 154–165, 189, 216, 222, 230, 231, 255, 267, 278

W

Walpole, Horace, 208–209, 211–213, 291

Walpole, Sir Robert, 131, 153, 158, 167, 181, 192, 204, 208, 211, 212

Warren, Mercy Otis, 223–225

Wheatley, Phillis, 292–294

Wieland, Christoph Martin, 242–243

William III, 90, 114, 120, 121

Wollstonecraft, Mary, 306–308

Wycherley, William, 67–68

Z

Zhu Yizun, 37–38